Severe Depres

This book is dedicated to my father,
Joseph C. Barker (1919– 85), whom I
was most fortunate to meet before he left:

Illnesses are almost always spiritual crises in
life in which older experiences, and phases
of thought, are cast off in order to permit
positive changes.

Josef Beuys (1921–86)

Severe Depression

A practitioner's guide

Philip J. Barker

Clinical Nurse Consultant,
Tayside Health Board,
and Honorary Lecturer,
University of Dundee,
Scotland

CHAPMAN & HALL

London · Glasgow · New York · Tokyo · Melbourne · Madras

Published by Chapman & Hall, 2–6 Boundary Row, London SE1 8HN

Chapman & Hall, 2–6 Boundary Row, London SE1 8HN, UK

Blackie Academic & Professional, Wester Cleddens Road, Bishopbriggs, Glasgow G64 2NZ, UK

Chapman & Hall, 29 West 35th Street, New York NY10001, USA

Chapman & Hall Japan, Thomson Publishing Japan, Hirakawacho Nemoto Building, 7F, 1-7-11 Hirakawa-cho, Chiyoda-ku, Tokyo 102, Japan

Chapman & Hall Australia, Thomas Nelson Australia, 102 Dodds Street, South Melbourne, Victoria 3205, Australia

Chapman & Hall India, R. Seshadri, 32 Second Main Road, CIT East, Madras 600 035, India

---

Distributed in the USA and Canada by Singular Publishing Group Inc., 4284 41st Street, San Diego, California 92105

First edition 1992

© 1992 Chapman & Hall

Typeset in 10/12pt Palatino by Excel Typesetters Company

Printed in Great Britain by St. Edmundsbury Press, Bury St. Edmunds, Suffolk

ISBN 0 412 38880 4   1 56593 051 7 (USA)

A catalogue record for this book is available from the British Library

Library of Congress Cataloging-in-Publication data available

Contents

Acknowledgements

This book is the result of a lengthy gestation. I began to think about its structure in 1981, completing the manuscript almost exactly a decade further on. During that time many people have influenced my beliefs about the nature of depression, and the value of all therapies for this timeless affliction. Some important conversations, chance encounters and hints at understanding have doubtless been forgotten with their passing. Some people are, for several reasons, unforgettable. To the following I extend my heartfelt thanks.

Without the support and insight of Rosemary Barker this project would not have been possible. My excuse was that the subject was a captivating one, requiring my earnest and unflinching attention. Her acceptance of my frequent distraction and unremitting obsession is greatly to her credit. I have been fortunate to have had the company of such a partner on my own journey of discovery.

Charlie Barker has, over this decade, stimulated my thinking on issues of gender, equality and the manipulation of power. How satisfying it is to observe that she reflects the ageless truth: the child *is* father of the man.

Annie Altschul owns the quietness that rests easy with wisdom. I heard her silence often and was reassured by the knowledge that she too was thinking.

Bette Harris deserves great praise for drawing me back to a keener appreciation of the necessary and sufficient structure of the English language.

I am grateful to Carol Miller for her attention to what, at times, was a confused manuscript.

Rosemary Morris, of Chapman and Hall, is to be thanked for her keen interest in the concept and patience during its production.

Hildegard Peplau provided me with a dozen ideas, hypotheses and issues for further consideration, in response to a single question. Her generosity of spirit is a match for her insight.

Graham Naylor was more helpful than he will ever know in letting me develop my art within his area of clinical responsibility.

John Drummond offered a critical appraisal of the draft manuscript that ultimately strengthened the text and our comradeship.

To the many people who have been depressed, and who have allowed me entry to their lives, I owe a special debt. Much of this book reflects the distant intellectualization of the long dark night of the soul. I hope that I have been sensitive to the lessons painfully learned. To the women of Ward 20 and the DRCU women's group, I extend my fraternal thanks. I was honoured to have always been so welcome.

I believe that I have led a fortunate life. I am blessed with the satisfaction of knowing the tiredness of approaching age each evening, and youthful anticipation with each new day. The simple effort of writing this book has returned me to my roots. To the architect of my rediscovery I owe the deepest thanks; whoever (s)he might be.

Sheldon Kopp's *Laundry List*, c.1970, is reprinted by kind permission of The Guilford Press, New York.

Preface

In common with most other people, writers have a tendency to 'give themselves away' in conversation. A carefully worded argument or, more likely, a chance remark can be taken as an indication of where the writer 'stands', what the writer's views are on the subject in hand. The subject of this book is sufficiently important to allow me to break with this tradition. Rather than leave the reader to interpret where I stand on severe depression, I shall admit my prejudices from the outset. I believe that this is necessary to frame the 'entry point' to the book. My views should not be taken as a key to severe depression. Compared with many of my peers, I know little. Compared with the sufferer, I know nothing. My views represent the key to my thinking on the subject of severe depression. My views are all this book can offer.

I wish no disrespect to my colleagues in the various helping arts when I say that people who suffer from severe depression are more often the object rather than the subject of psychiatric treatment. When people experience short-lived depression they are often described as 'depressed'. The longer the depression lasts, or the more treatments which are offered without success, the greater is the likelihood that the person will be described as 'a depressive'. The process by which people are overtaken or displaced by clinical syndromes, like some medicalized version of *The Invasion of the Body Snatchers*, has always eluded my understanding. The description of a person as a 'depressive' has the same ring of truth as descriptions of people as 'blacks', 'Jews' or 'simpletons': it tells us a little of where the person has come from (history), but nothing of their future (potential).

The professional treatment of the person as an object is a strategy for sparing our blushes, when we fail to be of much help. Only rarely do we acknowledge that our lack of success represents a true failing on our part. More often we dismiss the person and replace her with a diagnostic 'thing', largely of our (professional) creation. We have not failed the person and, we add sympathetically, the person has not failed herself: this 'thing' is bigger than both of us.

This book is about people who subjectively experience severe depression. It is not about severe depressives, and here I am not merely playing with words. I believe that all who wish to help people in such dire straits need to respect, and embrace, the person who experiences the distress. The person does not leave, go on holiday or, in anything other than a metaphorical sense, 'take a back seat'. We replace the person with a 'patient' at our peril. I have included very few case histories or other 'clips' from my conversations with people who have been depressed. Although such verbatim accounts provide a fascinating glimpse of the melancholic experience, many such accounts are already in print. My aim was to focus on the personal experience of depression, asking what lessons were to be learned by us, the practitioners. Helpers need to have some appreciation of what the experience of depression means to the individual. It may be more important that they know how to make sense of their experience of the depressed person's experience: that is one definition of involvement. Most of the ideas explored in this book derive from my involvement with the experience of depression. I hope that readers can build upon my fumbling understanding; that my travels might assist them to find their own way.

I also wish to acknowledge that most of the 'answers' to the problem of severe depression are either incomplete or inadequate. I intend no disrespect to those who are assumed to have made great discoveries concerning causes and treatment. It appears, however, that our undisputed knowledge of severe depression is a depressing subject in itself. It is also unclear to me whether any of the 'successful' treatments, such as ECT or drug therapy, seriously address, merely mask, or simply 'stamp out' the problem. The incompatability of 'existentialist' and 'biochemical' explanations of severe depression represents the gulf between professionals, in which patients are either rescued or lost forever.

In a sense, all treatments can be defined as successful *to a degree*: as Lewis Carroll's Dodo observed: 'Everyone has won and all must have prizes'. The helping package which represents the focus of this book acknowledges this, at the same time recognizing that this is a fact of our own creation. The helping package I shall describe operates on several levels: I use the term 'holistic' by way of convenient shorthand, not because I am certain that this is a meaningful term. More correctly, the approach I shall discuss could be called a *multimodal* approach to severe depression. People who suffer severe depression witness a highly complex experience: they may be 'disturbed' on every level from their basic biological rhythms, like sleep, to their belief systems. In this book I try to remember this and shall try to offer an adequate, though hardly all-inclusive, response.

Finally, I think that it is important to confess that I have never suffered from a clinical depression of any description. Like many others who grew up as 'only children', I developed a keen sense of the loneliness and confusion of childhood, yet rarely understood why I felt such distress. Such experiences bred in me an enquiring mind and a tendency for reflection and critical self-analysis which, I hope, have served me well. At several points in my life I have been desperately unhappy: such low spirits, however, never undid me in the way they appear to undo those who are depressed. I continue to experience 'swings of mood', sometimes apparently of my own creation, often for no particular reason. My swing from liberated excitement to grim despondency invariably comes to rest easily between the two extremes. I count myself most fortunate that I can be positively fuelled by a heightened sense of energy, and can learn from my darker moments. That I have never witnessed directly the pathology of such experiences may be part of the reason why I am interested to help those who have.

I make these observations merely to acknowledge the difference between the author and the subject of this book. I have devoted a significant part of my professional life over the past 15 years to working with people who are severely depressed. Although we shared the understanding that I was there to be of help to them, I gained much from the experience that I would find hard to express. Any observations made in this book on the meaning of severe depression, and on meaningful ways of responding to such an experience, I owe to the sufferers with whom I have been fortunate to work. Given the state of my knowledge, this is a debt which I am unlikely ever to repay.

The book is in two parts. I begin by reviewing the history of ideas concerning depression, in an effort to balance the pathological perspective, so beloved by practitioners, with the human perspective best known to those who have witnessed the disorder. In Chapter 2, I review some of the psychological theories which appear relevant to the clarification of the sufferer's experience, and which provide a base for developing a therapeutic rationale. In Chapter 3, I outline an alternative paradigm of depression, which attempts to integrate existing knowledge. Such a paradigm might begin to recognize the complexity of its subject, albeit with limited predictive power. Chapter 4 outlines some of the principles of the practitioner's art. This is supplemented in Chapter 5 by my suggestions for using the skeleton self-help guide, which forms the basis of Part Two. I conclude with a backward glance at the paradigm in practice, along with some thoughts of possible pastures new. I have supplied notes at the conclusion of each chapter in an attempt to make the text accessible to at least two audiences. The reader may choose, therefore, whether or not to pursue the extensive theoretical and therapeutic literature, or to consider some of the wider issues stimulated by the subject.

Throughout the text I shall refer to the depressed person as 'she', wherever reference to an individual is appropriate. I do so partly in acknowledgement of the statistical fact that women represent a greater proportion of sufferers and, in some cases, might experience an unnecessary degree of suffering as a result of the thoughtlessness of men. As I have already observed, I have spent a substantial proportion of my professional life working with women who are severely depressed: they have been, and continue to be, a significant glimmer of light in my professional darkness. It seems only fitting that I should retain my personal relationship with those women who have been my teachers, by continuing to refer directly to them in this book.

Newport-on-Tay, 1992

Foreword

My qualifications for accepting the invitation to write the foreword to this book include half a century of nursing patients, teaching students to nurse patients and the experience of having been a patient suffering from severe depression. All of these serve to support Phil Barker's argument that our understanding of the problems of severe depression is incomplete and inadequate.

Listening to Phil Barker over a period of some years and reading what he has to say on the subject have helped me personally and professionally to develop my thinking and understanding, to open up new perspectives and, most importantly, to introduce hope into a field of endeavour generally characterized by gloom and despondency.

Depression is one of the most common disorders. People of all ages are actual or potential sufferers. Not only those who experience depression but all those in contact with them, friends, relations, informal and professional helpers, are caught up by the devastating effects of severe depression.

All those who aim to understand issues of health and disease, all who study the biological or psychological functioning of human beings, all who are interested in social welfare and the structure of society will sooner or later have to concern themselves with the enigma of depression. I believe this book is for all these people. Whatever the starting point of understanding, the writer's profundity of thought will provide challenge and stimulation for every reader. All will emerge wiser as a result.

The book is primarily about helping people to manage their own experience of depression and about the way sufferers and professionals can learn from each other. It demonstrates that, in spite of the feeling of helplessness, people suffering from depression can effectively assume personal responsibility for thoughts and actions.

Sufferers from depression may be tempted to start with Part II (Chapter 6), a self-help guide designed to assist them to do just that. This section addresses sufferers in a direct and personal way, encouraging a step-by-step approach to the solution of their problems. Phil

Barker acknowledges, however, that sufferers may lack motivation and the power of concentration to persevere and that they may need professional help. One can only stress Phil Barker's own advice: 'Do not expect too much too quickly!' Perhaps, as is the case with many instruction manuals, sufferers will only come to appreciate the quality of the advice when they are no longer in need of it. At that point they should join other readers in studying the first part of the book.

Chapters 1 and 2 provide a masterly exploration of the nature of depression, the medical and psychological perspectives, a survey of literary and artistic interpretations. These lead to the exposition of an integrated model of severe depression in Chapter 3, which forms the basis for a helping framework. From there, helpers and sufferers can jointly embark on a plan of action.

Chapter 4 is the manual for professional helpers. It allows them to reach an understanding of the cognitive process of depression. The author develops this as his favoured approach to the acquisition of the necessary skills and for the establishment of a helping relationship.

The writer does not claim that his approach is the only possible one nor that his understanding or conclusions are final or optimal. On the contrary, readers are invited, through the hard work of a radical re-examination of their position, to reach their own solutions. This is the reason why I believe that readers will have a thoroughly rewarding and enlightening experience.

Annie T. Altschul CBE, FRCN, BA, MSc, RGN, RMN, RNT
Emeritus Professor of Nursing Studies, University of Edinburgh

Publisher's note

The ideas, procedures and suggestions contained in this book are intended to be supplementary, rather than an alternative, to psychotherapeutic intervention provided by an appropriate mental health practitioner.

Chapter 1

The mellow horn of the pensive soul

INTRODUCTION

The emotional witness

This book is about the potential management of the experience of depression. In the next chapter, I shall consider some of the suggested causes of this depression. In Part II, I shall discuss a structure which might form the basis for helping people to reduce the negative effects of depression. In this chapter, however, I shall explore the depressive experience: what it means to the person who is depressed, and what it means to the professionals who describe, define and attempt to 'treat' it. How similar, or different, are these two 'views' of depression? What can the professional helper learn from the sufferer, and what might she learn from us?

What, exactly, do people mean when they say they are *depressed*? Dictionary definitions suggest that the depressed person has been: 'pressed down; lowered; brought down; humbled; abased or dispirited'. Such examples reflect the metaphorical status of 'conditions' like depression: the person feels as if some Thing has 'pressed her down' or 'taken the spirit' from her. She may well have no idea of what this Thing is which 'depresses' her; does it come from within her 'self' or has it attached itself to her, sapping her strength, extracting all her 'goodness', leaving only some kind of shell, or worse, some kind of 'ill'? What is clear is that this Thing can, and does, affect her: she has witnessed the experience.

The psychiatric eye is focused also upon the effect of depression: what it does to the person. A multitude of conflicting theories are at our disposal, each purporting to 'explain' the Thing which causes depression. One fact is clear to the psychiatric observer: people who are depressed experience a disturbance of affect; it is their emotional disposition which is 'pressed down or lowered'. When people talk about feeling depressed, psychiatrists describe and ultimately define these feelings, through diagnosis, as one form of affective disorder or another. For sufferers, however, if not also for those who live with or care for them, depression involves more than a mere disturbance of emotional disposition. Unhappy people the world over increasingly describe their low spirits as 'depression'. This may be yet another example of medicalization of everyday life*. People who are severely depressed, however, witness a wholly different kind of experience: one which is pervasive, spreading to every corner of their being. They may experience disturbing physical sensations; distressing emotional feelings; an upset of normal 'intellectual' and physical functions – such as loss of concentration, poor memory, upset sleep and eating patterns, loss of interest in sex and, most of all, an all-embracing torpor or weakness. Although this weakness can be physical, it can often appear spiritual in character. 'Unhappiness' may lie at the root but may also, paradoxically, be the least of their troubles.

People who are depressed emphasize the function of their experience. Typically, this is expressed in metaphorical terms:

> Depression is a weight, it drags me down, it grounds me.
> Depression is a wall encircling me, encapsulating me; it is a space from which there is no escape.
> Depression is a desolate landscape, it is a nowhere land, where I am noboby and my life amounts to nothing.

These are the three most common metaphors which people have used to describe to me their experience. In the most severe cases these metaphorical torments can assume even more grotesque proportions: the sufferer believes that she is being punished for her sins, or that her brain is melting. These experiences, characterized by their air of unreality will, clinically, be defined as 'delusional'. Although resembling some surreal nightmare, all such depressive depictions possess a reality which often is hard to express. To the physiologists and genetic scientists who seek an explanation for depression in some physical form, derived from some genetic link, these metaphors are superfluous to requirements. Scientists, like the best objective observers, often see

---

*Ivan Illich has offered the most infamous critique of the negative aspect of medical services. His criticism that 'the medical establishment has become a major threat to health' was based upon his concerns for the rise in medically induced illness (iatrogenesis), the dehumanizing nature of medical specialism, and the excessive, and inappropriate, use of medical intervention. Illich, I. (1975) *Medical Nemesis: The Expropriation of Health*. London, Calder and Boyars.

only the form, or appearance, of depression. The sufferer is in touch with depression's function: she knows what it does to her. For the sufferer, these metaphors define the true meaning of depression: metaphor offers a hyper-real description. The sufferer's experience of depression may not tell us why, but it tells us vividly what is the nature of the beast which so torments her. The meaning of depression is to be found in the experience of it. To paraphrase Marshall McLuhan, 'the message is in the medium'.

Depression: the illness

People who study, care for, or offer treatment to the depressed person have only a vicarious awareness of the experience. They can see and hear only how depression presents itself. It is unsurprising, therefore, that professionals are so interested in defining the form of depression, through symptom categories and diagnostic classifications. Classification systems, like the International Classification of Diseases (ICD) and the Diagnostic and Statistical Manual (DSM IIIR), offer a security to professionals faced with a distressed, and perhaps distressing, 'patient'*. The disturbing behaviour of the person is reduced, at least in psychiatric eyes, when it is explained in terms of this or that 'condition'. It could be argued that classification of psychiatric conditions differs little from the classification of medical conditions, like cancer or diabetes; or the classification of plants or species in the natural sciences. If such classifications served only to describe experiences such as depression, this would be correct. It is assumed, however, that classification systems, such as psychiatric diagnosis, explain the experience: why people are depressed and what this means in human terms. This major assumption has frequently been called into question.

The past 30 years have witnessed much debate over the definition of 'mental illness' in general. Are the experiences of severely depressed people illnesses, diseases, disorders, or are they simply variants of human behaviour: 'problems of living'? The distinction might be seen as unimportant: people who are severely depressed are so disabled or disadvantaged by their mental problems, it is as if they were ill or otherwise physically disadvantaged. Later in this chapter I shall dis-

---

*Diagnosis in the United Kingdom involves the use of the ICD. The American classification system, DSM IIIR, continues to gain popular support, largely because of its greater specificity, and multi-axial perspective. World Health Organization. (1978) *Mental Disorders: Glossary and Guide to their Classification in Accordance with the Ninth Revision of the International Classification of Diseases*. Geneva WHO; and American Psychiatric Association. (1980) *Diagnostic and Statistical Manual of Mental Disorders III*. Washington APA.

cuss some of the popular scientific concepts of depression. Many such concepts are based upon the view that depression is a disorder which can be understood from a medical perspective, in the same way that diabetes or cancer (two other largely unsolved medical riddles) can be understood. We cannot begin to consider the importance of these concepts, however, without first asking why depression should be thought of as an 'illness' requiring 'treatment'.

The idea that depression is a disease is an ancient notion refined significantly by the German psychiatrist Emil Kraepelin. To Kraepelin depression was an unwelcome occurrence in the life of a person who possessed a specific 'constitution' which facilitated the growth of the depressive disease process. Kraepelin set in motion the descriptive process which sought to categorize 'depressions' in much the same way that botanists, like Linnaeus, classified plant life. In Kraepelin's view the natural history of the illness, its form, onset and course, all served to assist the diagnosis. In crude terms, Kraepelin assumed that the 'disease' existed independently of the person, whom it subsequently afflicted and affected. Viewed from this perspective, depression is similar to any form of malignancy or infectious disease*.

This overtly 'biological' approach to psychiatric disorders like depression is greatly respected. Medical treatments, such as antidepressant drugs and electroconvulsive therapy, derive from this tradition and numerous clinical studies attest to their usefulness; a view often supported by the experience of sufferers. Whether or not such studies or treatments actually tell us anything about the meaning of depression is another question. This book is not, however, about the medical diagnosis of depression. Neither is it about the 'treatment' of the medical disorder of depression. Here I shall address, all too briefly and simplistically, the human experience of depression and shall suggest ways by which 'supporters' of the depressed person, professionals, partners, family and friends, can make themselves useful. I shall suggest also, with the greatest temerity, how people who are depressed might help themselves to confront, manipulate or otherwise deal with their experience. The guidance contained in the subsequent chapters is based upon the assumption that, for the depressed person, the metaphor is the reality.

---

*Arieti observed that Kraepelin's description of depressive illness owed much to Aretaeus, who predated him by 17 centuries. Aretaeus was the first to associate mania and depression, considering them both part of the same disease process. More importantly, he may have been more accurate than Kraepelin by noting that 'recovery' did not denote 'cure'. Arieti, S. (1974) Manic-depressive psychosis and psychotic depression. In Arieti, S. (ed.) *American Handbook of Psychiatry, Vol III*. New York, Basic Books.

Depression: the metaphor

In her celebrated essay *Illness as Metaphor*, Susan Sontag (1977) discussed the depiction of illness as a metaphor in our culture, using cancer and TB as classic, historical examples. Sontag argued that giving disease a 'meaning' was a punitive act; the meaning invariably being a moralistic one. Karl Menninger (1963), the neo-Freudian psychoanalyst, saw illness not only as what the world had done to the sufferer but, 'in a larger part it is what the victim has done with his world, and with himself (*sic*)'. Such 'psychologizing', in Sontag's view, suggested a false form of control of experience: experiences over which people had little or no control. Such 'psychological understanding undermined the "reality" of a disease' (Sontag 1977, p55). Later in the essay, Sontag narrowed the focus of her contempt of such 'psychologizing':

> . . . every illness can be considered psychologically. Illness is interpreted as, basically, a psychological event, and people are encouraged to believe that they get sick because they (unconsciously) want to, and that they can cure themselves by the mobilization of the will . . . Psychological theories of illness are a powerful means of placing the blame on the ill.   (Sontag 1977, p57)

Sontag's argument is powerful where 'disease' is synonymous with a disorder of the normal vital processes: cancer, in any form, epitomizes disease both in process and outcome. The disorder is tangible. The disease precipitates, in virtually every case, a psychological disorder linked either to the physical experience of distress or the expectation of death. Even the most abject physical disorder, therefore, has psychological concomitants. However, for people to use these psychological factors to 'bring' such an illness 'upon themselves' would require not only a perverse kind of 'will', but also the exercise of a powerful magic.

People who are severely depressed can be seen as 'diseased' in the sense that they are not 'at ease' and clearly are in an 'unhealthy condition'. That definition is stretched near to breaking point where it is assumed, also, that this 'unhealthy condition' is symptomatic of an underlying physical disorder: even one not yet clearly identified. Some forms of depression may involve a disruption of the normal physical functioning of the sufferer. Whether or not such changes are the 'cause' or the 'outcome' of depression remains unclear*. More import-

---

*In a series of deplorable laboratory experiments, dogs were exposed to painful electric shocks. Having no means of escape, the dogs eventually submitted to their fate, becoming apathetic and lethargic. In presentation, these animals appeared much the same as the severely depressed person. Physical changes, such as anorexia and 'staring' coat, were also observed. At post mortem, changes in the brain structure were also recorded.

antly, there are indications that other factors of a psychological or social nature may also be involved. If this is true then the origins of mental 'illnesses' like depression may be quite different from illnesses like cancers, which arise *mainly* from a physical cause.

Thirty years ago, Thomas Szasz's view that mental *illness* was a myth was tantamount to heresy. Today, the idea that *mental* illness per se does not exist has become almost a commonplace (Moore 1975). Our description and classification of all 'forms' of mental disorder is something we should not take for granted. In Kendell's view, this is an argument which, if considered logically, must be applied to all forms of disease:

> . . . (all) diseases are merely concepts, man-made abstractions justified only by their convenience and liable at any time to be adjusted or discarded. (Kendell 1983a)

Kendell drew our attention to the danger of assuming that that which we have 'described' necessarily exists: the condition of 'depression' may exist only because we have constructed it. This view is largely in keeping with Szasz's view that mental illness does not exist, but is a metaphoric illness. He accepts that certain states which commonly are called mental illnesses can look like physical illnesses. For instance, both depression and diabetes involve suffering. Since they 'look alike', and diabetes *is* a disease, depression also must be a disease. In Szasz's view, this illustrated the 'category mistake' described by the British philosopher Gilbert Ryle (1949): it is like saying that eagles and bats both fly, therefore they are both birds. In Szasz's view, even if we could show that 'mentally ill' people were suffering from a disease of the brain, we could not, legally, treat them against their will:

> Treating them involuntarily would still require that they be declared insane as well. (Szasz 1987, p169)

Szasz paraphrased Voltaire's famous remark that, 'If God did not exist, it would be necessary to invent him', by suggesting that psychiatry has done the same with the concept of 'mental illness'. He has argued that the science of psychiatry has replaced the revelations of traditional religion. Religious texts the world over have described the role and function of priests, prophets and myriad messiahs, all capable of unravelling the mysteries of life. In these more secular times, we turn to a

---

The hypothesis was subsequently offered that some of the biological changes in depressed persons might be the long-term result of psychosocial stressors. Seligman, M.E.P. and Maier, S. (1967) Failure to escape traumatic shock. *Journal of Experimental Psychology*, **74** pp1–9.

variety of psychiatric workers to find answers to questions which once might have been deemed spiritual in nature. In Szasz's view psychiatry now masquerades as a 'pseudo-religion', providing unnecessarily grandiose explanations of, for example, the workings of the unconscious mind. Psychiatry promotes the view that life is:

> ... a dark mystery; that our personal problems cannot be understood by common sense, intelligent inquiry, and some earnest effort; that the secrets of our inner life or unconscious mind can be penetrated ... only by a few select adepts.   (Szasz 1987, p360)

Not only is all of this false in Szasz's view, it is also counterproductive. It leads to the disenfranchisement of people: the concept of mental illness is used to 'explain away' certain human predicaments and to justify social policies. The 'pseudo-science' of psychiatry also is unnecessary since:

> Understanding why people act the way they do – what they value and what gives their life meaning – is far easier than understanding the atomic structure of matter or the chemical composition of [the] stars.   (Szasz 1987, p360)

The irony of acknowledging Szasz's caveats while writing yet another book on depression, based upon my experiences as a psychotherapist, does not escape me. Such ironies may, however, have played a constructive role in maintaining my interest in the personal, as opposed to pathological, nature of depression, and may have arrested my own temptation to construct elaborate explanations of that of which I have no direct experience.

BEYOND THE SLOUGH OF DESPOND

Loss: metaphor and reality

The true meaning of depression is known only to those with first-hand knowledge of that experience. People recognize that clapping applause or kicking a ball are very different actions: quite distinct experiences. These actions involve simple relationships between different parts of ourselves, or between ourselves and inanimate objects. Even a person born without hands or feet knows what clapping or kicking 'means' and can describe these actions in a 'sociocultural' sense. Such vicarious knowledge, however, scarcely touches upon the experience of such actions.

Depressed people also describe relationships between parts of themselves, or between themselves and the outside world, inanimate or living. These relationships describe their feelings about themselves or the world. These feelings depend, usually, upon a special kind of vision: the world of the depressive is seen as a bleak landscape; the person herself as an empty shell or a crooked shadow. It is all too easy to dismiss such vision as a cruel distortion: to say that too liberal a use of metaphor has exaggerated the case. An alternative view is that the depressive's vision is painfully accurate: too painful for us so-called normals even to contemplate. To those of us gifted with ordinary vision, these are cruel distortions of reality. Our 'concrete reality', itself a metaphor, is distorted by the depressive's special metaphor. She talks 'as if' this was the case; we, who are 'in touch' with reality, know that this is untrue. To reinforce our answer to the depressive riddle we turn to the common consensus. We assume that the majority view represents 'reality'; by implication, minority, eccentric views are distorted, probably by some kind of disease process of which we are as yet uncertain.

The view that a solid, concrete reality exists is part of the problem of depression. When people talk in metaphoric terms about the 'darker side' of life, or of their 'true natures', we get scared. Aristotle defined metaphor as consisting of 'giving a thing a name that belongs to something else'. Thomas Szasz, the arch-critic of traditional psychiatric diagnosis, pointed out that dictionaries define the words *literal* and *metaphoric* as opposites, one being an antonym for the other. Thus, when we describe someone as love*sick* or home*sick* we are using metaphor. We are not suggesting that such people are sick in the sense that they are suffering from an infection: this would involve literalizing the metaphor, accepting the two 'sicknesses' as one. Instead, we are saying that it is *as if* these persons were physically sick. For Szasz, the use of metaphor as a means of expression is wholly appropriate. Indeed, he describes how metaphor is a fundamental part of everyday communication. He warns, however, against forgetting that they are only metaphors (Szasz 1987, p135). Those who are lovesick, homesick or sick of life are indeed sick but to confuse such sickness with a physical sickness is, surely, to miss the point.

It might appear trite to suggest that people comment on their view of themselves or their world in an effort to understand, not because they have arrived at any significant conclusions. Perhaps when depressed people describe their experience they are grappling with just that kind of understanding. Depression, in common with many other mental disorders, involves a disturbance of the 'mind'. This is not quite the same as saying that it involves a brain disturbance (which may or may not also be the case). The metaphor of the mind represents an attempt to embrace a substantial concept in a single word. When a person fears that she is 'losing her mind', she does not fear the loss of her brain. To assume that one thing literally means the other confuses the issue and, more importantly, fails to understand the communication which has been made. Metaphor plays a vital role in describing things which cannot adequately be expressed through more literal language.

The absurdity of translating metaphors into more literal or simpler terms is rather like summarizing a Shakespearian tragedy in a single sentence, or explaining a joke, which usually results, in metaphorical terms, in 'killing' it. Most artists fight shy of explaining their work for this very reason. Samuel Beckett's play *Waiting for Godot* has been analysed repeatedly and exhaustively in an effort to reduce it to a few short and simple lines of meaning. When asked who or what was meant by 'Godot', Beckett replied: 'If I knew, I would have said so in the play' (Schmieder 1958). In a sense, Beckett is not free to reveal the meaning, especially if it would mean 'killing' that which he has created. His answer may well leave us wondering if he was seeking only to obscure the meaning further; or perhaps the true meaning had been summed up in those few casual words? The medium conveys the message: change the medium and the message also is transposed. Metaphor allows for creative expression on one side and creative interpretation on the other. The speaker communicates her meaning, without denying the listener an opportunity to invent an interpretation. As it is in art so, also, it may be in life.

Divine inspiration or hellish insight?

What relevance have the views of writers and artists to any serious consideration of depression, or indeed any emotional ill? What function does art serve, however, if not to express that which we consider important but which, as non-artists, we are unable to express ourselves? Susan Sontag believed that the provision of such assistance was the prime function of the artist:

> For the modern consciousness, the artist (replacing the saint) is the exemplary sufferer. And among artists, the writer, the man of words, is the person to whom we look to be able best to express suffering.   (Sontag 1967)

A vast body of literature supports the age-old argument that suffering and art are inseparable: indeed, that the former begets the latter. The Babylonians believed that demons had taken possession, and the Hebrews that depression derived from guilt and divine retribution. These fearful interpretations did not come to prominence again until the Middle Ages, when Martin Luther, ravaged by melancholy in later

life, ascribed it to the 'work of the devil'. The Ancient Greeks introduced a more positive philosophy of psychological derangement. In
Aristotle's estimation, all great thinkers, poets, artists and statesmen
were of 'melancholic temperament'. Mental illness added to rather
than detracted from a personality. This was based largely upon an
observation that a poet by the name of Marascus wrote excellent poetry
when manic, but was wholly mediocre when well (Zilboorg 1941). Not
all Greeks were quite so positive. Homer, commonly taken to represent
the healthy-minded joyousness of Greek literature, clearly had occasion
to despair, if not of life, then at least of his own kind, commenting
cheerlessly in the *Iliad* that: 'Nothing is more wretched than man of all
that breathes and creeps upon this earth'.

The interpretation of psychological suffering as a function of creativity
derives from the Ancient Greeks' concept of *furor divinus* ('godlike
rage'). Madness and art were connected, given by the gods. Plato
asserted that good poetry owed nothing to the rules of art; where the
poet was inspired, he was, as it were, possessed by a spirit not his
own. Indeed, nothing worth calling poetry could be composed until
the poet became, 'as it were, mad'. In *Phaedrus*, Plato placed a condition on the function of this mental suffering, believing that: 'Madness,
provided it comes as a gift of heaven, is a channel by which we receive
the greatest blessings'. This idea was revived by the Neoplatonists of
the Renaissance, and later by Dostoevsky and Nietzsche. The artist's
heightened consciousness, according to Dostoevsky, allowed him to
see unbearable truths about the tragic nature of the human condition:
'too great a lucidity *is* a disease'. In Nietzsche's view it was necessary
to 'make oneself sick, mad, to provoke the symptoms of derangement'
in order to become 'superhuman, more terrible, wiser'. The saint, the
prophet, the poet and the artist, all received this 'dangerous gift . . .
(which) threatened to topple him into the abyss of insanity (Meyers
1987). The poet, according to Kierkegaard, could not be anything other
than 'an unhappy man who in his heart harbours a deep anguish'.

The view that madness can be a gift as well as a punishment sur-
vives to this day in much literary criticism. Jeffrey Meyers described
how Robert Lowell and his circle of American fellow poets, Randall
Jarrell, John Berryman, Theodore Roethke and Sylvia Plath, believed
that their:

> madness [depression and manic-depression] could inspire great
> poetry, that pain and suffering were intrinsic to art, and that the
> artist sacrificed himself to achieve his vision.   (Meyers 1987, p16)

Their belief in the supremacy of intuitive, metaphorical feeling over the
logic of the intellect was in sympathy with Freud's notion of the power
of the unconscious. In this context, Jarrell noted that:

A feeling in the Dark
Brings worlds, brings words, that hard-eyed Industry
And all the Schools' dark learning never knew.

Whether or not he had insight into his eventual suicide is less clear, for he concealed his depression beneath a cultivated and controlled exterior. In many respects, the successful, angst-ridden artist was the one who destroyed himself. In this sense, Jean-Paul Sartre saw himself as a failure: 'In order to achieve authenticity, something has to snap'. Sartre's unsteady progression towards a natural death rendered him distinctly inferior to Gaugin, van Gogh and Rimbaud, all of whom drove themselves to destruction (Meyers 1987, p19).

The perception of the melancholy temperament as an arm of creative expression was characterized at great length by Robert Burton (1577–1640), whose 500 000 word classic, *The Anatomy of Melancholy*, took 20 years to write. The curious admixture of despair and enlightenment was obvious to him. Despite his view that, 'hell on earth . . . is to be found in a melancholy man's heart', there was 'naught so sweet' as melancholy; and he viewed the 'vile rock of melancholy' as one of the milder, but frequent forms of creativity*. Burton's Elizabethan age became known as the age of melancholy. Shakespeare, his contemporary, projected many appreciations of psychological disturbance, among them melancholy, and showed how little modern psychology is able to improve upon his descriptive talent. In *As You Like It*, he anchored the depressive experience firmly in the voyage through life, processed by regular doses of introspection:

It is a melancholy of mine own, compounded of many simples, extracted from many objects, and indeed the sundry contemplation of my travels, which, by often rumination, wraps me in a most humorous sadness.

Romancing despair

The idea that such distress should be a prerequisite for artistic creation offends common sense, and may be seen as a 'romantic' fiction. Wordsworth inaugurated the English Romantic movement, which represented a literary tradition which turned sour but which had a secure pedigree, especially within literature. Wordsworth tried to clarify how this 'gift/punishment' worked in his own case. In so doing, like many artists before him, he anticipated the 'cognitive' psychotherapists with

---

*For a summary of Burton's magnum opus, see Burton, R. (1621) The anatomy of melancholy, what it is. In Hunter, R. and Macalpine, I. (1964) *300 Years of Psychiatry*. London, Oxford University Press.

his observation that suffering came not so much from the world, but from the poet's 'construction' of the world:

> The Poet . . . [feels distress] though no distress be near him, save his unmanageable thoughts.

There existed, also, an inescapable price which Wordsworth or any poet would be charged for pursuing this vocation:

> We Poets in our youth begin in gladness
> But thereof come in the end despondency and madness

These sentiments were echoed by Wordsworth's contemporary Byron, who believed that:

> There is something, I am convinced, in the poetical temperament, that precludes happiness, not only to the person who has it, but to those connected with him.

The English Romantic movement, represented in particular by Wordsworth and Coleridge, developed an intellectual position which emphasized feelings for external nature which was much in keeping with the worship of nature of the Ancient Greeks. The movement laid great store by their reflections on the mysterious apprehension of the 'otherness' of the universe, and their relationship with it. This led them to question the whole nature of perception. The eyes of the poet may be the clearest 'windows on the soul'. As a result they were able to see more clearly both the splendour and the darkness of the world. The infatuation with despair led Gerard de Nerval (1805–55), the French romantic poet, to depict melancholy as a black sun:

> I am the darkly shaded, the bereaved, the inconsolate, the prince of Aquitaine, with the blasted tower. My only star is dead, and my star-strewn lute carries on it the black sun of melancholy.

Such melancholy, however, defeated the whole purpose of life according to John Dryden, who believed that: 'It is better not to be than to be unhappy'. The melancholic's tendency to shy away from life was explained by Shakespeare, who observed: 'Oh how bitter a thing it is to look into happiness through another man's eyes'. Such unhappiness could be compounded by a sense of desolation, described in almost 'clinical' detail by St Ignatius Loyola as:

> a darkening of the soul, trouble of mind, movement to base and earthly things, restlessness of various agitations and temptations, moving to distrust, loss of hope, loss of love; when the soul feels herself thoroughly apathetic, sad, and as it were separated from her Creator and Lord.　　　　　　　　　　　　　　　　　　　　(Loyola)

The unremitting nature of that dark shadow, cast over the world as well as the soul, represented to Gerard Manley Hopkins, the nineteenth century English poet, a 'world-sorrow' from which there was no escape.

> No worst, there is none. Pitched past pitch of grief,
> More pangs will, schooled at forepangs, wilder wring.
> Comforter, where, where is your comforting?
> Mary, mother of us, where is your relief?   (Cumberledge 1952)

When the depressed person speaks of the 'pain' of depression, this too is metaphorical. However, as Longfellow acknowledged, the likeness may be all too real:

> A feeling of sadness that is not akin to pain, resembles sorrow only as mist resembles rain.

Other writers have seen melancholy as more of a mixed blessing. Thomas Gray (1716–71), in his *Elegy Written in a Country Churchyard*, saw melancholy as a 'pensiveness' and 'heightened sensibility', encouraging a great capacity for feeling, for others as well as for himself. The theme of 'heightened sensibility' is reflected in contemporary psychological research: depressives may well see the world for what it really is, without the rose-tinted spectacles of non-depressed people (Sackheim 1983). Such modern empirical studies appear to span the centuries, validating the Platonic view that depression is a curious gift. Recipients of the 'gift' might well agree with Byron that:

> [it] is a fearful gift: what is it but the telescope of truth, which brings life near in utter darkness, making the cold reality too real?

Such telescopic vision can transform the depressed person's reality: 'There is no longer any past for me; people appear so strange; it is as if I could not see any reality; as if I were in a theatre; as if people were actors; and everything were scenery' (James 1981). Tolstoy encountered a similarly perplexing fate when he began what he called his 'arrest'. It was as if he knew not 'how to live' or 'what to do'. The metaphor of such an experience surely did not escape him. In his fiftieth year, enjoying great success, financial stability, creative and physical maturity, he could find no reasonable meaning to his life. The literal, incontestable truth, which occurred first to him in the form of a fable (metaphor), was framed in the universal question:

> What will be the outcome of what I do today? Of what I shall do tomorrow? What will be the outcome of my life? Why should I

live? Why should I do anything? Is there in life any purpose which
the inevitable death which awaits me does not undo and destroy?

(James 1981, p161)

Seeking the light

Tolstoy found an answer, like many before him and since, in religious
faith. For many melancholics, the loss of meaning and hope leads to a
spiritual path, whether this is one of discovery or invention. The loss
of hope is endemic to most severe depressions. The bleak vision of
the world and the future may be acutely accurate, as already noted.
The historical assumption that depressed people are possessed by
'unreasonableness' expressing itself in irrational thinking may be untrue in most cases. The depressed person's view may be painfully
accurate: she may need to temper this realism if life is to become
bearable.

In this sense the pursuit of 'hope' is vital to those who feel hopeless
and helpless. People who appear, by the assessment of their own
experience, unable to control the world, their interaction with it or
even the limits of their emotional responses to the vagaries of experience, are inclined, perhaps rightly, to feel helpless. Such helplessness
breeds hopelessness, as Vaclav Havel has observed:

Hope is not a feeling of certainty that everything ends well.
Hope is just a feeling that life and work have a meaning.

(Morrow 1990)

The expectant nature of hope places it very close to faith in meaning.
Our faith represents the complete trust that what we hope (or expect)
to happen, will happen. The religious person extends faith and hope to
cover expectations which lie beyond this life, whereas the atheist's
faith remains earthly in nature. The processes of hoping and having
faith, however, are no different. When people become seriously depressed, they are no longer certain that they can control the simpler
things in life, far less those which rest on faith and hope. When
helplessness engenders hopelessness, suicide often seems the most
appropriate action. The interaction between such feelings and our
biological selves is a vital one: literally so. For Tolstoy faith was one of
the forces by which men live. Its absence, the state of anhedonia,
meant collapse (James 1981, p481).

The American novelist William Styron has written of his chance
rescue from just such a collapse (Styron 1991). Having decided that the
pain of his depression was too much to bear he resolved to kill himself.
On the soundtrack of a film playing on television, Styron heard the

voice of a woman practising Brahm's *Alto Rhapsody*. This triggered a childhood memory of his mother, who died when he was 13, singing the same piece. The song, especially Goethe's words, was an evocation of hope, rising from gloom and despond. The recognition of this symbolic hope accompanied Styron's realization that he could not kill himself and so he called to his wife for help. In a review of Styron's 'memoir' of his depressive experience, Anita Brookner, also a novelist, suggested that part of the mystery of depression is its incommunicability, observing that even Styron, 'an accomplished novelist', is not altogether informative about his condition (Brookner 1991). This may have been true of Styron. It would be patently false, however, to suggest that the tongues, far less the intellects, of all sufferers from depression are silenced by their experience.

When the depressive experience is profound, the sufferer may well be literally retarded; communicating in monosyllables, if at all. The sufferer is, however, acutely sensitive to the experience; indeed, like that other acute emotional experience, panic, the sufferer chokes on the experience. It seems likely that little of the wealth of literature describing depressive experiences was actually written in the teeth of the storm. However, come the calm, many do recollect and remember only too well. During such calm periods Franz Kafka combined his talents for writing and introspection to describe, *par excellence*, the inner world of the depressive with rare insight and power. In Bemporad's view, Kafka's writings 'permit a rare and unforgettable glimpse into the inner world of melancholia' (Arieti and Bemporad 1980). Kafka, perhaps more than any other modern author, characterized life's ironies, the helplessness of the individual and the awesome nature of power: concerns which Aaron Beck was much later to translate into the negative cognitive triad – defeatist thoughts concerning self, world and future. Writing represented Kafka's salvation: unable to communicate directly his fears of responsibility and earthly pleasure, he was able to write about them, albeit in a metaphorical mode. He returned, repeatedly and obsessively, to the same themes, as though exorcizing the haunted shadows of an unhappy childhood and a miserable adulthood. 'Kafka's demons were purged [however] not on the psychoanalytic couch but by the relentless, clear-eyed explorations of the nethermost limits of his being' (Hall and Lind 1970).

The painful ascent

Brookner has also suggested that Dürer's engraving *Melencolia*, which graces the cover of this book, is the most striking image of depression ever produced; and is an apposite symbol for the 'despond' encountered by Styron. The central figure sits, 'heavy-limbed and defeated, sur-rounded by abandoned emblems of her study, her features thickened and made sullen by inertia, the spell under which she has fallen' (Brookner 1991). We should not leave this section without clarifying what Dürer might actually have intended by this image, for I believe that it carries a timeless message across the centuries to those sorely afflicted today.

The probable meaning of *Melencolia* caused great speculation in its day, unlike most of Dürer's prodigious output. The feeling of melan-choly reaches the viewer immediately and, in Knappe's view, the inscription itself serves to conceal rather than reveal the meaning. One interpretation is that Dürer recognized that, in addition to a morbid, inferior kind of melancholy, there existed a superior form, characteristic of thinkers and artists. Dürer's *Melencolia* is not an image of despair at the limitations of human knowledge, or indeed even a symbol of bottomless sadness. Instead, it represents an image of inspired listen-ing, of sensitivity to the mysterious language of the imagination, com-pared with which the instruments and other pieces of scientific appara-tus which litter the scene are useless and of no real importance*. Viewed from this perspective, the image can be seen to represent a challenge to materialism and all the other 'false gods' which might divert us from the chosen path. The ladder is a powerful symbol for the hope of ascent to the upper sphere of this world, rather than the next. The melancholy spirit has, therefore, access to this enlightenment and, if necessary, can be borne by her two 'wings': knowledge and magic. Knowledge, of course, represents that which we know and understand; magic, that which we know works but, as yet, do not understand why.

Dürer's image may, therefore, be a fitting symbol for the depressed person, though not for the reasons given by Brookner. Some depressive experiences arrive unexpectedly, cause great distress and, when they depart, leave the sufferer with no more than a sense of relief. Other depressive experiences also insult and injure but, by virtue of their discomforting presence, cause the individual to re-appraise, re-evaluate or otherwise adjust her world or her relationship with it. With the passing of the depression may come a legacy of understanding, albeit one acquired at great emotional cost. Many survivors of the slough of despond find it difficult to say what, exactly, helped them through their darkest hours. In this sense the power of magic remains with us.

I warn the reader against the interpretation that depression is some-

*My interpretation owes much to Knappe's analysis and insight. Knappe K.A. (1965) *Dürer: The Complete Engravings, Etchings and Woodcuts*. London, Thames and Hudson.

how good for people. Randall Jarrell spoke for all sufferers from depression when he observed with stark honesty that:

Pain comes from the darkness
And we call it wisdom. It is pain   (Meyers 1987, p179)

I acknowledge only that whatever passes for wisdom rarely is offered free. The melancholic, like those who suffer other slings and arrows of outrageous fortune, is privy to an experience which most would deny entrance. I admit only that the depressed person who can own this experience may survive the wiser. Some acquire the wisdom that, should the experience be repeated, it would be appropriate to bring their life to an end (Altschul 1985).

Neither do I lay claim to any understanding of the significance of the melancholic metaphor. I suggest only that it is foolhardy to ignore this special description of depression, or even to expect that this should be translated into a more literal form. People give a name to 'one thing' that already belongs to 'another thing' because it is *as if* this were the case. If a person believes that she is drowning, the helper's first task is to acknowledge her plight. Whether she is drowning in a river or in problems of her own imagining is irrelevant: the experience, within her own skin, is real. The true helper offers assistance unconditionally. Helpers have a responsibility to acknowledge that people know their own experiences better than anyone else: they do not lose that knowledge through the process of depression, or any other form of 'mental' disorder. Indeed, the knowledge of oneself may be ludicrously and painfully heightened, as we shall discuss later.

This section has addressed the direct experience of depression. The science of psychiatry is obliged to adopt a more oblique perspective. Psychiatry's attempts to describe and define human behaviour has used much the same methodology as prevails in the classification of plants and other natural forms. Much that carries the title 'pathological' is only unusual, or infrequently occurring. It could also be argued that the difference between 'normal' human behaviour and patterns of 'mental disorder' is like the difference between flowers and weeds: when a flowering plant grows where it is not desired, it is a weed – otherwise it is a flower. The characteristic behaviours of two boxers in a ring and two men fighting in a public house differ only in style and perceived appropriateness. Similarly, the anguish and soul-searching of the poet (or artist in general) is considered appropriate: where such emotional distress occurs in 'mere mortals' it is pathological. Hence the great confusion which results when attempts are made to distinguish 'creativity' and 'pathology' when both are possibilities within the same person, such as the artist.

Having spent a considerable proportion of my formative adult life among the 'artistic' fraternity, and having been required to offer psychotherapy to a number of emotionally 'ailing' artists, this conflict intrigues me greatly. As I begin to experience for myself the doubts concerning true self-worth, the inevitability of death and the extinction of the spirit, I begin to see this conflict as illusory. Pain is experienced as pain, whatever we care to call it. We might complain that life (or our experience) does not work out the way we had hoped. But, as Leonardo acknowledged:

> Experience never errs; it is only [our] judgements that err by promising effects such as are not caused by [our] experiments.
>
> (Taylor 1960)

THROUGH A GLASS DARKLY: DESCRIBING THE DEPRESSIVE EXPERIENCE

Acceptable anguish or pathological pain?

There are many ways of classifying or categorizing the kind of melancholic experiences described so far. Depressions commonly occur, however, in three main forms.

People can become depressed suddenly and fleetingly when, for example, precious belongings are lost in a fire or they are sacked from their job. The hurt, sadness and sense of loss associated with such events may come and go for a time, only to submerge or evaporate as the person rebuilds the life which once appeared so badly damaged.

People can also become depressed suddenly and seriously when, for example, a child dies or a relationship founders. The acute pain of such an experience can lessen through time, but may require the additional support of friends, confidantes or a professional counsellor. Some would argue that it is not appropriate to redefine such experiences as depression. In 1988, an aircraft was blown out of the sky by a terrorist bomb over the Scottish town of Lockerbie. Many people died. Friends and family of the dead from Lockerbie, and around the world in the case of the airline passengers, were devastated (Raphael 1986; Salter 1990). Those people, as well as members of the small town who had not been directly bereaved, experienced a kind of depression which will ease with time, though it will never be erased. It seems fitting that most memorials to those who have met a premature and communal death, such as on the battlefield, carry the inscription 'Lest we forget'. Such losses are incorporated, almost literally: they become part of the person, who rarely forgets.

Such experiences of loss thread their way through the history of all peoples: the loss of family, friends, homelands, treasures and, under some political regimes, the loss of rights of worship, basic human dignity, even of hope itself. The experience of such losses can be harrowing, painful and grotesquely disturbing. The criticism of the use of the term 'depression' here involves a concern that the experience might, somehow, be explained away or dismissed. The implication that depression is pathological might, therefore, diminish the political or personal human significance of the experience. I am sympathetic to the view that such responses may be no more or less than the natural human reaction to loss: a loss which should be respected as natural, normal and appropriate. We may well devalue such experiences by classifying them as 'depression': the assumption being that they are abnormal or inappropriate reactions to certain aspects of the business of living*.

A third kind of depression is our concern here. In addition to the characteristics of the acute forms noted above, severe depression possesses an enduring quality. In medical language such depressions are described as **chronic**: the distress is persistent or recurrent, it does not go away by itself and it rarely submits to the ameliorating effect of time. When it does depart, this may be temporary: the disorder may, characteristically, involve many recurrences of the same kind of emotional and 'life' problems. Severe depression also involves a sense of 'loss', which differs in character from the other two depressed states. Commonly, severe depression involves a loss of self-esteem or self-worth. The person also suffers **anhedonia**, the loss of the ability to enjoy life. These combined losses produce a complex form of despair. People who are severely depressed see no obvious way to 'cut their losses', to ease their disappointment or to salve the pain of rejection, whether this is actual or metaphorical.

These three different but overlapping states represent a form of human misery which has been called the common cold of psychiatry. Depression is, as Seligman (1973) observed, both 'familiar and mysterious'. These experiences may overlap to form a continuum of affective experience: extending from the tinges of sadness felt by anyone confronting unhappy events or memories to the life-threatening forms of morbid depression, which can be associated not only with suicide but with child neglect and abuse. The severity of more extreme forms

---

*Two valuable insights into the 'business of living and dying' are provided by Rosemary and Victor Zorza's account of the protracted death of their daughter from cancer, *A Way to Die: The Story of Jane Zorza* (1980), London, Andre Deutsch, and Gollwitzer, H., Kuhn, K. and Schneider, R. (1974) *Dying We Live: Letters Written by Prisoners in Germany on the Eve of Execution*. Glasgow, Fontana/Collins.

of depression, coupled with the helplessness of the sufferer, are the commonest indications for treatment.

The depression considered in this book would be classified as **primary**: the emotional disturbance is the central problem. A range of **secondary** depressions also exists. In these cases the emotional disturbance is a function of another disorder. Some neurological disorders and brain diseases show an associated depression: specific forms of epilepsy, Huntington's chorea, Parkinson's disease, muscular dystrophy and cerebellar atrophy. Some endocrine disorders can also be complicated by depression: most frequently this involves the thyroid gland, less often the parathyroid or in diabetes. Depression can also be a side effect of certain drugs, such as steroids, phenothiazines and butyrophenones. When these drugs are discontinued the depression disappears.

THE CREATION OF AFFECTIVE DISORDER

A disturbance of disposition

Severe depression appears to be as old as humankind itself. Hippocrates of Cos (c.460–c.377 BC) appears to have been the first to recognize depression, which he called *melancholia*. He believed that madness involved a 'corruption of the brain'. Within the brain arose 'our pleasures, joys laughter and jests, as well as our sorrows, pains, grief and tears'. When the brain was 'moistened' by black (*melan*) bile (*choler*), melancholy was the result. He also described a quite distinct emotional state which he called *mainesthai*: this 'madness' we know now as mania (Flew 1964). By the second century AD the Greek physician Aretaeus of Cappadocia was suggesting an explicit relationship between melancholy and the apparently opposite emotional state of mania. These roots lead directly to the twentieth century when these primitive yet valuable notions of depression formed the basis of what we now call 'affective disorder'.

The term **affect** derives from the Latin word for 'disposition' and is used to suggest a person's mood or inner feelings at any given moment. Logically, states of anxiety should be included in this classification, but historically it has been confined to extreme forms of sadness (depression) or happiness (mania).

The semeiology, or description by symptomatology, of affective disorder has long been seen as the Achilles heel of scientific psychiatry (Berrios 1985). Finding a common language to describe 'affectivity', as distinct from disorders of thinking or behaviour, has bedevilled psychiatrists ever since Kraepelin began this task almost a century ago*. We are aware of our emotions, we can describe them through use of our cognitive (thinking) processes and we are aware of how emotions are interconnected with our actions. These observations, however, do not take us far in clarifying exactly what feelings are, never mind in establishing the 'seat of the emotions'. Emotion means literally 'the movement of the mind'. The traditional assumption was that the mind was passive and was only aroused by some activating agent: the result being affection or passion. This ties in with the view that feelings play only a secondary role in the definition of human nature, an idea which dates back almost to the Ancient Greeks. Since at least the nineteenth century it has been argued that 'thinking' is the principal arousing agent, at least in the production of disturbance of affect. Gaining consensus on this is, however, fraught with difficulty, not least because of the vagueness of the term itself. We take for granted the complexity of the word 'feeling': a wide and highly abstract family of statements about subjective experience which includes not only mood but sentiment, passion, emotion and propensity*. Where affective disorder is concerned, feelings are defined usually in a negative manner: feelings are whatever thought and behaviour are not (Berrios 1985). The uncertainty over what exactly feelings are results in our continued emphasis upon 'disturbance of thought or behaviour', in our efforts to explain affective disorder.

The birth of the blues

Depression occupies a special place in the history of mental disorder since it can be traced back to the earliest written records of humankind. Most ancient myths and numerous biblical stories describe characters who might today be classed as depressives. Job, the Jewish patriarch, suffered cruelly but interpreted this as a divine test; one which he translated into the 'testament' of his faith. Job's 'comforters' serve also as an early illustration of the futility of 'therapy': Job's spontaneous 'cure' owed no direct debt to his comforters, and may illustrate the serendipitous nature of remission. This list of illustrious melancholic

---

* Other significant figures were Bleuler (1906), Chaslin (1912) and Ribot (1897): see Berrios (1985).
* Much of our present-day consideration of this aspect of 'mental life' stems from William James' article 'What is an emotion?'. In this, James challenged the conventional wisdom, which assumed that emotions created some outward expression, such as facial expression. He argued instead that 'our feeling of the (bodily) changes as they occur *is* the emotion'. Gregory, R.L. (ed.) (1987) *The Oxford Companion to the Mind*. Oxford, Oxford University Press, pp219–20.

sufferers continues with the second Roman emperor, Tiberius Caesar; Louis XI of France; Abraham Lincoln; and Winston Churchill, among many others. Churchill referred to his depression as a 'black dog', a thinly veiled reference to the fearful presence of melancholia which is steeped in folklore*.

Hippocrates' description of the 'melancholic' personality suggests an even older history. In the 25 centuries since Hippocrates coined the term 'melancholia', descriptions of the 'symptoms' of affective disorder have remained almost constant (Zilboorg 1941). Indeed, depression has often been viewed as the most singular manifestation of insanity. This was true at the time of the Renaissance, and persevered until the seventeenth century when all forms of psychological distress were described as 'melancholy'. By the eighteenth century, 'spleen' was identified as both the disease and the organ responsible for the disorder. Only with Kraepelin did we begin to describe the syndrome which we know today as affective disorder. Kraepelin was assisted greatly, however, by his eighteenth and nineteenth century predecessors, whose combined efforts brought the 'demonic' Middle Ages to a 'scientific' end. Kraepelin's main contribution was to impose a sense of order on colleagues who were 'floundering helplessly around in a morass of symptoms for which they were unable to find any common denominators' (Braceland 1957). The 'age of enlightenment' which paralleled the scientific revolution of the seventeenth and eighteenth centuries had begun to look upon mental illness as a function of physiological disturbance, rather than demonic possession. Kraepelin, through his resolute pursuit of the scientific method of medicine, paved the way for the development of the concepts of depression which we know today.

More recent descriptions

Affective disorder is the universal modern label for a class of disorders where mood disturbance is both prominent and fundamental. Where this disturbance is severe it is often described as an affective *psychosis* (Kendell 1983b), the equivalent of Kraepelin's original term 'manic depressive psychosis' (Kraepelin 1921). The prominent feature of any affective disorder is a phasic change in vitality: psychologically, both thinking and emotion are flattened; physically, the person loses natural 'drives' for food and sex. In mania, these features are reversed with the

---

*The reference to the 'black dog' is probably related to the 'fiend' still dreaded in many country places. The term 'dog' has, historically, a fearful connotation. Shakespeare used a similar reference in *Julius Caesar* (iii, 1) to describe the horrors of war: 'let slip the dogs of war'.

person showing an increased activity, heightened mood (elation) and the acceleration of cognitive function (such as 'flight of ideas').

Although much debate surrounds the explanation of the causes of depression, there is general agreement on the common signs and symptoms. The person complains of or exhibits:

- sadness or depressed mood;
- weight loss and poor appetite, or weight gain and increased appetite;
- sleep disturbance, especially difficulty in falling asleep, not return-ing to sleep after wakening during the night, early morning waken-ing, and, in some cases, a desire to sleep a great deal;
- change in activity, becoming either lethargic or agitated;
- loss of interest and enjoyment of usual activities (**anhedonia**)
- loss of energy and experience of fatigue;
- negative self-concept; self-reproachfulness, feelings of worthlessness and guilt;
- difficulties in thinking, decision-making or concentration;
- recurrent thoughts of death or suicide (Shaw *et al.* 1982).

Despite their desperate nature we should not forget that recovery from affective disorder is, almost always, complete; no matter how long it may last or how often it recurs. Unlike other major mental disorders, such as schizophrenia, sufferers do not decline in function or suffer lasting defects. Distinctions between 'natural' and 'clinical' forms of depression can be made on the basis of how the sufferer deals with the experience. The melancholy of a natural depression may stem from some unpleasant life event. The psychological pain eases with time, although in some cases this may be a very long time indeed. The sufferer from a natural depression is often left a legacy of understand-ing or psychological growth. The person feels 'more of a person' by virtue of the experience. More pathological forms of depression may involve a similar experience of sadness: this may, however, appear to be an exaggerated response to the precipitating event. The disruption of the sufferer's life may pass, only to recur fitfully, each recurrence re-creating, perhaps even intensifying, the pain of the first experience*.

The extremes of emotion: manic depression

Although their reported 'symptoms' have remained unchanged for 25 centuries, theoretical views of depression have changed repeatedly,

---

*Some psychoanalysts distinguish **anaclitic** depressions, which involve passive, depen-dent, immature relationships from **object-loss** depressions, which are characterized by retardation, inhibition and self-blame. Gibson, R.W. (1967) *Crosscurrents in Psychiatry and Psychoanalysis*. Philadelphia, J.B. Lippincott Co., p26.

perhaps inconsequentially. Such changes may say more about the theorizer than the presentation of the patient (Zilboorg 1944). The relationship between the extremes of sadness and happiness, and the way in which some appeared to swing from one to the other, has long been of interest. Falret first distinguished between melancholia and 'episodic' depression, when he coined the term *folie circulaire*, making the important parallel observations that the disorder appeared to run in families and most affected women. Kraepelin extended the 'scientific' view of mental disorder by distinguishing between dementia praecox, later termed schizophrenia, and manic depressive insanity: this latter term included all fluctuations of mood, as well as *folie circulaire*, melancholic and manic states – whether occurring only once or repeatedly (Braceland 1957). Although such a diffuse classification now appears reckless, Kraepelin's intention was to argue that all psychiatric disorders had an (as yet) unidentified organic basis and, like other physical diseases, would follow a predictable course. The distinction between manic depressive psychosis and dementia praecox (schizophrenia), in terms of the effects on the functioning of the person, was a prime example of this model in practice. Kraepelin saw manic depressive psychosis as unrelated to the sufferer's environment and life style; the cause was rooted firmly in heredity, constitution or metabolism. Similar expositions of faith in a unicausal 'medical model' persist to the present day.

Endogenous and exogenous depression

Kraepelin's concept of psychiatric illness as a mental equivalent of physical disease was rejected by some of his contemporaries. Adolf Meyer was dissatisfied, specifically, with the notion that depression arose from some 'unidentified' physical cause. He suggested instead that an interaction existed between some precipitating factor or life event, and the constitutional make-up of the individual. This conflict of opinion perseveres almost to the present day. Traditionally, some depressions have been described as 'reactive' or **exogenous** stemming from an apparent aversive external life event. Where such an environmental 'trigger' was not so obvious, the term **endogenous**, or arising from within, was used. Although the distinction between endogenous and exogenous was popularized by Kraepelin, the term may originate from Bonhoeffer's description of diseases of the brain caused by external toxins (Arieti and Bemporad 1980). Arieti has suggested that American psychiatry overemphasized the concept of reaction in depression, neglecting to acknowledge Meyer's emphasis upon the hypothetical defect within an individual, which might be stimulated by environmental factors.

Meyer's view of the person as a psychobiological whole is the significant ancestor of today's holistic movement. Working with his wife, who was America's first psychiatric social worker, Meyer argued that psychiatric illnesses such as depression were responses to life problems, determined to different degrees by genetics, the person's physical constitution and the social situation in which the person lived*. His work with Clifford Beers, an ex-patient, led to the creation of the mental hygiene movement, the antecedent of our contemporary primary care, preventive and advocacy programmes. Meyer's psychobiological model has special relevance to depression but, as I shall discuss shortly, has been adapted to form the basis for an alternative medical model, of relevance to all forms of 'illness', whether physical or mental. Increasingly, theorists have urged the abandonment of the term 'endogenous', suggesting, as it does, that some depressions are free from environmental influence.

Binary and unitary theory

Although various depression classifications exist, the commonly held view is that there is little to choose between them (Kendell 1976). The Research Diagnostic Criteria (RDC) was developed as a system for classifying nine distinct depressive states, the most important being **unipolar** and **bipolar** major depressive disorder, and **endogenous** major depressive disorder*. This system splits Kraepelin's 'manic depressive insanity' into two categories of recurrent mood disturbance: either unipolar or bipolar. When recurrent depression or mania only is evident, the disorder is classed as unipolar. Where depression and mania alternate, the term 'bipolar' is used. Although this convention is commonly accepted it has been argued that almost one half of people diagnosed as unipolar will become bipolar in subsequent episodes

---

*Meyer emphasized that a depressive reaction was just that: a **reaction** to something. The aetiology of depression involved, in his view, a constitutional make-up (predisposition) and a precipitating factor. He believed that too much emphasis was placed upon heredity and constitutional factors, to the virtual exclusion of the acknowledgement of external influences. His interest in the precipitating factors was reinforced by his belief that this alone could help us learn how to 'strengthen the person that he may become resistive'. Meyer, A. (1908) The role of mental factors in psychiatry. *American Journal of Insanity*, **65**, p39.

*The American Psychiatric Association's *Diagnostic and Statistical Manual* (DSM IIIR) has nine classifications of depression. These are heavily influenced by the RDC – Research Diagnostic Criteria. Spitzer, R.L., Endicott, J. and Robins, E. (1978) *Research Diagnostic Criteria for a Selected Group of Functional Disorders* (3rd edition). New York, New York State Psychiatric Institute.

(Perris 1966), suggesting that this is an as yet incomplete classification system (Shaw *et al*. 1982). Many British psychiatrists, aware of such an eventuality, often classify all forms of recurrent and severe depression as manic depressive psychosis (Naylor 1987).

The unipolar/bipolar distinction is only one of the dichotomous classification systems used to date. Others have included the distinction between primary and secondary; reactive (exogenous) and endogenous; and psychotic and neurotic depressions. One would expect all these diagnoses to have some prognostic power, in keeping with other medical diagnoses, accurately forecasting the course of the disorder. Although some prediction of the course and outcome of the illness is possible, these systems appear to be most useful as a means for classifying symptoms and for testing their hypothetical cause. These dichotomous classifications stem from Kraepelin's original description of two depressive types: manic depressive psychosis and psychogenic depression. The distinction between 'psychotic' and 'neurotic' depressions evolved in American psychiatry (Levitt *et al*. 1983). In Britain, Aubrey Lewis advanced the argument that such dichotomous distinctions represented no more than the extremes of a continuum of severity of depressive illness. In his view, 'depression' was a single disorder which ranged from very severe forms (such as manic depressive psychosis) at one extreme to milder forms of 'dysphoria' at the other.

The binary classification was used to suggest that some forms of depression were wholly biologically based and that others had psychological roots. In effect, some depressions were thought to result from a straightforward disturbance within the person, over which she had no control. Other depressions were linked to 'life events', a euphemism for virtually anything other than 'internal' events. Recent studies have suggested, however, that Lewis' view of the distinction between situational, or **reactive**, depression and the endogenous variety is invalid (Ariskal 1979; Garvet *et al*. 1984). Increasingly, the term major depressive disorder is used where the depression is both severe and recurrent. Such depressions may arise either from endogenous or exogenous causes. Even the binary distinction between bipolar and unipolar is considered suspect as, rather than being seen as different disorders, they may represent mild and severe forms of the same disorder. Although the two disorders may have a common aetiology, each might be triggered by different sources: these might be either environmental or genetic factors (Revely and Murray 1984).

How common is affective disorder?

Although depression has been recognized for thousands of years and studied scientifically for centuries, no single form of classification is universally accepted. The various classifications alluded to above all define and measure slightly different 'things'. Studies of the prevalence rates for depression provide only a vague picture, often because different studies employ different forms of classification. American studies have reported, for example, rates of depression of approximately 3% and 5% for men and women respectively (Weissman and Myers 1978). A British study described almost 5% for men and 9% for women (Bebbington *et al.* 1981), whereas in Australia the rates have been much lower – around 2.5% and 6.5% (Henderson *et al.* 1979). Despite these differences one picture is consistent: women sufferers from depression greatly outnumber men*. The prevalence rates also vary between subpopulations of the same community. Urban, working-class women, with children at home, have 2–3 times the expected rates of depressive episodes, with up to 25% higher annual prevalence rates in some groups (Taylor and Taylor 1989).

A different appreciation of the scale of affective disorder can be obtained from hospital admission and re-admission rates. In Scotland, for example, affective psychosis (i.e. severe depressive disorder) accounted for 20% of all women and 11% of all men admitted to hospital in 1984. Of those being admitted for the first time, almost 13% were women and less than 8% were men; for re-admissions the proportions were 24% and 12% respectively (Information Services Division 1986). It should not be forgotten, however, that it is acknowledged that women are more likely than men to report depressive experiences (Weissman *et al.* 1974) and that psychiatrists are more likely to diagnose depression in women than in men (Chesler 1972).

Some comunity-based studies add further weight to the argument that severe depression is the most significant form of psychiatric disturbance. One such study found that more than 60% of people showing severe forms of emotional distress fulfilled the criteria necessary for a psychiatric diagnosis. Of these, 4% were eligible for a diagnosis of mild depression and 22% for various diagnoses such as anxiety, phobia, panic, somatization or drug abuse. Thirty-five per cent were, however, eligible for a diagnosis of major depression (Boyd *et al.* 1982). Taken as a whole, these figures demonstrate the awesome status of severe depression. In addition to its frequency, depression ranks close behind coronary artery disease, hypertension and chronic bronchitis as a major cause of serious morbidity. As many as 6000 people commit suicide each year, as a function of depression. These figures do not include the significant population of 'sufferers' who are not diagnosed. Increas-

---

*Generally speaking, women sufferers from depressive disorders outnumber men 2:1. One specific exception exists in manic depressive psychosis, where the male/female distribution is almost equivalent.

ingly, it is recognized that people presenting various problems involving physiological malaise with no detectable physical cause may be suffering from depression (Hiday 1980). The scale of the psychiatric 'common cold' in the late twentieth century suggests that the Western world may have entered yet another Age of Melancholy (Jablensky 1987).

Clinically depressed or simply distressed?

Studies of the extent of depression in the normal population are confused, however, by the uncertainty over the dividing line between 'normal' unhappiness and 'pathological' misery. The implication of this dilemma has been described clearly by two major figures in the field:

> without some diagnostic criteria for who is 'in' or 'out' of a diagnostic class, such as depression, it is not possible to decide whether a given person or group of persons are clinically depressed as distinct from unhappy and discontented because of social deprivation or the frustration of their personal wishes.
>
> (Weissman and Klerman 1980)

Mirowsky and Ross (1989) are representative of the significant lobby of dissenters unhappy with the rigidity of psychiatric diagnosis. They acknowledge that:

> a person who feels bad is real, the person's feelings are real, the psychiatrist's act of classifying the patient's problems is real, the consequences of the psychiatrist's act of classifying are real. However, the entity, 'diagnostic depression', is *not* real. It is a linguistic pigeonhole into which some cases are placed.   (p29)

One of Mirowsky and Ross's objections to psychiatric diagnosis is that all such classification systems mistake the shape of the pigeonhole for the shape of reality. In philosophy, this mistake is known as 'reification' or the fallacy of misplaced concreteness (Srole and Fischer 1980): treating an abstract idea as if it had material existence. Mirowsky and Ross make the very important observation that deciding whether someone is 'in or out' of a class, such as depression, discards very important information about similarities and differences between the person diagnosed and other people. Given two 'unhappy' people, one may be diagnosed as depressed, the other (who fails marginally to meet the depression 'cut off' criterion) is not. Despite having something in common (unhappiness), they are deemed to be quite different: 'depressed' and 'not depressed'. The classification is quite 'black and white'. Take two other people: one happy and fulfilled, the other miserable and demoralized. Neither meets the criteria for 'depression': they are therefore deemed to be similar – not clinically depressed. Mirowsky and Ross argue that the available diagnostic systems fail to acknowledge the similarities of the first two people, and the stark differences in the second example. Their alternative, to describe and measure 'distress', has the appeal of including as much information as possible, at the cost of discarding our long tradition of diagnostic classification. Maybe what needs to be discarded is our traditional reliance on the 'false dichotomies and fake certainties of language' (de Bono 1991).

An integrated view of severe depression

Traditional medical approaches to illness have led us to believe that a single cause should exist for any disorder, like depression. This view, the search for a **unicausal determinant**, stems from the influence of traditional physical sciences. It assumes that singular 'cause-and-effect' relationships can be identified for any set of circumstances. The notion that depression is influenced, at least in part, by internal, constitutional factors, whether induced genetically or by some other freak of organic functioning, is the oldest explanation. Although Hippocrates' concept of the four 'humours' now seems crude, our scientific models of depression are but a refinenment of his ideas, after 2000 years reflection, rather than a genuine alternative. The idea that depression might arise wholly from non-physical causes is a fairly recent concept, if one excludes the age-old concept of demonic possession.

Four important theories have developed in the past century, each of which has made a significant contribution to our understanding of 'how' depression might develop, and 'what' might be offered by way of treatment. These theoretical models might be seen as extending from the broadest consideration of the role of the environment to the narrowest interpretation of the workings of the brain.

Reinforcement theory suggested that people become 'dysphoric' as their level of positive reinforcement declined, complemented by a con-current increase in unpleasant 'life events'*. **Interpersonal** theory extended these ideas, focusing more specifically upon the role of 'disturbed' interpersonal relationships (Coyne 1976). **Cognitive** theory narrowed the focus further, implicating the 'thinking style' of the

---

*The most elegant example is to be found in Lewinsohn, P.M., Weinstein, M. and Shaw, D. (1969) Depression: A clinical research approach. In Rubin, R.D. and Franks, C.M. (eds.) *Advances in Behaviour Therapy*. New York, Academic Press; and also Lazarus, A.A. (1968) Learning theory and the treatment of depression. *Behaviour Research and Therapy*, **6**, pp83–9.

sufferer: negative cognitive structures allegedly distorted the person's experience, resulting in negative consequences for mood (Beck 1967). **Biochemical** theories have focused on changes occurring in the neuro-transmitter system which subserves emotionality, sleep regulation and motor activity. According to the biogenic amine hypothesis, depression arises from a functional deficit in one or more of the neurotransmitter amines at critical synapses in the central nervous system (Bunney and Davis 1965; Schildkraut 1965).

Each of these theoretical models has a corresponding 'therapeutic' model: behavioural therapies aim to increase pleasurable events (Lewinsohn 1974); interpersonal therapy aims to develop more positive interactions (Klerman and Weissman 1982); various cognitive therapies aim to establish more constructive styles of thinking (Ellis and Harper 1961); and drug therapy aims to resolve the hypothetical neurotrans-mitter deficit (Paykel 1982).

The past two decades have witnessed a proliferation of theoretical model-making in depression, these four groups representing the major schools of thought. Each school claims to have identified a single causative agent which might account for the onset of a depressive episode. It may be that each of these models is correct. A wide range of factors might contribute to a depressive episode, from the widest aspects of a person's relationship with the environment to the specific function of neurotransmitters. The search for the Fundamental Truth, which might explain the origins of all depressive experiences, may be a futile exercise. The answer may well be: 'there are many answers!'. In Chapter 3, I shall consider a more flexible way of examining the possible causes of depression: an integrated model which takes account of the possible effects of a variety of influences. This alternative to the search for a single-cause model has been hailed as the modern successor to the age-old medical model (Engel 1977; Gordon 1990). I shall examine it from a more practical viewpoint, in an effort to find a more effective way of living with the disabling effects of severe de-pression. Whatever we wish to call It, however we wish to describe It, no matter how often we try to dismiss It, one inescapable fact remains – depression 'is'. Our task would appear to be to respond construc-tively. Where does our perception of depression, either as sufferers or observers, lead us 'to'? (de Bono 1991).

The psychiatric description of depression, witnessed through the ever-increasing development of classification systems, represents the use of language to establish the 'truth' of depression. Using everyday words to which we attach special, technical meanings, we hope to depict, and by some magic or sleight-of-hand, reveal the true meaning of depression. We should not forget the other possibility: that by increasingly clever use of language we have lost sight of the fact that we are still treating an abstract idea (depression) *as if* it had a material presence. We should not forget, either, that the English language has very limited powers of expression, especially when it comes to describing human perception. The language itself may impose restrictions on our already restricted perception of the sufferer's experience. The experience of depression may be a more complex affair than the mere diagnosis of depression, the illness. The human experience of depression may be the 'sum' that is greater than all of the 'parts' of the experience. Depression may be the Thing which transcends the 'disorder'.

I began this chapter by considering what depression might mean for the sufferer. The history of the past 2500 years indicates that it is very difficult to gain any kind of consensus on the naturalistic description of affective disorder. Such a consensus is possible. We, the observers, have the capacity to agree upon what we have observed. Whether that which we have observed is anywhere near the true meaning of the experience of depression is, however, a very moot point. We may only have established what depression means for us, the non-depressed. This may represent the limitations of language as a vehicle for unearthing 'the truth'. Some truths may be impervious to the analytical tool of even our finest, most rigorous and technical language. Those who would seek to help the sufferer from severe depression may find the armour of humility more useful than the sword of true knowledge.

REFERENCES

Alloy, L.B. and Abramson L.Y. (1979) Judgement of contingency in depressed and non-depressed students; sadder but wiser. *Journal of Experimental Psychology*, **108**(4), 441–85.

Altschul, A.T. (1985) There won't be a next time. In Rippere, V. and Williams, R. (eds.) *Wounded Healers: Mental Health Workers' Experiences of Depression*. Chichester, John Wiley.

Arieti, S. and Bemporad, J. (1980) *Severe and Mild Depression: The Psychotherapeutic Approach* (Chapter 17). London, Tavistock.

Ariskal, H.S. (1979) A biobehavioural approach to depression. In Depue, R.A. (ed.) *The Psychology of the Depressive Disorders*. New York, Academic Press.

Bebbington, P.E., Hurry, J., Tennant, N., Sturt, E. and Wing, J.K. (1981) Epidemiology of mental disorders in Camberwell. *Psychological Medicine*, **11**, pp561–79.

Beck, A.T. (1967) *Depression: Clinical, Experimental and Theoretical Aspects*. New York, Harper and Row.

Berrios, G.E. (1985) The psychopathology of affectivity; conceptual and historical aspects. *Psychological Medicine*, **15**, pp745–58.

de Bono, E. (1991) *I Am Right – You Are Wrong: From this to the new renaissance; From rock logic to water logic*. Harmondsworth, Penguin.

Boyd, J.H., Weissman, M.M., Thompson, D. and Myers, J.K. (1982) Screening for depression in a community sample; understanding the discrepancies between depressive symptoms and diagnostic scales. *Archives of General Psychiatry*, **30**, pp771–8.

Braceland, F.J. (1957) Kraepelin; his system and his influence. *American Journal of Psychiatry*, **114**, p871.

Brookner, A. (1991) Sloughing off despond. *The Observer*, 3rd March.

Bunney, W.E. and Davis, J.M. (1965) Norepinephrine in depressed reactions. *Archives of General Psychiatry*, **13**, pp483–94.

Chesler, P. (1972) *Women and Madness*. New York, Doubleday.

Coyne, J.C. (1976) Toward an interactional description of depression. *Psychiatry*, **39**, pp28–40.

Cumberledge, G. (1952) *Poems of Gerard Manley Hopkins* (3rd edition). London, Oxford University Press.

Ellis, A., and Harper, R.A. (1961) *A Guide to Rational Living*. Hollywood, Wilshire.

Engel, G.L. (1977) The need for a new medical model; the challenge for biomedicine. *Science*, **196**, pp129–36.

Flew, A. (1964) *Body, Mind and Death*. Problems of Philosophy series. New York, Macmillan.

Garvet, M.J., Tollefson, G.D., Mungas, D. and Hoffman, N. (1984) Is the distinction between situational and non-situational primary depression valid? *Comprehensive Psychiatry*, **25**(3), pp372–5.

Gordon, J.S. (1990) Holistic medicine and mental health practice; toward a new synthesis. *American Journal of Orthopsychiatry*, **60**(3), pp357–70.

Hall, C.S. and Lind, R.E. (1970) *Dreams, Life and Literature; A Study of Franz Kafka*. Chapel Hill, University of North Carolina Press.

Henderson, S., Duncan-Jones, P., Byrne, D.G., Scott, R. and Adcock, S. (1979) Psychiatric disorders in Canberra; a standardized study of prevalence. *Acta Psychiatrica Scandinavica*, **60**, pp355–74.

Hiday, V.A. (1980) View from the front line; diagnosis and treatment of mental health problems among primary care physicians. *Social Psychiatry*, **15**, pp131–6.

Information Services Division (1986) *Scottish Health Statistics 1985*. Edinburgh, Common Services Agency for the Scottish Health Service.

Jablensky, A. (1987) Editorial: Prediction of the course and outcome of depression. *Psychological Medicine*, **17**, pp11–19.

James, W. (1981) *The Varieties of Religious Experience* (10th impression), pp158–9. Glasgow, Collins/Fount.

Kendell, R.E. (1976) The classification of depressions; a review of contemporary confusion. *British Journal of Psychiatry*, **129**, pp15–28.

Kendell, R.E. (1983a) Diagnosis and classification. In Kendell, R.E. and Zeally, A.K. (eds.) *Companion to Psychiatric Studies*. Edinburgh, Churchill Livingstone.

Kendell, R.E. (1983b) Affective psychoses. In Kendell, R.E. and Zeally, A.K. (eds.) as above.

Klerman, G.L. and Weissman, M.M. (1982) Interpersonal psychotherapy; theory and research. In Rush, A.J. (ed.) *Short-term Psychotherapies for Depression*. New York, Guilford Press.

Kraepelin, E. (1921) *Manic Depressive Insanity and Paranoia*. Edinburgh, Livingstone.

Levitt, E.E., Lubin, B. and Brooks, J.M. (1983) *Depression; Concepts, Controversies and Some New Facts* (2nd edition). Lawrence Erlbaum Assoc, London.

Lewinsohn, P.M. (1974) The behavioural study and treatment of depression. In Hersen, M., Eisler, R.M. and Miller, P.M. (eds.) *Progress in Behaviour Modification (Vol. 1)*. New York, Academic Press.

Loyola, St Ignatius. *Spiritual Exercises* (First week – 'Discernment of Spirits'). Cited in Cumberledge, G. (1952) above.

Menninger, K. (1963) *The Vital Balance; The Life Process in Mental Health and Illness*. New York, Viking.

Meyers, J. (1987) *Manic Power; Robert Lowell and His Circle*, p18. London, Macmillan.

Mirowsky, J. and Ross, C.E. (1989) *Social Causes of Psychological Distress*. New York, Aldine de Gruyter.

Moore, M.S. (1975) Some myths about 'mental illness'. *Archives of General Psychiatry*, **32**, pp1483–97.

Morrow, L. (1990) Essay. *Time*, September 17th, p104.

Naylor, G.J. (1987) Personal communication.

Paykel, E.S. (ed.) (1982) *The Handbook of Affective Disorders*. New York, Guilford Press.

Perris, C. (1966) A study of bipolar (manic depressive) and unipolar recurrent depressive psychoses. *Acta Psychiatrica Scandinavica*, Supp. 194.

Raphael, B. (1986) *When Disaster Strikes; A Handbook for the Caring Professions*. London, Unwin Hyman.

Revely, A. and Murray, R.M. (1984) The genetic contribution to the functional psychoses. In Crown, S. (ed.) *Contemporary Psychiatry* (Chapter 2). London, Butterworths.

Ryle, G. (1949) *The Concept of Mind*. London, Hutchinson.

Sackheim, H. (1983) Self-deception, depression and self-esteem; the adaptive value of lying to oneself. In Masling, J. (ed.) *Empirical Studies of Psychoanalytic Theory*. Hillsdale, New Jersey, Lawrence Erlbaum Assoc.

Salter, D. (1990) Lockerbie and after; an examination of the myths and metaphors of managers and workers in a disaster. *Changes*, **8**(4), pp311–21.

Schildkraut, J.J. (1965) The catecholamine hypothesis of affective disorders; a review of supporting evidence. *American Journal of Psychiatry*, **122**, pp509–22.

Schmieder, A. (1958) Waiting for Beckett. *Chelsea Review*, Autumn.

Seligman, M.E.P. (1973) Fall into helplessness. *Psychology Today*, **7**, pp43–8.

Shaw, D.M., Kellam, A.M.P. and Mottram, R.F. (1982) *Brain Sciences in Psychiatry*. London, Butterworths.

Sontag, S. (1967) *Against Interpretation and Other Essays*. London, Eyre and Spottiswood.

Sontag, S. (1977) *Illness as Metaphor*. New York, Farrar, Strauss and Giroux.

Srole, L. and Fischer, A.K. (1980) 'To the Editor.' *Archives of General Psychiatry*, **37**, pp1424–6.

Styron, W. (1991) *Darkness Visible*. London, Jonathan Cape.

Szasz, T. (1987) *Insanity; The Idea and Its Consequences*. New York, John Wiley.

Taylor, J. and Taylor, D. (1989) *Mental Health in the 1990s; From Custody to Care?* (p8). London, Office of Health Economics.

Taylor, P. (1960) *The Notebooks of Leonardo da Vinci*. New York, American Library.

Weissman, M.M. and Klerman, G.L. (1980) 'In reply.' *Archives of General Psychiatry*, **39**, pp1423–4.

Weissman, M.M., Klerman, G.L. and Paykel, E.S. (1974) Treatment effects on the social adjustment of depressed outpatients. *Archives of General Psychiatry*, **30**, pp771–8.

Weissman, M.M. and Myers, J.K. (1978) Rates and risks of depressive symptoms in a US urban community. *Acta Psychiatrica Scandinavica*, **57**, pp219–31.

Zilboorg, G. (1941) *A History of Medical Psychology*. New York, W.W. Norton & Co.

Zilboorg, G. (1944) Manic depressive psychoses. In Lorand, S. (ed.) *Psychoanalysis Today*. New York, International Universities Press.

Chapter 2

Fragile insights:
some psychological views
of depression

By these gates entering, which cloudy show,
I from the touching lustful world did go;
And, faring on – need none, the way to ask –
Saw in a water, there, my face sans mask . . .
Let not your prophets and diviners deceive you . . .

(De La Mare 1984)

It was noted in Chapter 1 that an acceptable definition of depression remains elusive. A range of depressive disorders exist: the extent to which they belong to the same 'family tree' continues to provoke dispute*. Most people with serious depression are treated by a medical practitioner supported, to varying degrees, by a range of other health care professionals. The layperson can be excused for assuming, therefore, that all forms of mood disturbance represent a depressive condition equivalent to physical forms of illness: possessing distinct diagnostic characteristics; needing, and responding to, medical intervention.

Increasingly, the concept that depression can be explained causally in terms of the influence of any single factor is called into question. In Chapter 3 the process by which these 'psychosocial' factors interact with the physical dimension of the person herself will be discussed further*. In this chapter, some of the psychological and social dimen-

---

*For a discussion of the proliferation of definitions of depression, see Kendell, R.E. (1976) The classification of depressions: a review of contemporary confusion. *British Journal of Psychiatry*, **129**, pp15–28.
*The current interest in 'biopsychosocial' models of mental health has been influenced greatly by Engel's call for an alternative to the traditional medical model; Engel, G.L. (1977) The need for a new medical model: a challenge for biomedicine. *Science*, **196**, pp129–36. For a more 'holistic' interpretation, see Gordon, J.S. (1990) Holistic medicine and mental health practice: toward a new synthesis. *American Journal of Orthopsychiatry*, **60**(3), pp357–70.

sions of depression will be considered, albeit briefly. I acknowledge that the mere act of observing depression from this psychosocial perspective represents a prejudiced viewpoint. Depression, in common with all other experiences, can be viewed from a number of perspectives. The 'seven hills of Rome' provide a metaphor for the disagreements and distinctions which might exist between various models of depression. It could be said that a view of Rome is possible from any of the hills, indeed that any one offers the 'best' view. The ultimate counterclaim lies in the view that is gained from the very 'heart' of the city: from the very experience of being within its streets. In choosing to look at depression from a specific 'psychosocial' angle, I am aware that this offers no better view than any other angle: it is, however, the view which I can reach and which affords me, a blinkered professional, some sight of the person who is depressed.

Cause and effect – curing the myopic tradition

The predominant focus of the scientific investigation of depression has been upon explaining this emotional disorder as a function of some underlying physical state. This sustained interest has spawned numerous theories which purport to explain depression in terms of: some form of genetic transmission, cerebral amine metabolism, or the effects of endocrine function or electrolyte metabolism*. Despite these not inconsiderable advances on the 'biophysical' front, the theoretical jigsaw of the causation of many forms of depression remains incomplete. The explanation of distressing or disturbing behaviour as a form of disease began with the nineteenth century discoveries of pathology and bacteriology. The acceleration of interest in this form of explanation reached its zenith in the 1970s when, as Rose, Lewontin and Kamin (1988) observed:

> . . . biological determinist arguments have increasingly been heard insisting that the explanation for the symptoms of all social ills, from violence on the streets through the poor education of children to the expressed feelings of the meaninglessness of middle-aged housewives, must be located in the brain dysfunction of the individual concerned.

The work of scientists intent upon 'reducing' the explanation of a complex phenomenon such as severe depression to the effect of some singular physical event seems short-sighted, to say the least. Scientific

---

*For a useful discussion see Shaw, D.M., Kellam, A.M.P. and Mottram, R.F. (1982) *Brain Sciences in Psychiatry* (Chapter 15). London, Butterworths.

enquiry has long cherished the ambition of explaining all phenomena in the most elegant, or simple, terms, ever since William of Occam proposed his 'principle of parsimony'. The principle, popularly known as Occam's Razor, prompted the British psychologist Don Bannister to observe that it could be used to shave off excess explanations, but could also 'cut the throat' of any self-respecting theory.

The most extreme form of depressive disorder, manic depressive psychosis, might serve as a good example of the inadequacy of 'reductionist' explanations. This disorder has long been assumed to result from genetic transmission producing a distinct biochemical 'fault'. Studies of identical twins who suffered from manic depressive psychosis have noted, however, that some twins have been unipolar, experiencing only depressive *or* manic episodes, whilst the others were bipolar, exposed to *both* manic and depressed episodes. Where twins are monozygotic, the result of fertilization of a single ovum by a single sperm, the two 'individuals' are genetically identical, always of the same sex and typically of strikingly similar appearance. It might be expected, therefore, that 100% concordance would exist between the twins, if manic depression is a 'genetically transmitted' disorder. The fact that this has not been demonstrated has led some authorities to conclude that environmental influences of one kind or another must play a part in the causation of severe depressive disorders (Bertleson *et al.* 1977). In Kendell's (1983) view, environmental factors must play some part, however small:

> . . . if they did not the concordance between monozygous twins would be close to 100% and the illness would develop at a similar age, and pursue a similar course in both.

The idea that the 'environment' acts upon people, who may or may not possess some kind of 'vulnerability', to produce a variety of forms of mental disorder derives from Meyer's work, as noted in Chapter 1. The specific role of the environment in the 'creation' of depression, however, has been recognized at least since Freud's publication of *Mourning and Melancholia* in 1917 (Freud 1957). In Freud's view children who lost a parent at an early age felt guilty for surviving the deceased, for not having prevented the death, and even for believing that the death was somehow 'wished'. It is now thought unlikely that any one event, however, traumatic, can effect depression in later life. If such events have any effect it is likely to be weak and not restricted to depression. The effect of other 'loss states', such as childbirth where the fetus breaks its special link with the mother, and hysterectomy where the capacity to bear children is lost, have also been studied.

However, if these explain anything it can only be how certain kinds of depression occur in some women.

Many conceptual models exist within psychological theory, each of which claims to explain the cause of depression, and which serve as the bases for various schools of psychotherapy. Although all deal with one form of experience or another, over the past 30 years increasing attention has been paid to the joint processes of 'perception' and 'judgement' as correlates of depressed mood*. More recently, studies have focused upon the person's perception of events as significant 'stressors', or potential threats to psychological homoeostasis or equilibrium. An eclectic, interactional, psychotherapeutic model has emerged from this emphasis which, given its focus upon the relationship between thinking and mood, can reasonably be called 'cognitive'*.

Cogito ergo sum

Aaron Beck was one of the first modern writers to challenge the view that depression involved only emotional elements. He rejected, specifically, the idea that any impairment of thinking resulted from affective disturbance (Beck 1963). Psychological studies had found no evidence of abnormalities in cognitive processes when formal psychometric tests were applied to depressed people. It was assumed, therefore, that thinking style played no part in the genesis of depression (Schafer 1948).

Several cognitive models have been described in the past 20 years, each postulating a relationship between specific cognitions and depressed affect. The theories summarized here represent distinct sociological, psychological and psychiatric viewpoints. Each suggests that emotional reactions are mediated, or brought about, at least in part, by thought – a view which has much in keeping with the much older tenets of Stoic philosophy*. Despite this common theme, however,

---

* For a seminal paper in this respect, see Beck, A.T. and Hurvich, M. (1959) Psychological correlates of depression. *Psychosomatic Medicine*, **21**, p50.

* The proper meaning of the term **cognition** is the use or handling of knowledge: such 'knowledge' being the 'sense' we make of the information supplied by our senses. In this 'sense', we construct 'knowledge' using sensory information from both present and past, as in memories. These can be manipulated to produce 'knowledge' of events which have not occurred, as in fantasies. The term derives from the Latin *cognoscere*, to learn. Gregory has suggested that it may also be related to *gnomon*, the shadow-casting rod of a sundial, which measures the heavens from shadows. Gregory, R.L. (ed.) (1987) *The Oxford Companion to the Mind*. Oxford, Oxford University Press.

* For a careful consideration of the debt owed to Aristotle by contemporary 'cognitivists', and a critique of the philosophical underpinnings of cognitive therapy, see Walters, P. (1990) Between existence and construction: A comparison of the 'models of man' of Aristotle and Beck. *Nexus 1990*, **1**(2), pp31–40.

each model expresses differences which influence its practical application in a psychotherapeutic context.

The social model

Depression has long been associated with the concept of loss (Freud
1957; Bowlby 1985). A relationship between certain losses (such as
death of a parent, divorce or child leaving home) and the onset of
depression has been observed by a number of researchers. Brown
and Harris' (1978) sociological study of women in a London borough,
whom they described as suffering from various kinds of depression,
extended this loss concept by identifying the role of 'social status' as
one determinant of the women's reaction to such critical life events. By
rating the 'contextual threat' of events, and the degree of long-term
difficulty, Brown and Harris showed that chronic life problems, such as
bad housing and problems with in-laws, represented a special kind of
life event which was more common in 'depressives' than in other 'non-
depressed' people they studied. They also identified four **vulnerability
factors** which, although not direct causes of depression, heightened
the risk where critical life events were evident. These factors were:

- the early loss of mother;
- involvement in the care of young children;
- absence of a confiding relationship;
- lack of a full or part-time job.

A subsequent attempt to replicate the London study in Canada confirmed the relationship between threatening life events and depression,
where a confiding relationship was absent, but failed to support the
role of social class, employment and parental status. To what extent
this reflects a cross-cultural difference is unclear.

The findings of the London study provided the basis for a cognitive
model of depression which Brown and Harris acknowledged was no
more than 'speculative'. In their view the patient's **appraisal** of her
world was of primary importance. Women in particular became demoralized when they could not fulfil the 'role identity' demanded by
the prevailing culture: when they could not behave in the manner
expected, by others or by themselves. The concept of the mother who
cannot cope assisted greatly in the escalation of prescriptions for tran-
quillizing drugs like diazepam (Valium) in the 1960s: these were popularly termed 'mother's little helper'. In Brown and Harris' view, when
women were obstructed, by severe or longstanding life problems, from
fulfilling their culturally appropriate 'plans of action', they were de-
prived of sources of reward or value. Brown and Harris saw this as

a symbolic loss, equivalent to that most commonly associated with Bowlby's ideas. It is clear, however, that their ideas have much in common with the reinforcement loss hypothesis used by some behaviourists to explain the onset of depression (Lewinsohn 1974).

In addition to the issue of 'appraisal', Brown and Harris also speculated about the role of the woman's perception of her control over her circumstances:

> . . . loss may be of *faith in one's ability* to attain an important and valued goal [emphasis added].   (Melges and Bowlby 1969)

When a woman could not conceive of ever restoring her source of value or self-esteem, they argued, she would experience a feeling of hopelessness, especially where memories of some previously unresolved event are re-activated. The vulnerability factors have the effect of lowering self-esteem: they generate a pessimism over the woman's ability to control her world. Brown and Harris speculated that low self-esteem would generalize this sense of hopelessness, leading to **denial**, in an attempt to suppress the painful emotions. Their inevitable release would take the form of depression.

Although critics of this model have noted the apparent conflict between the 'appraisal' and 'denial' of hopelessness (Bebbington 1985), empirical evidence for such co-existence has been offered by other researchers (Horowitz *et al.* 1980).

The psychological model

The concept of hopelessness noted by Brown and Harris had been addressed earlier by Seligman's 'learned helplessness' model. Using as his basis a series of experiments involving the administration of 'inescapable shocks' to dogs (Seligman and Maier 1967), Seligman developed the hypothesis that the depressed person fails to learn adaptive ways of dealing with painful events, learning 'helplessness' instead. He thought that if a person failed repeatedly to control her environment, as his dogs had failed to escape the painful electric shocks, she would construe herself as 'helpless', unable to alter a highly unsatisfactory state of affairs. Believing that her behaviour lacked meaning, she would become passive, expressing feelings of misery and hopelessness. The meaninglessness of the depressed person's existence, described so differently by the earlier existentialist literature*, was redefined by Seligman in a more direct sense: if her actions on the

---

*For a specific existentialist discussion of the nature of emotion, see Sartre, J.P. (1957) *Existentialism and Human Emotions* (trans. B. Frechtman and H.E. Barnes). Secaucus, New Jersey, Castle.

world failed to realize 'what she had intended', her behaviour was, essentially, *meaningless*.

Seligman first saw this model as highly specific, addressing only the person who was:

> . . . slow to initiate responses, believing himself to be powerless and hopeless, and [who] sees his future as bleak.
>
> (Seligman 1975, p81)

The model dealt with specific rather than generalized pessimism: 'specific to the effects of one's own actions (ibid, p86). The pessimism involved three deficits:

- failure to control events, resulting in a *motivational* deficit;
- erroneous expectations of repeated failure in the future, representing a *cognitive* deficit;
- the *emotional* deficit of depressed mood.

This model was criticized, perhaps appropriately, for its basis in animal experiments*. As a result, revised versions of 'learned helplessness' were developed*.

The reformulated model of Abramson and her colleagues is the most significant of these (Abramson *et al.* 1978). This model placed greater emphasis upon the concept of **attribution**. In their view, if someone fails to control some event in their life, they tend to ask why this is so. The answer determines how widespread and long-lasting will be the effect of this 'failure' on the person's self-esteem. By introducing the **locus of causality***, the reformulated model distinguished be-

---

*Two influential critics were Blaney, P.H. (1977) Contemporary theories of depression: critique and comparison. *Journal of Abnormal Psychology*, **86**, pp203–23; and Depue, R.A. and Monroe, S. (1978) Learned helplessness in the perspective of the depressive disorders: conceptual and definitional issues. *Journal of Abnormal Psychology*, **87**, pp3–20.

*For examples of the original reformulations, see Abramson, L.Y., Seligman, M.E.P. and Teasdale, J. (1978) Learned helplessness in humans: critique and reformulation. *Journal of Abnormal Psychology*, **87**, pp49–74; and Miller, I.W. and Norman, W.N. (1979) Learned helplessness in humans: a review and attribution theory model. *Psychological Bulletin*, **86**, pp93–118. The reformulated model has been further redefined as the **hopelessness** theory of depression; see Abramson, L.Y., Metalsky, G.I. and Alloy, L.B. (1988) The hopelessness theory of depression: does the research test the theory? In Abramson, L.Y. (ed.) *Social Cognition and Clinical Psychology: A Synthesis*. New York, Guilford Press; and Abramson, L.Y., Alloy, L.B. and Metalsky, G.I. (1988) The cognitive diathesis-stress theories of depression: toward an adequate test of the theories' validities. In Alloy L.B. (ed.) *Cognitive Processes in Depression*. New York, Guilford Press. For a summary of this as yet unidentified subtype of depression, see Alloy, L.B., Abramson, L.Y., Metalsky, G.I. and Armitage, S. (1988) The hopelessness theory of depression: attributional aspects. *British Journal of Clinical Psychology*, **27**, pp5–21.

*The term **causality** is essentially philosophical, referring to the 'perception' of causative events. Current interest derives from the work on the 'attribution of causality' of the American social psychologist, Fritz Heider (b. 1896). See, for example, Heider, F. (1946) Attitudes and cognitive organisations. *Journal of Psychology*, **21**, pp107–12.

tween the person's perception of the *task as impossible* and the perception of the *person (self) as incompetent*. If the person believes that nobody could have controlled the situation, a feeling of helplessness will ensue. If, however, the failure is attributed to some deficit within herself, she will feel incompetent, producing a lowering not only of mood but also of self-esteem.

Acknowledging the deficits of the original model, Abramson and her colleagues explained the pervasiveness and chronicity of depression by describing a number of dimensions of attribution. Helplessness will be pervasive and chronic, they argued, if the person attributes failure to stable factors, which are seen as unlikely to change across time, or to global factors which are seen to apply across a wide range of situations. The dimension of controllability was used further to explain guilt: if the person thinks that she could, or should, have controlled the situation, she is likely to feel guilty. In their view, feelings such as guilt were no more than a subset of low self-esteem.

Abramson and her colleagues emphasized that their attributional model provided sufficient, but not necessary, conditions for depression. Their reformulated model responded to many of the criticisms of Seligman's original theory of learned helplessness: specifically, it offered an explanation of why depression should persist over time, and how this might generalize across situations by interpretations of experience. In this sense it has been described as elegant, precise and sufficiently complex to account for people's response to their circumstances (Bebbington 1985).

The psychiatric model

Beck's cognitive model stemmed from his disenchantment with traditional psychoanalysis; in particular with the idea that depression arose from a need to suffer (Beck 1967). The model had a number of influences: Adler's individual psychology (Adler 1927); Kelly's personal construct theory (Kelly 1955); and Ellis' rational emotive therapy (Ellis 1962). All of these emphasized the role of the person's 'construction of reality'. Given that Beck's cognitive model had such disparate influences, clearly it did not represent a wholly novel formulation of emotional disorder. Beck was sufficiently realistic to acknowledge that cognitive formulations of reality could be traced back as far as the Ancient Greeks. Indeed, the scientific analysis of the 'construction of reality' has a long pedigree within this century alone. As psychoanalysis was developing its toehold as the definitive explanation of the production of human emotion and behaviour, Vaihinger reminded us that reality existed only in our experience of it: that the experience of reality was mediated by cognitive processes. When people talk about their experience of the world, they merely assume that their experience is real:

> It must be remembered that the object of the world of ideas as a whole . . . is not the portrayal of reality – this would be an utterly impossible task – but rather to provide us with an instrument for finding our way about more easily in the world.
>
> (Vaihinger 1924, p15)

In order to 'find our way about' or make sense of our world, we label our experiences in specific ways; attributing certain qualities to specific experiences; for example, when people say that sugar is sweet:

> Where is the sweet that is ascribed to the sugar? It exists only in the act of sensation . . . Thought not only changes immediate sensation thereby, but withdraws further and further from reality and becomes increasingly entangled in its own forms. By means of the creative faculty . . . it has invented a Thing which is supposed to possess an attribute. This Thing is a fiction, the Attribute as such is a fiction, and the whole relationship is a fiction.
>
> (ibid, p167)

The age-old philosophical question, 'Are things real or do we merely "invent" them?', is vital to the area of emotional disorder, and especially depression. People who are severely emotionally distressed often appear to witness a world which differs markedly from our own. Their view of themselves, as part of that world, is also often darkly different from our perception of them. Suggesting that the world, or the person, is not really bleak, depressing or pointless is itself pointless. Their sense, or perception, of the world is the only reality they will ever know; their senses tell them a different story*. Beck extended these earlier concepts in a cognitive model which was based upon systematic clinical observation and experimental research (Beck and Greenberg 1974; Beck *et al.* 1980). His observations, both clinical and experimental, clarified for him why depressed people adopted this 'negative' view: why they constructed a depressing sense of their world which, ultimately, they adopted as their central experience.

In Beck's view, psychopathology is present when a person engages in distorted thinking which deviates from what most people would consider to be a realistic way of interpreting 'reality'. It was clear that Beck saw the need to define depression in medical and normative

---

*The same is true, of course, for us. They cannot fathom why *we* should own such a positive outlook on what, from their perspective, is such a bleak landscape. That outlook is, however, all that we know, at least for the present.

terms*. He saw three specific classes of distorted thinking in depression, which he called the 'cognitive triad':

- a negative view of self;
- negative expectations of the environment (or world);
- negative expectations of the future (Beck 1970).

In Beck's view, the depressed person saw the world as making unacceptable demands, putting insurmountable obstacles in her way. She also saw herself as inadequate, diseased or defective: expecting that the future would bring only further difficulty, suffering and failure.

Specific 'schemas', or belief systems, were also identified within the model. It was hypothesized that these had their origins in childhood experience. When a critical life event is encountered, these schemas – which process the experience of the event – stimulate particular dysfunctional interpretations of the event:

> A schema may be inactive for long periods of time but can be energized by specific environmental inputs.
>
> (Beck *et al.* 1980, p13)

Such 'prepotent dysfunctional schemas' could be triggered by a range of inappropriate events and, in depression, could lead to the loss of control over thinking processes. In severe depression, the person's dysfunctional thinking becomes autonomous, operating independently of external events. In common with other theorists, Beck also noted the role of loss:

> . . . after experiencing loss (either as the result of an actual, obvious event or insidious deprivations) the depression-prone person begins to appraise his experiences in a negative way.   (Beck 1976)

In short, some people become depressed as a result of single, major, traumatic events; others from a succession of minor, distressing losses. The theory suggests that a number of discrete thinking errors, involving faulty information processing, maintain the cognitive triad and the supporting dysfunctional schemas. Beck observed, for example, how the depressed person tends to:

1. perceive events in highly 'black-and-white' terms, using highly polarized values (employing the 'thinking error' of *dichotomous thinking*);

---

*For a careful consideration of the 'medicalization' of 'extraordinary' behaviour, see Sedgwick, P. (1982) *Psycho-Politics*. New York, Harper and Row; and more recently, Hill, D. (1990) *Madness: The Politics of Schizophrenia*. London, J.M. Dent.

2. isolate negative events from their natural context (*selective abstraction*);
3. give support to the negative view of the event, despite evidence to the contrary (*arbitrary inference*);
4. use single negative events to prove a general rule (overgeneralization);
5. scale events up or down in value or potency to demonstrate failure (magnification or minimization);
6. perceive events as highly personal despite the absence of evidence to support this (personalization);

These particular styles of thinking were described by Beck as 'primitive', rather than moderate, multidimensional and 'rational'. Such thinking, he argued, involved attributions of self-blame: these carried a highly absolutist, as well as moralistic, tone. In his view, people remained depressed over time by persistently using negative thinking, which was stimulated by dysfunctional schemas which, in turn, stimulated further emotional distress.

A review of the cognitive models

Although these three models discuss depression from distinct perspectives, four discrete attitudes thread their way through the models. Although given differing emphasis, and often descriptions, the models suggest that depression involves:

1. a lowering of self-esteem;
2. helplessness or hopelessness;
3. self-blame;
4. the concept of 'imposition' or 'burden'.

The role of self-esteem was addressed by all three models. Brown and Harris suggested that this was linked to ideas of self-confidence and mastery, ideas which were echoed in Beck's 'negative view of self' and Abramson's locus of causality, where the person perceived herself as incompetent. The concept of hopelessness or helplessness existed in very broad terms in the models of both Beck and Brown and Harris. Garber reinforced the value of Abramson *et al.*'s view that helplessness can function as a distinct theme, noting that:

> . . . it is possible to be helpless without being hopeless, but it is not possible to be hopeless without simultaneously being helpless.
>
> (Garber *et al.* 1980)

Self-blame, prominent in Beck's model, is not stressed by Brown and Harris and is translated by Abramson *et al.* into the concept of controllability, albeit without the moral tone engendered by the imperative nature of Beck's 'shoulds and musts'. Finally, both Beck and Brown and Harris emphasize the role of 'imposition': the person who sees herself as a failure is (according to 'depressive' logic) a burden on others.

These common threads were reinforced by Bowlby (1985), who noted that Seligman's learned helplessness theory is highly compatible with his own concept of loss in the genesis of depressive disorder (*sic*) (ibid, p247) and also that Beck's theory of depressive disorder 'is cast in the same mould' as his own view of the role of cognitive biases (ibid, p249). These comments were important since Bowlby represented not only a significant individual voice on the genesis of emotional distress, but also a significant link with the older tradition of psychoanalysis. Bowlby's studies involved an extension of Freud's original research on loss in *Mourning and Melancholia*. He noted that the helplessness described by Seligman was very similar to the helplessness described by mourners. Despite his acknowledgement that Beck's data are explicable by his own theory, however, he emphasized the limitations of Beck's model: noting that no attempt was made to explain the actual function of childhood experience in the generation of negative schemas. Bowlby reserved most support, however, for the social model proposed by Brown and Harris which he viewed as 'of great importance for an understanding of depressive disorders' (ibid, p256). Bowlby's psychosocial model, and by implication those other psychological models he endorsed, emphasized the role of the person's relationship to life events in the aetiology of depression: this relationship is discussed later in this chapter.

It was noted in Chapter 1 that depression covered a wide variety of experiences. It could be argued that the three theoretical models reviewed here relate specifically to 'psychological' forms of depression, where the 'depressive' state occurs as a reaction to environmental or psychosocial events. If we assume that 'biological' forms of depression, such as manic depressive psychosis, exist solely as a function of the influence of factors within the individual (endogenous), rather than as a function of external (exogenous) influence, then the relevance of these cognitive theories is diminished considerably.

Bowlby noted, however, that acknowledgement of the importance of these cognitive, information-processing variables did not preclude the additional attribution of a significant role to neurophysiological processes (ibid, p261). He acknowledged that a relationship existed between abnormal levels of certain neuroendocrines, neurotransmitters and depression, but questioned the assumption that such a causal relationship always occurred in one direction: that is, that changes in neurophysiological processes always produced depressed mood. He suggested that the variation in the size and pattern of neurophysiological responses to psychological events could be accounted for, in part, by individual differences which may have a genetic base. He suggested further, however, that subjection to severely stressful conditions, especially during childhood, might effect a permanent change in the neuroendocrine system so that it becomes thereafter more or less sensitive (ibid, p262). The British physiologist Clive Wood has taken this hypothesis a stage further. He suggested that a person's 'attitudes' toward the world have a more significant effect upon her chemical make-up than has been realized:

> Until recently, the nervous and immune systems were thought of as completely separate. But the discovery of [these] lymphocyte receptors means that immunity is to some extent under mental control. What we think and feel is likely to influence our immune responses. So unhappiness gets into our cells by way of their surface receptors. (Wood 1990, a and b)

These views challenge the traditional notions that some depressions are distinctly endogenous, arising from within the person, whereas others are exogenous, the result of external influence. The interaction of 'mind' and 'body', in the form of the effect of thoughts and feelings upon the physical 'self', represents an altogether more complex model: one which may well be necessary to explain this extraordinarily complex phenomenon.

THE CONCEPTS OF ATTRIBUTION AND LOCUS OF CONTROL

Life events: the schools of hard knocks?

All three models described briefly above acknowledge that specific 'life events' play a part in the production of depression. It has long been considered that life events influence a range of mental disorders, as noted in Chapter 1. Although much research has been done on the effect of different life events in the precipitation of depression, often the design of these studies has been weak, making it difficult to come to any firm conclusions. Paykel (1983) noted that many studies used retrospective life events interviews. He suggested that when questioned, many people would try to recall events which might have influenced their depression: this has been described as the 'search for meaning' (Kendell 1983). Other researchers have argued that although the importance of life events in general, as a cause of depression, remained unclear, various studies had shown that 'quality of life' events, such as 'major losses', appeared to play a significant role (Findlay-Jones 1981). As was noted earlier, the person's perception of an event is her only link with the 'reality' of that event. This may explain why some people are distressed as much by the loss of a pet as others are by the loss of a spouse, child or partner.

The assumption that life events might 'trigger' or 'enhance' a depressive reaction has increasingly become accepted. Although the literature for mania is much less clear, there are indications that manic episodes may also be a form of 'maladaptive response' to life events. Ambelas studied 69 people admitted to hospital in a manic state and noted that a 'significant' life event had occurred in one-third of the group in the month before admission (Ambelas 1979). Kennedy and his colleagues studied a similar group: 85% of their sample experienced a similar life event in the four month period before admission (Kennedy et al. 1983). A matched control group admitted for orthopaedic treatment had less than half the number of life events. Furthermore, the people with mania rated 66% of their life events as 'highly undesirable', compared with less than 30% of the orthopaedic group.

These findings suggest that people who experience depression, mania, or both, may experience *more* 'life events' than other people. Statistically speaking, life may provide a greater proportion of 'hard knocks' to these people than to 'ordinary' mortals. Depressed people may also perceive these events as representing more of a 'threat' than would others not so predisposed to emotional disturbance. Such interpretations alone do not represent a serious challenge to traditional biochemical assumptions about the genetic base of depressive disorders, such as manic depressive psychosis*. They may indicate, however, that the genesis of both mania and depression is more complex than reductionist biomedical theories have thus far suggested. Traditional notions of life events, and their likely effects on health, as expressed by life insurance charts, are increasingly viewed with scepticism. In the case of depression, the significance of a life event does not appear to rest exclusively upon when, or even how often, it occurs. As the three cognitive theories illustrate, the process by which the person perceives and judges such events may be equally, if not more, significant in determining their impact upon the person's mood state.

---

*For some of the classic descriptions within this literature, see Angst, J. (1966) Zur atiologie und nosologie endogener depressiver psychosen. In *Monographen aus der Neurologie und Psychiatrie*, **112**, Berlin, Springer-Verlag; Bertleson, A., Harvald, B. and Hauge, M.A. (1977) Danish twin study of manic-depressive disorders. *British Journal of Psychiatry*, **130**, pp330–51; and Perris, C. (1966) A study of bipolar (manic-depressive) and unipolar recurrent depressive psychoses. *Acta Psychiatrica Scandinavica*, Supp. 194.

Attribution: giving meaning to the world

If life events do not have an 'automatic' effect upon people, how do they come to be affected by their circumstances? The concept of **attribution** has been used to describe how people perceive and explain what happens to them. Valins and Nisbett (1972) defined attribution as the 'process whereby the individual "explains" his world'. As a general rule, people implicate either factors within their control, such as their own behaviour, or factors such as the action of others, the weather, their physiological state or the effect of drugs, all of which clearly are beyond their immediate control.* In ordinary parlance, people who are feeling unwell might say that they have been 'working too hard'; their family is 'getting on their nerves'; they are 'under the weather'; they are 'one degree under' or feeling 'a little liverish'; or that their medication 'doesn't agree with them'.

Valins and Nisbett observed that people often seek the consensus of others to assist in such explanations, except where some aspect of their behaviour was deemed to be 'bad' or 'shameful' (Sarnoff and Zimbardo 1961; Schacter 1959). For example, people whose relationships or work performance are disrupted through heavy drinking often are aware that others might 'attribute' the cause of their problems to their drinking behaviour. Similarly, people whose behaviour offends some cultural taboo rarely make their practice public. This was true of most people who felt attracted sexually to their own sex; they attributed this 'urge' to themselves (their own behaviour, which they should be able to control). Since the practice of homosexuality was deemed, culturally, to be 'bad' and the explanation of the 'badness' was within their control, they experienced debilitating feelings of inadequacy, shame or 'abnormality'.

Studies of people who are depressed have documented similar feelings, especially of powerlessness and futility (Sackheim and Wegner 1986). In a study of suicide attempters, 'hopelessness' was identified as playing a key role in determining the suicidal act (Beck *et al.* 1975). The greater the degree of depression, the more prone the person was to expressions of self-blame, self-deprecation and feelings of guilt. When we are unwell, in any sense, we tend to say that we feel 'bad'. Where people feel 'depressed' they tend to attribute the cause of the 'badness' to some personal deficiency. Where the 'badness' is extreme, the responsibility is greatest, and the 'logical' solution is a 'death sentence'. It is worth noting that when 'good' or positive events occur, depressed people are likely to attribute these to external factors, which are beyond

---

* For the classic experiment, see Schacter S. and Singer, J. (1962) Cognitive, social and physiological determinants of emotional state. *Psychological Review*, **69**, pp379–99.

their control. Where 'bad' or negative events occur, these are attributed to internal factors, within the person (Rizley 1978). This led Seligman to the conclusion that 'a certain attributional style combined with bad outcomes causes depression' (Seligman *et al.* 1979). He did not rule out, however, the possibility that depressed people might attribute bad outcomes to internal, stable and global causes.

Sex differences in 'attributional style' have also been noted: when things go wrong depressed women tended to attribute blame to themselves, whereas men tend to blame others (Frieze 1975). This might account for the higher proportion of women suffering from depressive disorders: in some cases the incidence is almost three times as high for women as for men. Brewin (1986) suggested, however, that the relationship between cognitions and depression may be more complex and that **non-causal** cognitions (such as self-evaluative judgements), which are not seen as playing a direct role in 'creating' bad outcomes, may play a key role in the reduction of self-esteem. Where, for example, a person feels bad because she is 'rejected' by her partner, she might recognize (correctly) that the direct cause lies with her partner's behaviour. She might explain her partner's actions further by saying, 'He rejects me because he does not value me: he does not value me because I am valueless'.

It is clear that there is no 'biological' distinction between the sexes to account for this difference in attributional style. So why do men consistently 'explain away' bad outcomes whereas, in the same context, women take responsibility for actions which, clearly, are the responsibility of others? The objective explanation seems to lie in a sophisticated, if unwitting, form of social engineering. The task of therapy, therefore, seems to involve the near-Sisyphean task of overturning the effects of cultural conditioning.

Although Beck's original view was that a 'thought disorder' may be common to all types of psychopathology (Beck 1963), more recent research suggests that the thinking style of depressed people differs significantly from other patient groups. Sackheim and Wegner (1986) observed that when normal subjects were exposed to specific tests, they attributed 'successful' outcomes to themselves and 'failures' to the influence of factors outwith their control. People diagnosed as schizophrenic showed the same 'self-serving' bias. However, when depressed people were tested, they showed a quite different response: blaming themselves for failures and re-attributing success to outside factors, other people, luck, fate, etc. That study supported Beck's notion that where 'attributions of responsibility' were concerned, people with depression were characterized by a self-punitive bias. Other researchers have shown that depressed women undergraduates were more likely to use self-deprecating statements and then to use 'illogical' arguments to support these beliefs than were non-depressed undergraduate women (Cook and Peterson 1986). One conclusion is that 'depressives' are irrational, both in their beliefs and their justification. An important dispute exists, however, over the issue of 'irrationality' at both an academic and a clinical level.

The view that the depressive thinking style was irrational had been challenged by Lewinsohn and his colleagues (1980). He showed that when asked to evaluate their social performance, people who were depressed were more likely to rate themselves in a similar way to independent observers. Alternatively, non-depressed subjects were more likely to give themselves *better* ratings than independent observers. This finding, which has been supported by subsequent studies, is very disturbing: at least to non-depressed, 'ordinary' people. Depressed people appear to have a more accurate view of themselves than people who are not depressed. The problems appears to be one of 'depressive realism' rather than depressive 'irrationality'. Sackheim (1983) suggested that the goal of psychotherapy may not, therefore, be to encourage accurate *self-appraisal,* but may instead involve promoting the use of the cognitive distortions which characterize normal functioning.

Locus of control

Attempts to measure the extent to which a person perceives events as consequences of her own behaviour, and potentially under personal control, have been called 'locus of control' (Lefcourt, 1977). Locus of control describes how the person perceives events as a function of her own behaviour, or as a function of luck, chance, fate or some other factor outwith her control. To date, there has been only limited attention paid to the role of this concept in affective disorder in general.

One of the key measures in locus of control research is Rotter's *Internal–External Scale.* This measures the extent to which people believe they can control what happens to them (internal control); or believe that events are largely outwith their control (external control). The scale measures expectation of generalized reinforcement. Rotter cited a series of studies which provided strong support for the hypothesis that people with a strong belief in their capacity to control their own destiny are likely to be more aware of the way the environment shapes their behaviour. Such people place more value on coping skills. As a result they were, in Rotter's view, more sensitive to attempts to influence them (Rotter, 1966).

Rotter's scale was taken a stage further by Reid and Ware who developed a '3-Factor Internal-External Scale' (Reid and Ware 1974).

This scale tried to identify subcategories within the global 'internal' or 'external' measure. They identified 3 such sub-divisions:

- Fatalism, where the person attributed the outcome to luck or chance;
- Social Systems Control, where 'sociopolitical' factors were used to explain the event; and
- Self-Control, where the person attributed the outcome to her own actions.

Reid and Ware argued that people could have highly developed self-control scores, and that these could co-exist with attributions of fatalism or political powerlessness, and vice versa. This view was echoed later by Garber and his colleagues suggestion that 'hopelessness' and 'helplessness' were different.

Several studies have examined the beliefs of depressed people using these standardized loci of control measures. The suggestion that 'negative expectations' might play a key role in causing different kinds of maladjustment, such as anxiety or depression, is not new*. Failure to attain certain outcomes, or 'make things happen', might produce feelings of loss but only if the person defines them as essential or desirable. The way people describe their capacity to control such outcomes, and thereby reach necessary goals, is at the heart of the locus of control hypothesis. However, the experience of 'loss' need not result only in one form of emotional distress. Indeed, the complexity of affective disorder is echoed in Phares' observation that depression may:

> . . . represent a situation where the person realises that the achievement of valued goals is blocked and that the blockage may be relatively permanent. If the blockage is seen as temporary, anger or hostility is more likely. When the element of finality is present, the reaction is more likely to be depression.   (Phares 1976, p125)

In Miller and Seligman's view, depression resulted from learning that 'reinforcement' was independent of voluntary responses. Depression, they continued:

> . . . is a specific cognitive distortion of the perception of the ability of one's own responses to change the environment, rather than a general 'pessimism'.   (Miller and Seligman 1973)

In effect, the depressed person thinks that any 'personal' attempt to change the circumstances of her life will be futile. If the assumptions of this model are correct, highly 'externalized' people should be more susceptible to learned helplessness. Some support exists for a relationship between externality and depression (Abramowitz 1969): this has

---

*For a review of this literature, see Phares, E.J. (1972) A social learning approach to psychopathology. In Rotter, J.B., Chance, J. and Phares, E.J. (eds.) *Application of a Social Learning Theory of Personality.* New York, Holt, Rinehart and Winston.

been challenged, however, on the grounds that the 'pessimistic' wording of some external items and more 'optimistic' wording of internal items on the Rotter scale could account for this (Lamont 1972).

If the 'learned helplessness' hypothesis is translated into locus of control terms, we would predict that highly externalized individuals are unable to see themselves as capable of controlling outcomes: therefore they become depressed. Such a hypothesis would not, however, preclude the possibility that depression might originate from the opposite perspective; from high internality. Phares (1972) suggested that two kinds of people might suffer from depression: those who see 'negative outcomes' as their responsibility, and those who do not expect to attain valued goals or outcomes. This hypothesis supports Rotter's original speculation that a curvilinear relationship might exist between pathology and locus of control: people who are either extremely internal or external being maladjusted. Evidence of this curvilinear relationship can be seen in people with clinical levels of depression: those who are externalized feel helpless to control their plight and are sad; those who are internalized also feel sad, but this derives from guilt or anger stemming from a perceived failure to accept responsibility, or from sheer 'incompetence'. In this sense, one group may tell themselves that they are unable, incapable and therefore hopeless, whereas the others tell themselves they should have behaved differently and therefore have failed.

The distinction between people who blame themselves and those who blame others, noted earlier in terms of differences between men and women, can also be restated in locus of control terms. Molinari distinguished between congruent externals who did not expect their behaviour to have any influence on events, and 'defensive externals' who adopted externalized beliefs as a defence against feelings of personal failure. Depressed women, therefore, might be described as congruent externals, accepting blame for failure too readily; whereas men (defensive externals) are, perhaps, quick to blame others (Molinari and Khanna 1981).

The highly externalized individual might also be described as fatalistic, believing that nothing can be done to relieve or recover the situation. The externalized subject who experiences negative life events may feel powerless to control or otherwise cope with them. It has been suggested that some people expect a high proportion of 'malevolent outcomes'; these people are more likely to be depressed than those with a lower 'malevolence expectancy' (Gregory 1981). In a similar vein, Lefcourt (1981) reported that externals were:

> . . . more likely to report distress associated with life events, and that unpleasant events had a more lingering impact on moods exhibited by externals.

Many of these hypotheses were framed using mildly depressed student samples. Where clinical populations have been studied the picture is less certain. In a hospital study in which more than half of the group suffered from a 'psychotic depression', a significant relationship existed between externality and depression; this was strongest for the men in the study (Legget and Archer 1979). Other studies, however, have found only a mild relationship between depression and externality (Moore and Paollilo 1984) or none at all (Peterson *et al.* 1978). The discrepancy between these findings can be accounted for, at least in part, by the research method*.

More recently, it has been hypothesized that dysfunctional beliefs, in particular attributional biases, either result from long-term depressions or predispose the person to longer depressive episodes (Eaves and Rush 1984). Self-blame, in particular, may be a relatively stable and enduring characteristic of people predisposed to depression. Other researchers have suggested that dysfunctional attitudes may represent an important vulnerability factor: if such 'negative' beliefs are evident, even when the person is 'well', these might serve as a sign of likely future depressive episodes (Rush *et al.* 1986). Another important view is that where low self-esteem *and* depression are present, this may reflect a clash between what the person 'thinks she should be able to do' and what she 'actually does do' (Brewin 1986). These highly sophisticated investigations of self-blame and other attributional processes will ring bells for many who work with, or otherwise care for, people who are depressed. These three studies reflect an interest in the person's use of unconditional shoulds and musts, first described by Albert Ellis (1962). These moral imperatives not only generate intense existential pain but, if the person fails to deliver the necessary outcome, this pain is exacerbated by waves of guilt, demanding even higher standards by way of atonement.

DOES THE HEAD RULE THE HEART?

Each model reviewed in this chapter agrees that the way a person 'constructs' her view of the world, and her place within it, can predispose her to depression. Although each model emphasizes the role of information-processing, different researchers have used different interpretations of the concept of cognition. The models also differed in another important respect: how they were developed. The investigation of the social origins of depression used sociological field studies; the

---

*The differences between these three studies may be accounted for by the samples. Legget and Archer's sample was mixed-sex with mixed diagnoses, more than half with a psychotic depression. Moore and Paollilo's sample was 'non-psychotic' and Peterson *et al.*'s sample involved no less than 18 different diagnoses in 39 subjects.

learned helplessness work was based upon psychological laboratory experiments; and the cognitive therapy model emphasized studies of psychiatric patients. The result is three tales, each with a similar moral, but different heroes and villains. Although each model emphasized cognition, recognition was given also to loss of reinforcement. It was noted that 'reinforcement' might be defined as any pleasurable event but might equally be defined as 'any successful outcome', for example where a person needs to find (or create) a solution for a specific problem. Where pleasurable events, or necessary outcomes, were not forthcoming, 'loss' might be the resultant experience.

A further cognitive dimension was represented by the locus of control hypothesis: this also emphasized the idea of control over outcomes. This dealt specifically with the person's expectations of 'what might happen' if she did this or that. It was noted that, using this measure, studies of people with severe depression offer confusing results, due partly to design faults. More recent studies which have tried to resolve such problems suggest that women with a long-term history of severe depression are more fatalistic about life in general than 'normal' women (Barker 1988). A related study suggested that this depressed group might have similarly fatalistic views about the occurrence, and recurrence, of their depressive illness (ibid, Chapter 11). That view echoed Rosenbaum and Hadari's (1985) finding that people with depression expected events to be controlled by chance, whereas a sample of people diagnosed as paranoid expected 'powerful others' to exert influence over them. A related study by Walford-Kramer and Light (1984) showed a significant relationship between low 'mastery' scores, similar to Reid and Ware's 'self-control' factor, and depression.

The terms 'attribution' and 'locus of control' have been used in this chapter to describe further the information-processing aspect of cognition. Trying to clarify the meaning of cognition in this way is not, however, without its complications. Palenzuela (1984) noted that different investigators had a tendency to define locus of control in different ways. As a result, similar terms end up with different meanings, especially when locus of control is used to measure other constructs, like depression.

Similarly, some writers have confused attribution and locus of control. In this chapter an attempt has been made to clarify the difference between the two ideas: **attribution** involves people 'looking back' in an effort to explain things which have happened; **locus of control** involves people judging, in advance, what they think might be the relationship between different events. This distinction appears vital to the area of psychological therapy for people with depression. When people make 'attributions' they try to explain things which happened in the past, such as 'why' they became depressed. When people use the locus of control construct, they make predictions about 'what action' might cause 'what outcome' in the future. Most forms of therapy involve helping the person to change her behaviour, to produce outcomes which differ from those she experienced in the past. Assessing the extent to which the person thinks she can control such outcomes assumes a central position in the therapeutic process. The potential significance of psychological characteristics, such as 'high externality', for people with 'chronic' disorders like depression, was noted by Wise and Rosenthal (1982):

> ... [the] patient's illness beliefs may be determined by a cognitive style such as locus of control rather than by the actual severity of the illness.

Assessing the person from this psychological perspective had obvious implications for the 'patient' and for those treating her, since in their view:

> ... the externally located individual tends towards greater fear of vulnerability to illness, and has a greater conviction that he (*sic*) is ill, yet is less able to express anxiety and fear.   (ibid, pp252–3)

It may be that people who experience severe depression continue to think in a negative and fatalistic way, even when they are 'affectively well' (Barker 1988). The interaction of this defeatist thinking style with negative life events may play a central role in precipitating the recurrence of further depressive episodes. Where people are treated solely by drug therapy, their 'passivity', or 'helplessness' to control the depression, is heavily emphasized. The medical advice given to people with manic depression confirms their status as 'sufferers in remission' only:

> Lithium smoothes out disabling mood swings, gradually restoring normality . . . The impression of 'cure' is misleading, however. Lithium does not cure manic depression, but it holds it in check.
> (Camcolit Therapy Guide)

It is reasonable to assume that most, if not all, people diagnosed as manic depressive, and offered lithium therapy as part of their overall treatment, will also be offered this interpretation of their illness. It might be assumed that people who are encouraged to perceive their mood, if not their overall functioning, as permanently under the control of a simple chemical salt will also see themselves as unable to influence all kinds of personal, interpersonal and social events. If such depressions are not caused partly by learned helplessness, the treatment may produce an equivalent helplessness in the form of 'patient passivity'.

In Schopenhauer's view, madness was largely a problem of memory*. The wisdom of hindsight can often prove our undoing: if we were less able to recall past 'failed outcomes', we might perceive ourselves less as failures. Indeed, for many people, patients and normals alike, the recollection of the past disturbs our ability both to live in the present and to attack the future. We devote so much energy to recalling the past and planning for the future that we often lose sight of the fact that the present is the only reality. It is all too apparent that people become depressed as a result of some past event: whether this is recent or distant seems immaterial. Recovery from the depressive episode, however, cannot be reclaimed from the past, nor does it lie in the future. It begins in the here-and-now, in the reconstruction of the person's view of the world and her place within it. The difficulty for therapists of all persuasions, in structuring this learning situation, was described by Reynolds (1985). Writing of his patients, he noted:

> . . . they feel and think a great deal and do very little. What needs to be done often is to sit and map out a plan of action. My students often need to be prodded to find out about reality by acting on it and in it.

REFERENCES

Abramowitz, S.I. (1969) Locus of control and self-reported depression among college students. *Psychological Report*, **25**, pp149–50.

Abramson, L.Y., Seligman, M.E.P. and Teasdale, J. (1978) Learned helplessness in humans: critique and reformulation. *Journal of Abnormal Psychology*, **87**, pp49–74.

Adler, A. (1927) *Practice and Theory of Individual Psychology*. New York, Harcourt Brace.

Ambelas, A. (1979) Psychologically stressful events in the precipitation of manic episodes. *British Journal of Psychiatry*, **135**, pp15–21.

Barker, P. (1988) *An Evaluation of Specific Nursing Interventions in the Management of Patients Suffering from Manic Depressive Psychosis*, (Chapter 10). PhD thesis, Dundee Institute of Technology.

Bebbington, P.E. (1985) Three cognitive theories of depression. *Psychological Medicine*, **15**, pp759–69.

Beck, A.T. (1963) Thinking and depression. *Archives of General Psychiatry*, **9**, pp36–45.

*I am indebted to Peter Walters for drawing my attention to this and other historical precedents: Schopenhauer, A. (1958) *The World as Will and Representation* (3rd edition). (Trans. E.F.J. Payne). Vol. I, pp192–3; Vol. II, pp399–402. New York, Dover Publications.

Beck, A.T. (1967) *Depression: Clinical, Experimental and Theoretical Aspects.* New York, Harper and Row.

Beck, A.T. (1970) The core problem in depression: the cognitive triad. In Masseman, J. (ed.) *Science and Psychoanalysis.* New York, Grune and Stratton.

Beck, A.T. (1976) *Cognitive Therapy and the Emotional Disorders* (p129). New York, International Universities Press.

Beck, A.T. and Greenberg, R.L. (1974) Cognitive therapy with depressed women. In Franks, V. and Burtle, V. (eds.) *Women and Therapy; New Psychotherapies for a Changing Society.* New York, Bruner/Mazel.

Beck, A.T., Kovacs, M. and Weissman, A. (1975) Hopelessness and suicidal behaviour; an overview. *Journal of the American Medical Association,* **234**, pp 1146–9.

Beck, A.T., Rush, A.J., Shaw, B.F. and Emery, G. (1980) *Cognitive Therapy of Depression.* London, John Wiley.

Bertleson, A., Harvald, B. and Hauge, M.A. (1977) Danish twin study of manic depressive disorders. *British Journal of Psychiatry,* **130**, pp330–51.

Bowlby, J. (1985) *Attachment and Loss; Volume 3 Loss, Sadness and Depression.* Harmondsworth, Pelican.

Brewin, C. (1986) Internal attribution and self-esteem in depression; a theoretical note. *Cognitive Therapy Research,* **10**(4), pp469–76.

Brown, G.W. and Harris, T. (1978) *The Social Origins of Depression; A Study of Psychiatric Disorder in Women.* London, Tavistock.

Camcolit Therapy Guide (undated) (p3). The Lithium Information Service, Norgine Ltd., 116–20 London Road, Oxford.

Cook, M.L. and Peterson, C. (1986) Depressive irrationality. *Cognitive Therapy Research,* **10**(3), pp293–8.

Costello, G. (1982) Social factors associated with depression; a retrospective community study. *Psychological Medicine,* **12**, pp329–39.

De La Mare, W. (1984) *Behold This Dreamer: Of Reverie, Night, Sleep, Dream, Love-Dreams, Nightmare, Death, The Unconscious, The Imagination, Divination, The Artist and Kindred Spirits* (p381). London, Faber and Faber.

Eaves, G. and Rush, J.A. (1984) Cognitive patterns in symptomatic and remitted unipolar major depression. *Journal of Abnormal Psychology,* **93**, pp31–40.

Ellis, A. (1962) *Reason and Emotion in Psychotherapy.* New York, Lyle Stuart.

Findlay-Jones,R. (1981) Showing that life events are a cause of depression; a review. *Australia and New Zealand Journal of Psychiatry,* **15**, pp229–38.

Freud, S. (1957) *Mourning and Melancholia* (originally 1917) (pp243–58). London, Hogarth Press.

Frieze, I.H. (1975) Women's expectations for and causal attributions of success and failure. In Mednick, M.T.S., Tangri, S.S. and Haffman, L.W. (eds.) *Women and Achievement.* London, John Wiley.

Garber, J., Miller, S.M. and Abramson, L.Y. (1980) On the distinction between anxiety and depression; perceived control, certainty and probability of goal-attainment. In Garber, J. and Seligman, M.E.P. (eds.) *Human Helplessness: Theory and Applications.* New York, Academic Press.

Gregory, W.L. (1981) Expectations for controllability, performance attributions and behaviour. In Lefcourt, H.M. (ed.) (1981) See below.

Horowitz, M.J., Wilner, N., Kaltreider, N. and Alvarez, W. (1980) Signs and symptoms of post-traumatic stress disorder. *Archives of General Psychiatry*, **37**, pp85–92.

Kelly, G. (1955) *The Psychology of Personal Constructs*. New York, Norton.

Kendell, R.E. (1983) Affective psychoses. In Kendell, R.E. and Zeally, A.K. *Companion to Psychiatric Studies*. Edinburgh, Churchill Livingstone.

Kennedy, S., Thompson, R., Stancer, H.C., Roy, A. and Persad, E. (1983) Life events precipitating mania. *British Journal of Psychiatry*, **142**, pp398–403.

Lamont, J. (1972) Item mood-level as a determinant of I-E test response. *Journal of Clinical Psychology*, **28**, p190.

Lefcourt, H.M. (1977) *Locus of Control*. New York, John Wiley.

Lefcourt, H.M. (ed.) (1981) *Research with the Locus of Control Construct, Vol. 1*. New York, Academic Press.

Legget, J. and Archer, R.P. (1979) Locus of control and depression among psychiatric in-patients. *Psychology Report*, **45**(3), pp835–8.

Lewinsohn, P.M. (1974) A behavioural approach to depression. In Friedman, T.M. and Katz, M.M. (eds.) *The Psychology of Depression; Contemporary Theory and Research*. Washington, Winston.

Lewinsohn, P.M., Mischel, W., Chaplain, W. and Barton, R. (1980) Social competence and depression; the role of illusory self-perceptions? *Journal of Abnormal Psychology*, **89**, pp203–12.

Melges, F.T. and Bowlby, J. (1969) Types of hopelessness in psychopathological processes. *Archives of General Psychiatry*, **20**, pp690–9.

Miller, W.R. and Seligman, M.E.P. (1973) Depression and the perception of reinforcement. *Journal of Abnormal Psychology*, **82**, p82.

Molinari, V. and Khanna, P. (1981) Locus of control and its relationship to anxiety and depression. *Journal of Personality Assessment*, **45**(3), pp314–9.

Moore, T.W. and Paollilo, J.G.P. (1984) Depression; influence of hopelessness, locus of control, hostility and length of treatment. *Journal of Consulting and Clinical Psychology*, **54**, pp875–81.

Palenzuela, D.L. (1984) Critical evaluation of locus of control; towards a reconceptualisation of the construct and its measurement. *Psychology Report*, **54**, pp683–709.

Paykel, E.S. (1983) Methodological aspects of life events research. *Journal of Psychosomatic Research*, **27**(5), pp341–52.

Peterson, R., Sushinsky, I. and Demask, R.S. (1978) Are locus of control and depression related? *Psychology Report*, **43**, pp727–31.

Phares, E.J. (1972) A social learning approach to psychopathology. In Rotter, J.B., Chance, J. and Phares, E.J. (eds.) *Application of a Social Learning Theory of Personality*. New York, Holt, Rinehart and Winston.

Phares, E.J. (1976) *Locus of Control in Personality*. Morristown, New Jersey, General Learning Press.

Reid, D.W. and Ware, E.E. (1974) Multidimensionality of internal versus external control: addition of a third dimension and non-distinction of self versus others. *Canadian Journal of Behavioural Science*, **6**(2), pp131–42.

Reynolds, D.K. (1985) *Playing Ball on Running Water* (p34). London, Sheldon Press.

Rizley, R. (1978) Depression and distortion in the attribution of causality. *Journal of Abnormal Psychology*, **87**(1), pp32–48.

Rose, S., Lewontin, R.C. and Kamin, L.J. (1988) *Not in Our Genes: Biology, Ideology and Human Nature*. Harmondsworth, Penguin.

Rosenbaum, M. and Hadari, D. (1985) Personal efficacy, external locus of control and perceived contingency of parental reinforcement among depressed, paranoid and normal subjects. *Journal of Personality and Social Psychology*, **49**(2), pp539–47.

Rotter, J.B. (1966) Generalised expectancies for internal versus external control of reinforcement. *Psychological Monographs: General and Applied*, **80**(1), pp1–28.

Rush, A.J., Weissenberger, J. and Eaves, G. (1986) Do thinking patterns predict depressed symptoms? *Cognitive Therapy Research*, **10**(2), pp225–36.

Sackheim, H. (1983) Self-deception, depression and self-esteem; the adaptive value of lying to oneself. In Masling, J. (ed.) *Empirical Studies of Psychoanalytic Theory*. Hillsdale, New Jersey, Lawrence Erlbaum Assoc.

Sackheim, H. and Wegner, A. (1986) Attributional patterns in depression and euthymia. *Archives of General Psychiatry*, **43**, pp553–60.

Sarnoff, J. and Zimbardo, P. (1961) Anxiety, fear and social affiliation. *Journal of Abnormal and Social Psychology*, **62**, pp356–63.

Schacter, S. (1959) *The Psychology of Affiliation*. Stanford CA, Stanford University Press.

Schafer, R. (1948) *The Clinical Application of Psychological Tests*. New York, International Universities Press.

Seligman, M.E.P. (1975) *Helplessness: On Depression, Development and Death*. New York, W.H. Freeman and Co.

Seligman, M.E.P., Abramson, L.Y., Semmel, A. and van Baeyer, C. (1979) Depressive attributional style. *Journal of Abnormal Psychology*, **88**(3), pp242–7.

Seligman, M.E.P. and Maier, S. (1967) Failure to escape traumatic shock. *Journal of Experimental Psychology*, **74**, pp1–9.

Vaihinger, H. (1924) *The Philosophy of 'As If'* (p15). London, Routledge and Kegan Paul.

Valins, S. and Nisbett, R. (1972) Attribution processes in the development and treatment of emotional disorders. In Jones, E., Kanouse, D., Kelly, H., Nisbett, R., Valins, S. and Weiner, B. (eds.) *Attributions: Perceiving the Causes of Behaviour* (p137). Morristown, New Jersey, General Learning Press.

Walford-Kramer, P. and Light, H.K. (1984) Depression and mastery in women; differences according to personal characteristics. *Psychological Report*, **54**(3), p710.

Wise, T.N. and Rosenthal, J.B. (1982) Depression, illness beliefs and severity of illness. *Journal of Psychosomatic Research*, **26**(2), p252.

Wood, C. (1990a) Sad cells. *Journal of Alternative and Complementary Medicine*, **8**(10), pp15–17.

Wood, C. (1990b) *Say Yes to Life*. London, J.M. Dent.

Chapter 3

Between Scylla and Charybdis: an integrated explanation of depression

The system of punishment I was brought up with was relatively benign and straightforward. I was punished (i) for disobedience, (ii) for *what* I did wrong – that is, both for disobedience, which is wrong in itself, and for what, in being disobedient, I had done which I should not have done, because it was wrong in itself to do that, whether I had been told to or not. I was told not to do things only because it was wrong for me to do them. (Laing 1985)

INTRODUCTION

In the past 20 years, much has been made of the importance of the approaching second millenium: the New Age has arrived*. Much has also been made of the fact that the conclusion to the twentieth century represents a new 'Age of Melancholy'. I have alluded in Chapters 1 and 2 to the historical views of depression and some of our ways of explaining this phenomenon. Given that this book is focused upon helping people live with severe depression, I have emphasized models of depression which might be described as psychological in character: those which seem most plausible to me as a helper. In this chapter I shall try to take these explanations a stage further by proposing an integrated model of severe depressive illness: one which acknowledges

---

*In Holroyd's view, the 'radical and evolutionary changes in human consciousness and society' expected, in the 1970s, to be produced by the astrological shift from the Piscean to the Aquarian age, failed to materialize. Capra has a more optimistic view of the potential for 'turning the tide', and the kind of movements which might realize this. Holroyd, S. (1989) *The Arkana Dictionary of New Perspectives*. Harmondsworth, Arkana Penguin. Capra, F. (1983) *The Turning Point: Science, Society and the Rising Culture*. London, Flamingo Fontana.

the complexity of the experience, and which might be in keeping with the long-awaited 'new age'.

The meaning of depression is the expression of a personal, very special emotional experience. In this chapter I shall ask what exactly is being expressed through the person's emotion. I assume that people express their experience and understanding of their world through their emotions. 'Meaning' is the sense which we make of our world; a sense we express most often emotionally. What is different about the world of the depressed person? What do they experience and what do they understand by this experience?

We have spent most of the past 2000 years trying to put our scientific finger upon the single most important factor involved in the explanation of depression. This approach, assumed to represent traditional medical practice, may be seriously flawed in its basic methodology. At the end of the last century, we harboured the expectation that all functional mental disturbances, including depression, might be explained by an infectious diseases model. This concept of nervous disease has, largely, been abandoned. We tend now to favour the idea of 'sickness': the 'experience' that something is wrong (Susser 1990). We continue, however, to pin a significant proportion of our hope for a solution on the discovery of single causal agent, whether this be genetic, traumatic, psychological or social (Charlton 1990). Such 'explanations' say little, if anything, about the meaning of depression – at least, not in any personal sense. Within the past 15 years, the idea of the single causal factor – that x causes y – has been called into question[*]. It has been suggested that a more open-ended, multimodal model is needed to explain the various states which might be called 'un-health' (Engel 1977). Whether or not such an alternative will include the personal experience of depression remains to be seen.

EXPLAINING DEPRESSION: THE WISDOM OF HINDSIGHT

Alone in a crowd

The idea that people are greater than the sum of their parts is hardly new, but it attained an unprecedented popularity in the late 1960s. That decade might well be defined as the beginning of today's New Age movement. The post-war period saw an enormous acceleration of interest in comparative pyschology and religion, extrasensory perception, the occult, and virtually anything 'spiritual' (Bliss 1985). It

[*] De Bono would argue that this is only one way of looking at a problem. de Bono, E. (1991) *I Am Right – You Are Wrong*. Harmondsworth, Penguin.

seems likely that the popular psychiatric heroes of the time, such as R.D. Laing, attracted public interest largely for their exposition of the frailties of traditional psychiatric thought, and their embrace of a crude mix of humanism, hopefulness and hipness (Laing 1985).

The 1960s served as the decade within which many of the sacred cows were sacrificed and a significant commitment was made to the power of both the 'personal' (Dreifus 1973) and the 'interpersonal' (Capra 1988). The ground for that social revolution had been prepared by the ferment of the mid-1950s. In the wake of the Suez crisis of 1956, Britain experienced an unprecedented rise in illegitimacy, violence, and all sorts of crime. Suicide also rose sharply, highlighting the depth of the social crisis. The disenchantment with the established order followed a discrete trail through the 'Angry Young Men', mounting impatience with convention, tradition and authority – stimulated to a degree by the experience of unprecedented affluence – culminating in a teenage revolution and the establishment of a New Morality. These social transformations took place in the shadow of the nuclear deterrent: the emergent generation rightfully were described as belonging to the 'Bomb Culture' (Booker 1969). This disenchantment was paralleled in the USA of the 1950s by the Beat Generation*, reaching a climax in the outcry against the Vietnam war in the late 1960s and the political watershed of the Watergate affair.

What is the relationship between these sociopolitical events and the onset of our second 'Age of Melancholy'? A number of major epidemiological studies have shown that the risk of depression in the general population has increased *almost tenfold* since the Second World War. The average age for becoming depressed for the first time has reduced: for people born in the late 1930s, the average age is between 30 and 35; for those born in the mid-1950s, the average is between 20 and 25 (Reich *et al.* 1988). Although it has been argued that these trends indicate a 'genetic-environment interaction', there are strong arguments for perceiving this as a specific environmental effect (Seligman 1990)*. Perhaps the 'cause' of this escalation is 'modernity' itself, which Western people believe they 'enjoy', and which is so coveted by emerging Westerners, such as the people of the Soviet Union and the former German Democratic Republic. Support for this

* Wilentz described, succinctly, the history of the 'beats', their predecessors and myriad influences: Wilentz, E. (ed.) (1960) *The Beat Scene*. New York, Corinth Books.
* Ellison also noted that, 'people with strong religious faith report higher levels of life satisfaction, greater personal happiness and fewer negative psychosocial consequences of traumatic events'. Ellison, C.G. (1991) Religious involvement and subjective well-being. *The International Journal of Health and Social Behaviour*, **32**(1), pp80–99.

hypothesis exists in the observation that this trend is not a global phenomenon.

The incidence of depression has remained constant over the past 45 years in several societies:

- non-Western cultures, such as China;
- primitive modern tribes, such as the Kaluli in New Guinea;
- tight-knit communities, such as the Old Order Amish;
- stable rural cultures, such as specific rural counties in eastern Canada.

The observation that people born within the past 30 years are ten times more likely to become depressed than their grandparents possesses, therefore, one qualification: those people need to belong to a modern society*.

Seligman (1990) has argued that the 'overbalanced' promotion of the importance of the individual in modern society has led to an unprecedented growth of the ill we know as depression. The inhabitants of Western (capitalist) democracies increasingly are forced into joining an 'individualist' culture: where autonomy, personal control and responsibility are stressed over any collective or common good. Ronald Reagan spoke to a Wall Street audience, in the first term of his presidency, on the 'Age of the Individual'. This view was echoed some years later in Margaret Thatcher's famous pronouncement that 'society' did not exist – there was only 'individual responsibility'. In Seligman's view, belief in the individual self is viable only against a background of belief in a significant institution: religion, country or family. Many of those who have benefited from the increased affluence and political freedom of the past three decades have suffered, concurrently, the loss of God, country and family. When such people 'fail' or otherwise experience loss, they can no longer fall back on traditional social, national or spiritual supports. Without the buffer of these larger beliefs, the individual's helplessness and failure can, all too easily, become hopelessness and depair. In the contemporary parlance, the 'responsible' individual is left to 'pick up the tab': the buck finally stops at the fully isolated self.

These are in no way 'socialist' or anti-capitalist views. Economics is not the problem. Rather, it is the promotion of the individualist philosophy, which appears set to fracture a set of social values which have changed little since our ancestors huddled together in caves,

---

* This echoes Laing's comment: 'A child born today in the UK stands a 10 times greater chance of being admitted to a mental hospital than to a university'. Laing, R.D. (1967) *The Politics of Experience and The Bird of Paradise* (p87). Harmondsworth, Penguin.

sharing their fears and conveying, through mutual warmth, solidarity and reassurance (Bronowski 1977). It seems appropriate that depression should express itself through feelings of 'aloneness' and 'isolation'. The world inhabited by the depressed person is a limbo: literally, a place to which things of no importance or value may be relegated*. With the wisdom of hindsight, the need to arrest the erosion of the social context of human experience and to re-examine our relationship with the infinite becomes, like the 'green' movement, an increasing priority. Why save the planet if (Wo)Man is no longer able to enjoy the experience?

Holism: ambition and reality

These social developments have taken place against a wider backdrop of societal change, within which new ways of looking at human problems have gained popularity. In an effort to escape from some of the restrictions imposed by increasingly technological forms of health care, *holism* has re-entered the field. The interest in holistic and various other forms of alternative and complementary health care was central to the New Age philosophy, born of the 1960s. Thirty years on, however, holism possesses something of a dual identity. It connotes both an approach to the 'whole' person within the total environment, and a range of health-promoting strategies. This dual identity has proven particularly attractive to two groups: a section of the lay public which has grown increasingly health-conscious over the past two decades; and a section of the professional health care system disenchanted with the increasing reductionism of medical treatment. Both these groups are expressing a desire for a more integrated, individualized system.

Holism, however, is neither a new phenomenon nor the 'alternative' to medicine which often is assumed. The term was originally coined in an effort to develop a model of biological thought to challenge the mechanistic evolutionary theory of the nineteenth century*. The holistic approach has attracted considerable support within psychiatry. Indeed, some authors have suggested that the contemporary interest in the 'whole person' derives from four specific, American psychiatric developments. Benjamin Rush, the 'father of American psychiatry' who was central to the early nineteenth century's moral reform move-

---

*I am grateful to Janet S. for highlighting this metaphor: many depressed persons are, in her sense, on the edge of hell.
*The term *holism* was coined by Jan Christian Smuts in his (1926) book, *Holism and Evolution* (New York, Macmillan). The term derives, however, from a broader philosophical enquiry associated principally with Henri Louis Bergson (1964) *Creative Evolution*. London, Macmillan.

ment, emphasized the 'single, indivisible being' who was the patient. In the early part of the twentieth century, Adolf Meyer's 'psycho-biology' developed this theme further by focusing upon the person's reaction to his world; and the psychoanalyst William Alonson White defined psychiatry as the medical specialty which 'approaches the whole individual'. These developments led, albeit indirectly, to George Engel's contemporary reformulation of psychiatry as a 'biopsychosocial' discipline (Engel 1977).

The concept of holism is at least one stage beyond that of the biopsychosocial model, which considers the role of 'internal' physio-logical and biological factors and their interplay with various psycho-logical and social processes in the generation of any disorder. Holism adds the overarching concept of the 'spirituality' of the individual. Of even greater importance, perhaps, is the emphasis upon the unique, positive and active nature of the individual. Holism assumes that people can play an active part in the construction of their own health, not simply by avoiding disease. This view has attracted some criticism on the grounds that the person is being 'blamed' for becoming ill, or that holism denies the obvious effects which the environment can have upon an often 'helpless' individual (Crawford 1977).

It is difficult to justify the adoption of a holistic approach in terms of obvious measurable benefits, in the traditional scientific sense. Some authorities might even argue that such an approach would be wholly inappropriate. The holistic approach does, however, have some very important things to say about the 'person' who is the patient; and about the person's relationship with the therapist or carer. At this stage of our exposition, there may be some value in discussing a holistic alternative paradigm of severe depression, if only because so many of the traditional theories have tended to ignore the person entrapped by the disorder.

An alternative view of depression: why is this necessary?

The ideas which have been discussed so far represent values or beliefs concerning the nature and function of depression. In philosophical terms, these derive from specific **paradigms**: patterns which we con-struct to serve as a guide for our actions. Our interest in paradigms stems from Thomas Kuhn's (1970) argument that 'normal science' was built on a largely unquestioning framework, supported by fundamental theories or paradigms. This framework determines not only how experiments are designed, but also how findings are interpreted. In Kuhn's view, scientists of all persuasions deceive themselves by claiming that science is objective, rational and value-free. All scientists look at the world from a particular theoretical standpoint. Given that no common body of 'neutral' observations exists, it is almost impossible to decide which of the competing theories is 'correct'.

Part of our difficulty in 'explaining' depression and finding an appropriate form of treatment relates to this 'paradigm clash'. Among the paradigms emphasized so far have been the psychoanalytic, behavioural, social and biological. Each represents views of the nature and function of depression. Each has its own inherent belief system, which acts as a guide for the 'believer'. Psychoanalysts and behaviourists behave differently, by virtue of their beliefs. Although we talk in everyday parlance about the 'non-believer', such a position is impossible. One cannot *not* believe; one can only hold an alternative belief. The rejection of one position assumes the adoption of another. This holds true for depression, in keeping with all other forms of mental disorder. Although many psychiatrists have bemoaned the disturbing presence of those who do not, apparently, believe in mental illness, this also is an impossibility*. Rather, it is a case of some people not accepting one view, or paradigm, of mental illness*. As a result, whether they admit it or not, they express belief in an *alternative* paradigm, however vaguely this may be articulated. Or we might say that some people are 'pre-paradigmatic'; not having committed themselves to any view of a situation such as depression.

The anxieties of psychiatrists confronted by 'unbelievers' revolves around their **positivist**, scientific stance. Traditional psychiatric medicine assumes that a reality exists 'out there', driven by immutable laws, waiting to be 'discovered'. If psychiatrists believe that they have found important facts about the nature and function of depression, they may, rightfully, become upset when these 'findings' are disputed. This traditional scientific approach has changed little since the days of Archimedes. Positivist scientists continue to talk as if they were observing nature 'doing her thing' from behind a thick wall of one-way glass (Guba 1990). One wonders whether or not those distressed by the anti-psychiatrist 'ravings' of the past 20 years appreciate that there may be more than one way of defining reality.

*For a contemporary discussion of the psychiatrist's dilemmas, see Stewart, I. (1991) Psychiatry: on its best behaviour. In Barker, P.J. and Baldwin, S. (eds.) *Ethical Issues in Mental Health*. London, Chapman and Hall.

*The term **paradigm** should be interpreted flexibly. As Guba notes, to be 'intellectually useful' it should not be 'cast in stone'. He notes that Thomas Kuhn, who pioneered the promotion of our collective awareness of the concept, used the term in no less than 21 different ways. Masterman, M. (1970) The nature of the paradigm. In Lakatos, I. and Musgrave, A. (eds.) *Criticism and The Growth of Knowledge*, Cambridge, Cambridge University Press; Guba, E.C. (1990) The alternative paradigm. In Guba, E.C. (ed.) *The Paradigm Dialog*. London, Sage.

Alternative paradigms

There are a number of alternatives to the traditional positivist stance. Each involves a slightly different view of the nature of reality, and different ways of studying it. **Postpositivists**, for example, also believe that there is a 'reality' out there, but acknowledge that we may not know very much about it*. To the postpositivists, reality is essentially a 'social construction', dependent upon the way people perceive the world. This view is extended further by **constructivism**, which asserts that there are multiple realities: these derive from the personal experiences of individuals, or the consensus views of specific social groups. That different people see the world differently, from time to time and from place to place, does not mean that reality is constantly in a state of flux. Rather, people – individually or in groups – are involved in a process of construction, deconstruction and reconstruction, of what they *know* as reality.

The importance of acknowledging that all paradigms are human constructions, no more or less, cannot be overstated. This holds true for the study of all aspects of our world, depression included. All paradigms represent the way we *think* about the world. As a result, they reflect, inevitably, the values of the people who constructed them. Reality exists only in the context of a mental framework (**construct**) for thinking about it (Guba 1990, p25). This reality can only be seen through a window of theory, whether this is explicit or implicit. Inevitably, this window represents a value system. There is a case for taking a **relativist** position in this debate. Realities are multiple and exist in people's minds. If we are to develop a truly informed and sophisticated model, perhaps one way forward is through relativism.

Given that this book aims to take a practical approach to the helping process, the reader may be forgiven for questioning the relevance of such arcane philosophy. These considerations seem to me, however, to be central to gaining any kind of understanding of the world of the depressed person. We assume that depression exists 'out there' at our peril. Much of the discussion about what exactly depression is seems to be similar to any discussion about the nature of death. We can observe what happens to people when they are dying or are dead; we have developed various ways of describing the 'absence' of life. The 'exact' nature of death, however, is beyond our ken, at least for the present.

One could say that these considerations are *vital*. The pursuit of a paradigm of depression which is alive and which is a true, honest

* Popper, who claimed to be the person who killed positivism, acknowledged that his philosophy 'assumes a physical world in which we act', but added that it was also necessary to 'assume a social world'. Popper, K. (1976) The logic of the social sciences. In Adorno, T. (ed.) *The Positivist Dispute in German Sociology*: New York, Harper Torchbooks.

'reconstruction' of the event of depression must be our aim. We have discovered much which is relevant. We should not deceive ourselves by assuming that this is anything other than a partial description. We may be some way from knowing even all of the parts, never mind that magical entity, the *whole*, which is assumed to be greater than the sum of the parts.

A metaphor for life, death and depression

Let us assume that a person, or indeed a person's experience (such as suffering), is like a town. The town is set in a small valley, bordered by a number of hills, each of differing heights. How do we, the observers, gain a view of the town? How do we identify which of the hills will afford us the 'best' view? Each hill affords us a particular view. We can describe the town's general appearance; with the aid of a powerful telescope we can even see some of its activity, such as the ebb and flow of traffic. Will the highest hill, affording the most panoramic view, from which we study the town using our powerful telescope, provide us with the 'best' view? Or will it offer only one view?

This simple metaphor may illustrate the problem faced by researchers intent upon developing the ultimate scientific model of depression. Each hill affords its own, unique view. Some aspects of that view are shared with its neighbours. And so it is for the various 'scientific' models of depression: each studies the same phenomenon from a specific vantage point, sharing views with its neighbours but describing things which are 'unseen' by opposing viewpoints. Each possesses its own 'angle' on depression. Although these views are different, is any one more or less 'true' than the others? Alternatively, is the whole view only possible by adding each of the views to that afforded by the town dweller, at street level? Perhaps the 'whole view', or *truth*, is no more than a goal to be pursued, eluding our grasp, always just out of sight. Perhaps the concept of truth is no more than a synonym for helpfulness.

Linear explanations

Our traditional view of depression, in common with many other disorders whether psychological or physical, is *linear* in nature. It is assumed that event A acts upon event B, producing event C. In the case of the 'common cold', some viral agent (A) infects specific human processes (B) producing specific constitutional disturbances (C) such as inflammation of the mucous membranes of the nose and pharynx. The more complex the disorder, the more complex are the effects (symptoms). In general, however, this linear model purports to explain the creation of disorder through this three-stage process. We have noted in Chapter 1 how depression has been explained by everything from the effect of specific 'humours' (Hippocrates) to 'bereavement' (Freud). Although the specific 'causative agents' have changed across the past 2000 years, the assumed process remains largely unchanged:

$$A + B = C$$

Only recently have theorists begun to construct explanatory models which try to dispense with this traditional formulation. In the next section I shall attempt to illustrate a more 'wholistic' model of depression: its creation, maintenance and, hopefully, resolution.

EXPLAINING DEPRESSION: A WHOLE PERSON MODEL

Existing paradigms: attractive but deficient?

Although an exciting assortment of theoretical models have been developed to explain the development of depression, none has been able, so far, to predict depression. One might expect that 'medical' models would provide the clearest index of probable depression, especially where the disorder has already been identified in a family member. As we noted in Chapter 1, however, even where an identical twin develops a serious depression, such as bipolar disorder, the other twin will be affected similarly in only a proportion of cases. Even where we assume some genetic factor is involved in a 'biological' depression, the accurate prediction of who will be affected and how is sorely lacking. Great insights have been gained into the way depression works; however, the search for the common biochemical pathway, the 'holy grail' of biological research, remains inconclusive*.

Freud's discovery of the unconscious*, especially the concept of loss, served as an attractive explanation of the development of some depressions. It is clear, however, that most of his psychoanalytic followers abandoned his interest in the relationship between 'mental mechanisms' and neurobiology. As a result, much of contemporary psychoanalytic theory ignores, perhaps to its cost, the role of the 'physical' person who becomes depressed. The resulting explanatory models,

---

*It is acknowledged that different 'forms' of depression may exist. This is illustrated by the person's responses to different drugs. Stern, S.L., Rush, J.A. and Mendels, J. (1980) Toward a rational pharmacotherapy of depression. *American Journal of Psychiatry*, **137**, pp545–52.

*Ellenberger noted that it was more a case of re-discovery, the unconscious having been around, in one form or another, for a very long time. Ellenberger, H.F. (1970) *The Discovery of The Unconscious: The History and Evolution of Dynamic Psychiatry*. New York, Basic Books.

with some notable exceptions, tend to reduce the complexity of the depressed person to an outcome function of abstruse psychic phenomena*.

One of the most popular contemporary models, the cognitive hypothesis summarized in Chapter 2, claims that certain people develop dysfunctional attitudes about themselves, their world and the future; all of which predisposes them to a depressive episode under certain conditions. A number of studies suggest, however, that people who become depressed differ little in their thinking style from those who remain undepressed (Lewinsohn *et al.* 1981); and those who recover cannot be distinguished from people who have suffered from other psychiatric conditions, or those who have no psychiatric history (Wilkinson and Blackburn 1981). Another powerful assumption of the cognitive model is that depressed people engage in distorted cognitions. Empirical studies, however, contradict this view: the grim reality is that non-depressed people employ more distortion than their depressed counterparts. It has been suggested that people who become depressed have failed to develop the kind of defensive screen against harsh reality which most people routinely use (Layne 1983). These cognitive views are elaborations on earlier psychoanalytic views which also provided plausible descriptions, but which failed to predict who would or would not become depressed. Although depressed people clearly engage in specific forms of thinking, a significant question mark overshadows the assertion that dysfunctional cognitions cause depression.

At the risk of sounding certain, or appearing to oversimplify the situation, it has always seemed apparent to me that complex human problems like depression require complex explanations. By complex, I mean 'involving many parts'. Many complicated, unicausal and determinist explanations have been proffered to date, from the psychoanalytic to the biochemical. The narrowness of their vision appears, to me at least, to be their major weakness.

THE SPIRAL PARADIGM

A synergistic model

Some models of depression assume that factors within the individual or originating in past or present environments act upon the person,

---

*Bowlby pointed to 'real' rather than fantasy events as the basis for his model of vulnerability to depression. In Gilbert's view, he was closer, in this sense, to the behaviourists than to Freud or Klein. Bowlby, J. (1986) *Loss, Sadness and Depression: Volume 3 Attachment and Loss*. Harmondsworth, Pelican; and Gilbert, P. (1984) *Depression: From Psychology to Brain State* (p43). Hillsdale, New Jersey, Lawrence Erlbaum Assoc.

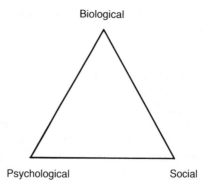

Figure 3.1 The personal pyramid.

who is characterized by passivity. Other models which assume that becoming depressed does involve the person limit their explanation to a narrow band of specific factors. Although rarely stated directly, many traditional models of depression assume that such problems arise from biological *or* psychological *or* social origins. Increasingly, it is argued that most mental disorders, if not also many physical disorders, arise from the interplay of biological, social and psychological factors: this does not exclude the recognition that one factor may be more influential than others.

Triple selves

This section explores an alternative paradigm for the development of depression, based upon assumptions about the nature of the person, as shown in Figure 3.1. The 'person' is depicted as the sum of at least three elements:

- the biological 'self': certain physical characteristics which process the production of emotional, cognitive and behavioural responses;
- the psychological 'self': the myriad processes which produce the images, thoughts, memories and fantasies associated with mental life;
- the social 'self': the relationships with individuals and groups which identify the person's position within a culture or society at large.

We might compare this paradigm to the well-known model for fire, which requires heat, fuel and oxygen: the removal of any one element extinguishes the fire. This model of the person assumes that these three elements are essential characteristics of the human state.

Considerable debate surrounds the question of whether or not depression is a 'biological' disorder. The question is, however, flawed. Our biology is involved, in various complex ways, in every event in our lives. The pleasures gained from hearing a concerto by Mozart, recalling a happy event or drinking a cup of tea are all biological pleasures. Depression, like happiness or despair – and every other experience, whether positive or negative – must also be biological. A more appropriate question might be, to what extent is depression *wholly* biological?

I assume that people are greater than the sum of their parts. I am aware of a headache, or of my legs walking. I am aware of images in my 'mind's eye' and of words being 'spoken' in my 'internal dialogue'. I am aware of specific 'rules' and 'duties' which influence my dealings with people. But who am *I*? The person *who* actually experiences these physical, psychological or social 'events' remains unclear. I concede, for the moment, that most people believe that 'they' are something other than the action and interaction of their parts. This **synergistic** representation suggests that the 'person' is the product of the collaborative working of at least these three elements: the combined forces of the individual elements being greater than the sum of their parts. The schematic presentation of this model suggests that these 'core' characteristics extend outwards in the case of some people, producing more rounded, adaptive individuals. For others, these core characteristics are more narrowly defined, producing individuals who appear more limited, less adaptive.

These core aspects of the person can be seen as strong or weak: exhibiting assets (strengths or immunities) or deficits (weaknesses or vulnerabilities). This model assumes that some people are born with a biological 'constitution' which will withstand significant life pressures, or 'stressors'. The less fortunate may own more vulnerable selves, which may buckle under the strain of certain degrees of stress. The psychological self develops as a function of 'learning'. Some people acquire means of dealing with the ups and downs of life (coping mechanisms), whereas in others such assets are less obvious. Finally, the social self also can be strongly defined or weakly constructed. Some people are supported by individuals with whom they share close, confiding relationships. They may be members of close families, perhaps supported further by friends and membership of social organizations (such as clubs, fraternities, religious bodies). All these provide direct or vicarious means of support.

People who survive the stresses of everyday living, or even extraordinary forms of trauma, may possess strong constitutions, well-developed coping strategies, or strong social support systems. This

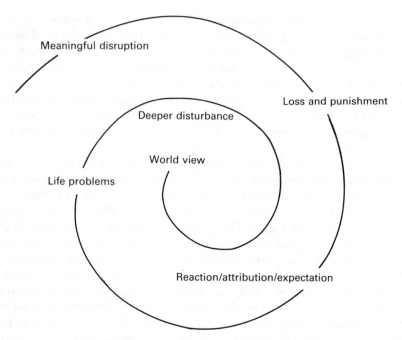

Figure 3.2 The spiral of severe depression.

paradigm assumes that the presence of all three may be the most significant predictor of 'immunity' from depression or, indeed, many other mental disorders. This paradigm is also unscientifically 'optimistic'. It assumes that even where people might be disadvantaged in one element, appropriate manipulation of the other elements can restore a balance.

This paradigm assumes, in line with Meyer's psychobiological hypothesis, that all forms of psychiatric disorder involve responses to specific events. Although in later stages of depression the person may be responding to a 'thing' of her own construction, initially the event is environmental in origin: it is a 'life event'. This response is mediated by the person's interpretations: what does it mean? The paradigm assumes that events disrupt the person's life style (upsetting, in some way, the stability of the 'triple selves'). The hypothetical process by which depression develops is illustrated in Figure 3.2.

Actions and interactions

The triangular model illustrated in Figure 3.1 lies at the heart of the alternative paradigm. This is the representation upon which the 'world' acts; and from which the person's reactions come. In considering how the model operates, imagine a spinning top viewed from above, with the illustrated spiral depicted on the top. As the top spins, it provides the illusion that the spiral is moving in and out, in constant motion. A naive viewer could not tell from 'where' the observed 'action' comes: does it 'go' from the inside out, or the outside-in? Does depression originate from within, or without? In terms of our hypothetical model, the answer to thie question is unimportant: the synergistic interaction between 'inner' and 'outer' carries the greatest significance.

The model assumes that all depressions have a beginning in the person's world. Some of these events, however, may be far removed, in time and place, from the beginning of an actual 'episode'. Such events serve as 'scene-setters' for depression. It is assumed that depression is always a response to the world: people are always depressed 'about' something, whether or not this is clear. The chain of responses to these life events produces a series of 'life problems' involving significant disruptions of the person on several planes of experience: behavioural, cognitive, affective and biological. In keeping with Thomas Szasz's (1974) 'existentialist' view, the resultant depression, like other 'mental illnesses', is a *problem of living*.

Overview of the paradigm

1. Meaningful disruptions

Certain life events disrupt the life of the depressed person because they are interpreted as actual or potential threats to the person's livelihood, life style or self-esteem. Although such life events are assumed to be the source of depression, they are defined by the person through psychological processes such as perception, evaluation and judgement, aided and abetted by social processes such as values, norms and customs. The events alone are meaningless. They become meaningful through the process of interpretation, emanating from the core.

2. Loss and punishment

All human interaction with the world can be reduced simply to positive and negative exchanges. Positive interactions strengthen, nurture or replenish; negative exchanges weaken, damage or retard the person's development. Some events restrict the 'life force', or remove supports or 'life enhancers'. Such restriction or withdrawal might be termed *loss*. Other events introduce experiences which are unpleasant or intolerable. These might be termed aversive events or *punishment*. Such events have no inherent meaning: this is provided by the interpretations noted above. Repeated criticism by parents might be viewed as punishment; the event is painful and we would avoid it if we could. Equally, we might call such criticism a loss of the respect, love and support which children expect or deserve (Lewinsohn *et al.* 1979). Such are the two faces of the life coin.

Such positive-losses and negative-gains can have a dramatic *or* gradual impact determined by the core processes which heighten or reduce the effect of similar events. Depending upon the construction, such events are interpreted as a loss (of satisfaction, value, pleasure, self-respect, etc) or the receipt of punishment (emotional pain, distress, unpleasantness).

3. Reaction, attribution and expectation

People respond constantly to everyday events, through various psychological/behavioural processes. Their perception of the effects of their responses influences their explanations of the meaning of such events. In turn, this influences their expectations of future events. People react constructively to disruption if they own 'problem-solving' or coping strategies or have the support of family and friends, who provide help and reassurance or otherwise 'share' the burden. People who face major 'losses' or 'punishment' and who own neither coping strategies nor social supports must begin to explain their plight, if only to themselves. 'Why me?' 'Why didn't that work?' 'What can I do now?' As we noted in Chapter 2, men tend to 'explain away' events, for example by blaming others; women tend to lay all the responsibility at their own door, in a heightened form of self-criticism. The kind of explanations and responses possible, in a short or prolonged crisis, depends on past experience and present support: both of these elements are derived from the core.

4. Life problems

Failure to deal constructively with life events produces a range of personal changes which underpin problems of living. If the person interprets her (re)actions as inadequate, she feels helpless; she may withdraw from situations linked with the event, however remotely, in a conscious effort to ease the distress or as an instinctive expression of defeat. Such withdrawal may parallel changes in interpersonal behaviour. Her evaluation may lead to the conclusion that she is inadequate, incompetent or substandard. Such evaluations fuel further self-criticism, encouraging feelings of worthlessness, which almost demand a retreat from normal social interaction. The disruptions experienced at this point represent the typical 'symptomatology' of depression: changes in behaviour, emotion and thought which appear 'pathological' to the professional observer who often assumes that such changes come 'out of the blue'.

5. Deeper disturbance

The person's emotional distress began with the initial experience of unusual degrees of loss and punishment. Her failure to respond constructively to these events aggravates this initial pain. Many of the strategies used to deal with distress, such as withdrawal, self-blame or isolation, merely add to the original list of losses. People who interpret their reactions in a particular way feel guilty. They may discontinue preferred activities, acting on the belief that they do not 'deserve' pleasure or satisfaction. This only compounds the original pain. People who interpret events differently may feel sad, and may discontinue the same preferred activities because they do not 'feel like' taking part in this or that. The result, however, is the same: further loss of satisfaction, compounding further the emotional distress.

6. World view

These hypothetical 'points' in the depression process are not separate entities, but are part of the person's continual construction of the world. All people are philosophers, attempting to make sense of their world and of their place within the Grand Design. This is done by use of **cognitive schemata**: learned patterns or frameworks used to process information about the world and its meaning. A half glass of water is described by one person as half full, by another as half empty. Each uses a different schema, which leads them to search their world differently: one looks for what is gone, the other for what is left (Ornstein 1986; Neisser 1976). These frameworks tie events together in our minds. They not only link our past experiences with present events, but influence how we 'discover' the world.

Such frameworks can also suggest attitudes towards life: the half glass example appears to distinguish an optimist from a pessimist. These frameworks represent the important, fundamental views the person has about herself, her world and life in general. The alternative paradigm assumes that, for the person who becomes severely depressed, either (i) a significant change occurs in an existing schema, or (ii) a negative schema, which has lain dormant, surfaces under certain conditions. In either case, the schema generates negative self-evaluations, pessimism about the future, and attributes the reasons for failure to personal inadequacies. In this hypothetical final stage, the person's 'struggle' with acute or chronic life events changes to an expression of defeat, within which she accepts that nothing can be done and that she is largely to blame for this state of affairs.

THE PARADIGM IN PRACTICE

1. Meaningful disruption

Life events – the context

The possible role of life events in the production of a depressive episode was noted briefly in Chapter 2. The paradigm assumes that depression is a function of something akin to stress. The important questions are: 'What kinds of stressors operate?' and 'How does the person interact with them?'. In general, such events can be divided into **macro-** and **micro**stressors, the former involving generalized events such as losing one's job or experiencing divorce, the latter more specific situations such as being criticized. Until fairly recently it was assumed that such life events were implicated only in the production of some depressions. It is now clear that life events are involved in some way in the generation of many, if not all, forms of depression*.

Interest in life events stems from the work of Holmes and Rahe, two physicians who appeared to demonstrate a connection between social-psychological stressors and physical illness*. Their readjustment scale identified events which required people to 'adjust to a new state'. Field studies suggested that physical illness increased in proportion to the sum of life events experienced in the previous year (Holmes and Rahe 1967). Holmes and Rahe believed that change itself was the important factor, rather than any psychological or social meaning attached to the

*Several studies describing a variety of events which could be defined as 'stressful', and which are associated with the precipitation of either mania or depression, are reviewed in Goodwin, F.K. and Jamison, K.R. (1990) *Manic Depressive Illness*. Oxford, Oxford University Press.

Despite the recognition that life events precipitate mania or depression, Goodwin and Jamison hypothesize that, as the illness unfolds, the process driving the onset of new episodes seems to become more autonomous, with stressful events contributing little or nothing. This hypothesis is analagous to the **kindling** theory: a process within the limbic system whereby initial activation gives way, over time, to a self-driven process; Post, R.M., Rubinow, D.R. and Ballenger, J.C. (1986) Conditioning and sensitisation in the longitudinal course of affective illness. *British Journal of Psychiatry*, **149**, pp191–201.

*Holmes and Rahe's work was an extension of Hans Selye's laboratory studies of the General Adaption Syndrome (GAS); Selye, H. (1976) *The Stress of Life*. New York, McGraw-Hill.

event. This assumption was, however, never fully tested. Their theory revolved around the concept of homoeostasis and adaptation: they believed that any event which destabilized the person would produce an adaptive form of biological adjustment. If interfered with, a spinning top will wobble but will regain its equilibrium. If the 'interference' is repeated, however, the top will go out of control and fall over. This crude analogy might suggest how the repetition of destabilizing events strains the body's adaptive capacity, resulting in illness. Holmes and Rahe referred to this environmentally stimulated strain as 'stress' (Holmes and Masuda 1974).

They restricted their speculative 'paradigm' to the province of physical illness. Other researchers, however, generalized wildly from their findings. The assumptions that anything which could cause psychosomatic illness could also produce emotional disorder has gained a strong foothold. The generation of emotional 'ills' seems to be more complex. In particular, the 'undesirability' of an event, as seen by the person, seems to be significant. Some events, such as marriage, retirement or childbirth, are highly destabilizing and require major changes in everyday life. Other events, such as abortion, do not demand such life changes but are nonetheless construed as undesirable (Haugh *et al.* 1979). Although Holmes and Rahe's work suggested that even positive events, such as success, marriage or promotion, could be stressful, research shows that psychological distress owes nothing to the influence of such 'desirable' changes. Emotional disturbance arises wholly from a surfeit of negative life events (Ross and Mirowsky 1979). The exact characteristics of a negative event are, however, less clear.

Life events – the process

It is not clear 'how' life events produce an effect within the biological self of the individual. The most common assumption is that such an effect is processed at a higher level of human functioning. Much everyday behaviour is performed automatically: we get up, shower, dress, eat breakast and travel to work without much formal thought*. People develop patterns of behaviour which dovetail with the demands of their environment. Life events which disrupt these 'automatic' behaviours bring additional demands, requiring more formal thinking; the need to plan, prepare, rehearse and problem-solve. The effect

---

*This has been described as 'scripted' behaviour, Langer, E.J. (1978) Rethinking the role of thought in social interaction. In Harvey, J., Ickes, W. and Kidd, R.F. (eds.) *New Directions in Attribution Research (Vol. 2)*, and Schank, R.C. and Abelson, R.P. (1977) *Scripts, Plans, Goals and Understanding*, both Hillsdale, New Jersey, Lawrence Erlbaum Assoc.

of life events is felt initially at the life-pattern level: the person is disturbed from following the everyday, routine, habitual behaviours. New demands are presented for which a pattern, or 'script', may not exist.

Life events in depression fall into three classes: multiple negative elements (macrostressors) such as losing one's job; focused negative events (microstressors) such as being criticized at work; and chronic difficulties such as poverty or relationship problems. Macrostressors have been called 'status loss' events since, invariably, they mark the transition to a position of lower status: the person experiences a loss of power, prestige or finances (Dohrenwend 1973). It seems inappropriate to try to measure the effect of any specific life event across different people in different situations. A single person who is made redundant loses money, esteem, authority and job satisfaction. A redundant parent experiences similar losses but may be expected to continue fulfilling parental obligations. In general, the parent who becomes unemployed can experience greater distress, since the demands of parenthood are not removed. The true effects of macrostressors, on a human level, involve changes in the individual's social status. These events are dependent partly upon the person's interpretation of their significance, and partly upon what they mean in social terms. The events do not possess any inherent negative qualities. Redundancy does not carry a specific 'weight' of distress; this is provided by the person or the culture. In some situations, a 'distressing' event may be viewed positively: redundancy or divorce may, for example, be interpreted as an opportunity to 'make a fresh start'.

Microstressors are also dependent upon interpretation for their effect. Most of the specific negative events experienced by depressed people also involve a perceived loss of social status: people describe being 'put down' by others, or feel that the event means that they have 'failed' or are somehow 'unworthy'. Repeated exposure to single negative events can be likened to a dripping tap, slowly wearing away the person's esteem.

The 'last straw' hypothesis

Chronic difficulties may provide a more significant index of the likely precipitant of a depressive episode than individual events. Poor relationships with colleagues at work, spouse or in-laws; recurrent bouts of minor illness; prolonged difficulties with studies; lack of work, finance or leisure time; the ongoing dependence of a family member suffering from a serious illness; all are examples of possible 'chronic difficulties'. Any single macro- or microstressor will, of course, assume wholly different proportions depending on whether or not chronic difficulties are also present. Mirowsky and Ross (1989) have argued that life events per se are a false index of possible precipitants of emotional distress. People can adjust to life events which become 'chronic difficulties': this does not mean that they become any less distressing.

Some things which appear to be 'events', such as being sacked or getting divorced, are actually part of a prolonged situation involving occupational or relationship difficulties. In Mirowsky and Ross' view, the concept of the life event is mythical: most stressors do not arrive 'out of the blue' but represent a change in potency of an existing stressor, to which the person may already have adapted. They dismiss the popular psychological tactic of developing inventories of life events or 'daily hassles' as trivializing the social causes of distress (Lazarus and Folkman 1984). In their view the true causes of psychological distress clearly are serious problems, not 'hassles'. Among these they cite inequality, inequity, powerlessness, dependency, isolation and lack of opportunity. These are the social sources from which flow the losses, failures and ongoing stressors that are interpreted as undesirable events.

It seems clear that 'events' are made meaningful by the interpretations of the individual and/or the social context. The 'events' which turn a person's ongoing difficulty (or misery) in the direction of a depressive episode may be akin to the proverbial straw which broke the camel's back. The last straw, on its own, possesses little significance. When added to all the other 'straws', it becomes an impossible burden.

Hypothesis 1 **The disturbance of depression begins with events which are rendered meaningful by personal interpretations, and/or the social values with which they are associated. These events may be the 'last straw' for the person and the 'first stage' in the depressive process.**

2. Loss and punishment

Meaning lost and pain gained

The meaning of life has been a recurrent theme so far in this book. I make no assumptions that depressed people are any more concerned than others about the meaning of their lives. It seems clear, however, that their lives appear more perplexing, less open to simple interpretations. If the meaning of their lives was ever clear, in the grip of depression such meanings become blurred, confused and, most importantly, may be challenged by the facts of everyday experience. The loss of 'meaning' may be one of the least tangible but most significant losses experienced in depression, associated with the acquisition of pain.

An uncomplicated definition of the meaning of life might be 'whatever a person is working towards, or fully involved with, at any point in time'*. Alternatively, one might define this as the purpose of life. Everyday activities, which may well be taken for granted, are significant parts of the greater configuration of our lives. Awareness of the significance, or 'meaning', of such mundane activities is often lost through necessary repetition. Awareness of the true significance of 'taking a bath', 'urinating freely' or 'drinking water' often emerges only when free engagement in these activities is denied. Only then do we become aware of the value of the ordinary. The contribution which such mundane actions make to the overall meaning of our lives becomes clearer. It seems significant that people who have experienced great privations come to cherish those aspects of life which are characterized by their ordinariness: walking on a pebble beach, smelling new-mown hay, watching the tide ebb and flow and hearing the sound of children at play*.

The joy of the ordinary

The Chinese writer Lin Yutang (1938) observed that 'all human happiness is biological happiness': a definition he might well have extended to include all sentient animals. In Yutang's view happiness was sensuous: it was not an abstract concept but a physical experience:

> To me the truly happy moments are: when I get up in the morning after a night of perfect sleep and sniff the morning air and there is an expansiveness in the lungs, when I feel inclined to inhale deeply and there is a fine sensation of movement around the skin and muscles of the chest, and when, therefore, I am fit for work;

---

*To the Chinese mind the meaning is even simpler: 'It is sufficient that I live – and am probably going to live for another few decades – and that human life exists. Viewed that way, the problem [the meaning of life] becomes amazingly simple and admits of no two answers. What can be the end of human life except the enjoyment of it?'. Yutang, L. (1938) *The Importance of Living*. London, Heinemann. The Western mind has often been dominated by the 'work ethic': 'The greatest use of life is to spend it for something that will outlast it'. James, W. (1981) *The Varieties of Religious Experience*. Glasgow: Collins, Fount paperbacks.

*These 'pleasant events' are derived from the diaries of John T. who struggled long and hard with both depression and physical disability.

or when I hold a pipe in my hand and rest my legs on a chair, and the tobacco burns slowly and evenly; or when I am travelling on a summer day, my throat parched with thirst, and I see a beautiful clear spring, whose very sound makes me happy, and I take off my socks and shoes and dip my feet in the delightful, cool water.

(ibid, pp122–3)

Yutang believed that his sensuousness was neither a personal idiosyncracy nor a oriental peculiarity. The American naturalist Henry Thoreau and his countryman the poet Walt Whitman provided Yutang with powerful occidental examples of the self-same philosophy. Thoreau, describing the pleasure he got from hearing crickets, observed:

First observe the creak of crickets. . . . They sit aside from the revolution of the seasons. Their strain is unvaried as Truth. Only in their saner moments do men hear the crickets.

And Whitman was in no doubt that his spirituality derived from his sensous exploration of sights and sounds:

For there is a scent to everything, even the snow, if you can only detect it – no two places, hardly any two hours, anywhere, exactly alike. How different the odour of noon from midnight, or winter from summer, or a windy spell from a still one!

Yutang noted that, just before his death, Lord Byron had told a friend that he had known only three happy hours during his whole life. This confused the sensuous Yutang:

Is it not plain . . . that the world is truly a feast of life spread out for us to enjoy – merely through the senses, and a type of culture which recognises these sensual pleasures therefore makes it possible for us frankly to admit them? (ibid, p132)

'Poor Byron', in Yutang's view, must have led an unbelievably miserable life, or was merely affecting the pessimistic culture of his time. Another possibility is that Byron had, like the severely depressed person, lost his awareness of all that he had done in his life. How does such loss happen?

Life disturbance

People who become depressed experience a disruption of ordinary living in which they are 'distanced' from their contact with the 'joy of the ordinary'. The disruption produced by life events distracts the person from everyday experience and introduces demands which she may be unprepared to meet. When people experience any loss – of relationships, money, employment, home, etc. – their attention is drawn, almost hypnotically, towards the resultant vacuum. Friends or family may be amazed that the person should wish to 'dwell' so much upon what is, patently, a painful experience. The person's absorption in her distress may partly be a function of her attempts to address the loss and partly a prolonged form of shock, inherent within which is the expression of disbelief. Any traumatic, aversive or otherwise painful event turns the person away from her natural supply of everyday, meaningful pleasures. The sun still shines, birds continue to sing and water maintains its capacity to slake thirst. The availability of such everyday pleasures, satisfactions and meaningful experiences, in most cases, remains unchanged. What does change, however, is the person's contact with these sources of meaning. If we compare loss to a flame, its double action becomes clearer: threatening to burn us (pain), while separating us from our safe ground (loss).

Hypothesis 2 **Meaningful life events are encountered, initially, as significant losses of positive experience, or the acquisition of unpleasant or aversive experiences.**

3. Reaction, attribution and expectation

Self-awareness – looking for explanations

The person who experiences some meaningful disruption of her life will always 'do' something in response to these events. Whether or not this is, ultimately, deemed to be useful, by herself or others, is less certain. Initially, she may respond automatically; later, more thought will be given in an effort to solve the problem. When it becomes clear that these reactions are failing to reverse the effects of the disruption, it is assumed that the person becomes more aware, both of what she is doing and what she 'thinks' about her actions.

How people 'make sense' of their lives depends greatly on how they 'attend' to the world. William James (1890) defined attention as:

the taking possession by the mind, in clear and vivid form, of one of what seem simultaneously possible objects or trains of thought.

James recognized that our perception of the world involved a complicated process of 'attention' and 'inattention'*. We 'take in' some

---

*Concepts of 'attention' typically emphasize the role of a hypothetical filter which determines how much information is passed through a 'channel' of limited capacity, for further processing. This filter 'selects out', for example, the voice of one person at a

things and exclude others. This is one of the key operations of the mind. People select information about the world and their relationship with it, using this to construct their 'world view'. This process is not always conscious. In addition to selecting between competing pieces of information, we distinguish between internal and external events. The alternative paradigm assumes that, at any point in time, attention is focused upon either the outside world (externally) or the self (internally) (Duval and Wicklund 1972).

There are strong indications that people who experience various forms of psychological disturbance attend more to themselves (self-focused attention) than to their environment: why they do so is less clear*. The layperson's advice to 'get out of yourself', 'take your mind off it' or 'stop dwelling on things' involves turning attention away from the self towards the environment. Such emotional first aid possesses an intuitive wisdom. When people experience a significant life event, such as failure, the natural reaction is to attend to the immediate internal experience; what does it mean and how does it feel? When such reflection is prolonged, however, it is likely also to prolong the person's distress (Greenberg and Pyszczynski 1986).

Although common in people who are depressed, such self-focused attention is not exclusive to depression. The special contribution made by self-focused attention towards depression appears to work in one of (at least) two ways:

1. As the person's attention turns inwards, this may trigger styles of thinking (schemas) which are dormant within the long-term memory. By 'reflecting' at length on a distressing experience, the person may activate styles of negative thinking formed in response to earlier negative life events; or
2. The person who becomes depressed may have a tendency towards self-focused attention, which is present in most situations. People tend to turn their attention back and forth, from the self to the environment, as an adaptive attentional process. Where attention is

party, excluding the many other audible stimuli which compete for attention. This process is controlled by long-term memory, with the result that 'recognizable' sounds or images will 'switch' the person's attention from one stimulus to another almost automatically. This blueprint of the attention process holds special significance for the study of depression. It is assumed that people who are depressed *selectively attend* to negative events, because they represent significant links with past negative experiences; Broadbent, D.E. (1958) *Perception and Communication*. Oxford, Pergamon Press. The concept of 'selective inattention', beloved by cognitive psychologists, probably owes its origins to Harry Stack Sullivan, the neo-Freudian psychoanalyst; Sullivan, H.S. (1953) *The Interpersonal Theory of Psychiatry*. New York, W.W. Norton and Co.
*Self-focused attention appears to be a feature of anxiety states, schizophrenia, psychopathy and substance abuse. Ingram, R.E. and Wisnicki, K. (1991) Cognition in depression. In Magaro, P.A. (ed.) *Cognitive Bases of Mental Disorders*. London, Sage

consistently self-focused, this may represent a cognitive weakness; a dysfunctional attentional pattern (Ingram and Wisnicki 1991).

Explanation – drawing inferences

If self-focused attention is one of the operations of the mind, what are its effects? The alternative paradigm assumes that the process of self-awareness, reflection or dwelling produces explanations of the meaningful disruption: what the event means to the person. Although several forms of explanation are possible, two related examples are of relevance to our discussion here: attributions and self-critical thoughts.

The concept of **attribution** stems from the philosophical work of David Hume (1711–76) and Immanuel Kant (1724–1804). Hume illustrated how people did not actually experience directly that *a* caused *b*. Instead, having observed, for example, that one event consistently precedes another, people infer that *a* caused *b*. Kant suggested later that such 'intuitions' are merely a passive process of sensibility, further acted upon by a process of understanding (Gregory 1987). Simply stated, in everyday life, people behave like scientists, trying to make their world more meaningful by attributing 'cause' and 'effect' relationships to events. The conclusion of Hume's view, in particular, is that any belief is as justified (or not) as any other. The person who believes that she has 'discovered' the cause of certain meaningful disruptions may only have found an explanation of her own construction.

Two forms of such attribution have been described (Chapter 2). The locus of control hypothesis assumes that people explain an event by attributing it to the effect of either some internal (self) or external factor (world). Attribution theory per se suggests that a 'stable-unstable' dimension provides a better illustration of how people explain their actions. Ability (self) and the scale of a problem (world) are examples of stable factors, and effort (self) and luck (world) are examples of unstable factors. The person uses such factors to explain events such as success or failure:

I failed because I wasn't good enough (self), or
I failed because the problem was too difficult (world).
I succeeded because I tried really hard (self), or
I succeeded because luck was on my side (world).

The reformulated 'learned helplessness' model of depression outlined in Chapter 2 incorporates both these forms of attribution: people who experience meaningful disruptions tend to attribute these to personal, stable and universal causes. People do not become depressed simply because they cannot cope with meaningful disruptions. Rather, depression depends upon the person's attributions of this lack of control. Attributing 'things which go wrong' to failings or weaknesses within herself lowers the person's self-esteem. Attributing causes to stable circumstances ('this is the way things are') makes it likely that the depression will be prolonged in nature. Attributing negative events to 'global' characteristics ('I have a weak personality', or 'I'm just not clever enough') compounds the personal failing further.

Explanation – crooked thinking?

Inextricably linked to these causal explanations are **self-critical statements**. As the person constructs her explanation of 'why' she has failed to cope effectively with some meaningful event, she 'refers' to her own failings, weakness or inaction. The person who becomes depressed is likely to be more critical of herself than any non-depressed person faced with similar circumstances. More importantly, the depressed person is likely to use a range of self-criticisms which strike their target with considerable emotional force. Typically, various parts of the 'self' are singled out for critical attention: her intelligence, body, sexuality, social skills, feelings and emotions, tastes, preferences, leisure pursuits, work or study habits (Nelson-Jones 1990). Through a 'personal dialogue' she will try to establish the meaning of her present situation. Since she has failed to cope with or resolve the problem, this means that she is:

deficient	incompetent	stupid	useless
a failure	inferior	unloved	weak
inadequate	pathetic	unwanted	worthless*

Some theorists believe that such self-criticism occurs against a broader canvas of 'self-defeating' thinking, arising from unhelpful views of the self, others or life in general. Albert Ellis believed that people who developed psychological problems, including depression, held rigid, personal rules characterized by 'musts', 'oughts' or 'shoulds'*. Ellis identified various 'self-oppressing' rules, all involving absolute demands on the person, others or the environment:

Demandingness: 'I must always be employed/loved/valued, etc.'
Perfectionism: 'I must never ever make mistakes/show weakness, etc.'

*These 'self-devaluing' statements were identified as of significance in determining vulnerability to depression; Teasdale, J.D. and Dent, J. (1987) Cognitive vulnerability to depression: an investigation of two hypotheses. *British Journal of Clinical Psychology*, **26**, pp113–26.
* Ellis challenged traditional psychological thinking with his, now famous, assertion that 'masturbation was not the cause of psychic ills, it was *mustabation*!'

Overgeneralization: 'I should get along with everyone.'
Self-rating: 'I ought to be successful at everything/anything I try; if not, it means I am a bad person.'
Catastrophizing: 'Things must get better, otherwise it will be just awful.'
Low frustration tolerance: 'I must improve/succeed/cope/get a new house; if not, I will kill myself.'*

In a similar vein, Aaron Beck (1974) believed that depressed people hold 'depressogenic assumptions'. These 'self-defeating' rules for living generate 'cognitive distortions', such as:

Arbitrary inference: drawing 'negative' conclusions, despite the absence of any obvious evidence to support this view; 'I failed once, this means I will never be successful'.

Selective abstraction: attending to one detail (usually negative) while at the same time often ignoring more relevant (positive) information; 'I'm just a mass of problems; I've got nothing going for me'.

Overgeneralization: drawing far-reaching conclusions on the basis of a single event, 'John says he can't stand me; nobody cares for me any more'.

Magnification and minimization: enhancing or diminishing the importance of events, typically in a self-defeating fashion; 'This is the worst thing that could ever happen to me,' or 'OK, I passed, but only just'.

Personalization: referring events to the self, even when there is no obvious connection; 'It was all my fault; or 'Everyone is depending on me'.

Absolutist, dichotomous thinking: describing events in extreme terms, like polar opposites; 'I lost my job; I'm a loser' (Beck *et al.* 1979)

In Beck's view people who become depressed tend to judge their experiences in a 'primitive' fashion. People who engage in more 'mature' thinking judge life events broadly, across a range of dimensions or qualities. However, the person who becomes depressed makes:

> global judgements . . . [using] primitive thinking [in which] the complexity, variability and diversity of human experiences and behaviour are reduced to a few crude categories.   (ibid, pp14–15)

---

*Ellis grouped these forms of 'self-disturbance' into two main categories. **Ego disturbance** involves self-oppression; **discomfort disturbance** implies emotional disturbance such as anxiety or depression felt when needs are not met. In Ellis' view, 'rational living' is only possible when self-acceptance and high tolerance of frustration are joined. Dryden, W. and Ellis, A. (1986) Rational-emotive therapy (RET). In Dryden, W. and Golden, W. (eds.) *Cognitive-Behavioural Approaches to Psychotherapy*. London, Harper and Row.

Although such views of the development of depression are commonly associated with the 'cognitive-behavioural-therapeutic' movement, interest in the role of 'thinking' in psychopathology has included eminent psychoanalytic theorists. Silvano Arieti (1970 and 1974) was one of the first psychoanalysts to recognize that depression might result from conflicts of ideas (cognitions) which are not reducible to the primitive or fundamental biological drives, as described by Freud. Arieti's **cognitive-volitional** school of psychotherapy emphasized the significant contribution made by (wo)man's higher aspects of development. In the case of depression, if not other forms of psychopathology, (wo)man appears to use her ideas about herself and the world in a wholly self-defeating manner. Therapists of a range of persuasions (from 'cognitive-behavioural' to 'cognitive-volitional') acknowledge that a change in thinking style is essential if the life problem of depression is to be resolved. Despite the implicit heresy, even some psychoanalysts have almost adopted a cognitive-behavioural position:

> Cure (*sic*) is the result of the patient altering his cognition in everyday behaviour outside the office. The task of therapy thus is to liberate the individual from his rigid distortions of the past and to make him receptive to the genuine novelty and flexibility of the future. (Bemporad 1980)

Expectation – the prospect of bleakness

These reflections on past events also determine the person's expectations for the future. If her explanation of past failures is in terms of some personal, unchanging weakness, it is 'logical' that she should expect to fail consistently in the future. This projected view of the self was described by Bandura (1977) as 'self-efficacy': the person's prediction of her capability to handle difficult situations in the future. The depressed person attributes her failure to cope effectively with past difficulties to personal failings which are unlikely to change. As a function of this explanation, she develops a negative view of the future: she expects that, confronted with similar demands, the same negative results will be repeated*. If such an outlook was not present

---

* It has been proposed recently that a specific 'hopelessness' depression may exist. The 'hopelessness' depression is characterized by (1) lack of energy, apathy and general reduction of psychomotor activity; 'There is no point'; (2) sadness. 'Nothing will change, the future is bleak'; (3) sleep disturbance, associated with rumination (brooding); (4) lowered self-esteem. Abramson, L.Y., Alloy, L.B. and Metalsky, G.I. (1990) Hopelessness depression: an empirical search for a theory-based subtype. In Ingram, R.E. (ed.) *Contemporary Psychological Approaches to Depression* New York, Plenum Press.

before, the person now adopts a pessimistic view of the future (Gutheil 1959).

The threatened species – alone, incompetent and powerless

Unlike our animal brethren, (wo)man possesses few, if any, inherited structures to help determine the 'best' actions in difficult situations. Other primates rely on instinct: (wo)man is guided by a special intelligence when making the 'right' choices. That special intelligence is **self-awareness**: knowledge not only of the world, but also knowledge *of* that knowledge (Fromm 1982). The alternative paradigm assumes that the person who becomes depressed is unable to respond constructively to meaningful disruption, for several reasons. More importantly, she *knows* that she is powerless and such self-awareness is an additional burden.

Powerlessness is especially, though not exclusively, evident among women. The feminist literature speculates that 'learned helplessness' might be the best explanation of the higher incidence of depression in women, who are both personally and politically powerless (Bernard 1973; Chesler 1972). Social rearing practices may encourage women to settle for a subordinate role. It may also, in some cases, predispose them to develop the self-critical thinking style noted above*. It may also be that, unable to contemplate facing the 'slings and arrows' of everyday life alone, many women settle for a submissive marital role; one which merely exacerbates their helplessness. A cynical, though not necessarily incorrect, view is that one partner's well-being is the other's depression. The likelihood of depression, in either partner, may be lowest in an 'equitable' relationship where both partners share decision-making. The more common scenario is the 'self-aggrandizing' relationship, where one partner tries to dominate the other in pursuit of personal well-being. That partner, almost invariably, is the dominant male.

Despite the impact of the women's movement, it seems clear that women do not simply believe that they are powerless: threats to their well-being exist within marriage or other permanent relationships and within wider societal forces which alienate and subjugate them (Mirowsky and Ross 1989, Chapters 7 and 8). The alternative paradigm assumes that the experience of meaningful disruption produces its own inimitable distress. The person's awareness of, and reflection

---

* The view has been advanced that little girls are *trained* to be helpless. Broverman, J.K., Broverman, D.M. and Clarkson, F.E. (1970) Sexual stereotypes and clinical judgements of mental health. *Journal of Consulting and Clinical Psychology*, **34**, pp1–7.

upon, her powerlessness to control this disruption can exacerbate such distress.

The alternative paradigm does not postulate that people construct the experience of depression directly: the assumption that 'crooked thinking' causes depression is too simplistic. It is assumed, however, that the initial experience of distress can be heightened; more fuel can be added to the emotional fire*. The alternative paradigm also acknowledges that the person is likely, in most cases, to have good reasons for her depression. Not only is she likely to experience significantly greater meaningful disruptions, she will have fewer social resources available to help her cope: she *is* alone, and under threat (Billings *et al.* 1983). It is assumed, however, that she adds the constructions that 'This is all my fault', and, 'Nothing can be done about it'*.

Hypothesis 3 **Rumination on the possible causes of emotional distress focuses attention on the 'self', is likely to be associated with self-critical attitudes, and leads to increases in feelings of distress.**

4. Life problems

The appearance of depression

At some stage, the original, internal experience of distress will be joined by external expressions of disturbance. The initial mood disturbance is augmented by specific biological, behavioural and cognitive disturbances: the 'picture' of depression begins to emerge. As she begins to appreciate, however accurately, her powerlessness, the depressed person begins to behave in ways which are 'appropriate' to such reasoning. If 'nothing can be done', why should she do anything?

---

*In a prospective study, Lewinsohn and his colleagues found that before becoming depressed, 'future depressives' showed no evidence of irrational beliefs or other forms of negative expectations or thinking. Nor did they perceive themselves to be powerless. Once depressed, however, such 'crooked thinking' was present as a *correlate* of depressed affect. Lewinsohn, P.M., Steinmetz, J.L., Larsen, D.W. and Franklin, J. (1981) Depression-related cognitions: antecedents or consequences? *Journal of Abnormal Psychology*, **90**, pp213–19.

*The significance of all such 'cognitive' explanations of distress is disputed. Studies suggest that depressed people do not make attributions spontaneously but only when asked for them, as in questionnaires. Hanusa, B.H. and Schulz, R. (1977) Attributional mediators of learned helplessness. *Journal of Personality and Social Psychology*, **35**, pp602–11.

Davison and Neale suggested that the psychologists' assumption that people *care* what the causes of their behaviour are may be flawed. 'Lay people may simply not reflect on why they act and feel as they do to the same extent that psychologists do'. Davison, G.C. and Neale, J.M. (1986) *Abnormal Psychology: An Experimental Clinical Approach* (4th edition) (p206). New York, John Wiley.

Such reasoning may inspire a retreat from everyday activity, associations and relationships: a physical and emotional withdrawal. Her overall presentation changes. Like many other mental health problems, friends and relatives only become aware that the person might be depressed when certain signals are emitted.

Behavioural effects

By this stage it may be possible to 'read' specific signals of depression. The person's reactions may become slower and more deliberate; she may appear indecisive; gestures may reduce to a minimum; speech may be slow and halting. She may become slightly stooped or may adopt 'retiring' postures withdrawing from the world. She may say that she finds things difficult, tiring or simply impossible. Less often, some people may show opposite reactions: becoming restless and agitated; pacing back and forth; fidgeting; complaining or repeatedly making vague expressions of unhappiness.

At the same time, the person begins to reduce further her involvement with everyday activities. Engagement in work, social and leisure activities all decline: these either are too 'demanding' or no longer 'satisfying'. A loss of 'interest' in sex is common, though not inevitable. Whether this is a 'behavioural' change brought about by the experience of emotional overload, or a 'biological' change stemming from some physical base remains unclear. Some compensation may be sought in alternative 'passive' activities: lying in bed, watching television, flicking through magazines or other 'light' reading. Gradually, engagement in these activities also fades. In the severely depressed state the person may describe a 'paralysis of the will'.

Biological effects

Changes also become evident within basic biological functions. The reductions in 'motivation', which are implied by the withdrawal from activity, are partnered by sharp reductions in energy levels. Even minor exertions may induce near exhaustion. Sleep may become disturbed: difficulty may be experienced in getting to sleep, with recurrent wakenings during the night or in the early hours. Less often, the person may sleep excessively. Such changes may be influenced by the ruminations and 'search for meaning' noted earlier: her thoughts may keep her awake or, once wakened, she may become absorbed in such thoughts. Alternatively, excessive sleeping may be a basic, instinctive form of withdrawal: hiding from the world and all its attendant problems. Appetite may also become disturbed: she either finds food unappealing, losing weight accordingly, or eats excessively, thereby gaining weight*.

Cognitive effects

The person's thinking may also change, both in form and function. The formative changes noted earlier, where she develops, or resurrects, a negative self-concept, are extended. Self-reproach and self-blame increase, bringing in their wake heightened feelings of worthlessness or guilt. At this stage many sufferers experience recurrent thoughts of suicide: a common rationale for such a desperate 'solution' is that she, or everyone else, would be 'better off'. Such **catalogic** thinking is the logic of despair*. At the same time, difficulties in thinking may also be experienced: concentration, memory and decision-making may all be affected.

These changes are insidious and complementary. They are encircled by a progressive flattening of affect: earlier experiences of frustration, anger, sadness and dejection turn now to isolation, boredom* or despair. In milder forms of depression, the person may cry often and for long periods. Where the experience of depression is severe, the person may feel like crying, but cannot. Some people who are severely depressed express strong wishes to be rid of this distressing state. Others, however, accept their fate. Feeding may be neglected to the point of starvation; inactivity extends as far as ignoring even basic needs; the person feels justified in believing that nothing in life is good, that death is preferable and that any attempt to improve her situation is

---

*It has been suggested that people who have been dieters react within depression by eating more, thereby gaining weight. Polivy, J. and Herman, C.P. (1976) Clinical depression and weight change: a complex relation. *Journal of Abnormal Psychology*, **85**, pp338–40. It may be that some people eat to elevate their mood. Liberman, H.R., Wurtman, J.J. and Chew, B. (1986) Changes in mood after carbohydrate consumption among obese individuals. *American Journal of Clinical Nutrition*, **44**, pp772–8. There would also appear to be a strong connection between disruption of eating and sleep. Bennet, G. (1988) *Eating Matters* (Chapter 7). London, Heinemann Kingswood.

*Distinctions should be drawn between suicides which are (1) **catalogical** – where the person feels helpless, fearful and pessimistic; (2) **logical** – where death offers a rational release from psychological or physical burdens; (3) **contaminated** – where death offers a transition to a better life (e.g. heaven) or a means of saving face (this may be culture-bound); (4) **paleologic** – where the thinking is guided by delusional or hallucinatory processes. Schneidman, E.S., Farberow, N.L. and Litman, R.E. (1970) *The Psychology of Suicide*. New York, Science House.

*Some people are affectively frozen: they report that they feel nothing. Everyone and everything appears to leave them cold. Joy, sorrow or pain do not appear to register. They experience a grey world, have no appetite for life and contemplate death as a passive option. Fromm (1982) believed that some such people may participate in violence or minor cruelty as a means of producing a source, however short-lived, of excitement. Also, Heath, R.G. (1964) *The Role of Pleasure in Behaviour*. New York, Harper and Row.

pointless. She may feel guilty about being alive, in the absence of any obvious 'reasons'. This person considers her mood entirely appropriate to what is an utterly hopeless situation: perhaps even believing that this is no more than she deserves*. The person who experiences this severe form of depression believes that she cannot extricate herself from such difficulties, and that no-one else can possibly help her*.

Hypothesis 4   **Failure to deal with critical situations stimulates 'problems of living' which are experienced on biological, behavioural, cognitive and affective levels, and which represent the 'symptomatology' of depression.**

5. Deeper disturbance

The downward spiral

Emotional distress was experienced first in an automatic, almost reflex form, when meaningful disruptions dislodged the person from the rhythm of her life. At that point she felt the disruption; the loss of satisfaction or meaning and the attendant emotional 'pain'. As time passed, without any obvious recovery or resolution, she began to construct her personal explanation of events, attributing her 'failure' to 'failings' within herself. Recognizing, albeit subconsciously, her helplessness, she tries to 'cut her losses' by withdrawing and hiding. Every depressed person is faced with Hamlet's dilemma:

> Whether 'tis nobler in the mind to suffer
> The slings and arrows of outrageous fortune,
> Or to take arms against a sea of troubles   (Hamlet, III, i)

The depressed person invariably sees only one viable option: to duck for cover. Unfortunately, this is likely only to increase the mental suffering induced by her outrageous fortune.

The continuation of these avoiding tactics leads indirectly to a deepening of her distress, especially if she continues to reflect upon her problems, and to evaluate how she is dealing with them. Nelson-Jones (1984) has proposed an elegant outline of the processes which contribute to this deepening crisis. Four specific ways of managing her

---

* In Bemporad's view, this person is experiencing a **psychotic** depression. Arieti, S. and Bemporad, J. (1980) *Severe and Mild Depression: The Psychotherapeutic Approach* (p60). London, Tavistock.
* Engel called this the **helplessness-hopelessness syndrome**. Engel, G. (1968) A life setting conducive to illness: the giving-up-given-up complex. *Bulletin of the Menninger Clinic*, **32**, pp355–65.

crisis may be taken, each of which accelerates the downward spiral. At this stage the developing 'career' of the depressed person becomes a headlong erratic rush.

1. Self-protection The person may deal with these painful disruptions by a cognitive form of self-defence. She may try to limit her recognition of the true meaning of certain events; that someone no longer loves her or that debts are accruing (**denial**). She may tell herself that there is nothing she can do; that this is not her responsibility (**rationalization**). She may block her awareness of the positive approaches made by others (offers of help, expressions of concern): to her these seem inappropriate (**defences against the good**). Because she now believes that she deserves 'her lot' she may turn 'good' experiences into 'bad' in order to maintain her negative self-concept (**distortion**).

2. Misattribution The person may rely increasingly upon the personal explanations of her distress noted earlier. Some people tend to avoid taking responsibility for their plight by blaming others; others take an excessive responsibility upon themselves. The person who is severely depressed is likely to review her progress in dealing with the meaningful disruptions, concluding that her 'failure' to find a solution is further evidence of her basic failings.

3. Unrealistic expectations By this stage the person has developed a strong belief in her own helplessness and incompetence. In reviewing her efforts to date, she sees only abject failure. In anticipating future problems, whether major or minor, she is convinced that she is inadequately prepared. Whether or not she really is inadequate is unimportant: she *thinks*, therefore she *is*! In reality, the person may only lack the confidence to experiment with various options. At the same time, however, she is overconfident that future events will be as threatening as she imagines. From such a viewpoint, the depressed person tends to look for possible hazards, to the exclusion of any possible gains which might be had. Such a negative view of future events further encourages her retirement from life.

4. Unrealistic rules In reflecting upon her plight and her failure to deal constructively with it, she continues to be influenced by the 'self-defeating' rules noted earlier. She feels ashamed because she has failed to live up to some 'gold standard' which, in all probability, has been defined by others. Women in particular often are defined by the media where rules concerning the 'ideal' mother, wife, lover and general object of sexual attraction are churned out with ceaseless regularity. Women who smack their children, burn the dinner, do not feel like having sex, have the 'wrong' kind of hair, complexion, body build, clothes, etc. feel guilty over what they deem to be *their* shortcomings. The depressed person does not stop to ask 'who' made these rules or 'why' they are to be obeyed. In addition to accepting as her own rules framed by others, she is totally unaware of the extent to which others may fail to abide by them*.

The emotional terrorist

The net result of these reflections is a form of emotional terrorism, through which the person begins to inflict serious damage. The alternative paradigm assumes that, for many people, a significant degree of 'outrageous fortune' exists. The severely depressed person does not aim for such self-abnegation. In Mirowsky and Ross' (1989) view: 'Some people are more distressed than others primarily because they are in difficult circumstances which their personal histories have not prepared them to master' (p181). At some point the person loses sight of the external nature of her distress; explanation becomes an internal, personal affair.

The person's relationship with herself becomes largely negative. She perceives herself to be weak, ineffectual, a failure, a potential hazard to friends, family or children. As such she is more likely to experience 'self-hatred' than anything remotely resembling 'self-love'. Such a damaging relationship with the self rarely ends there. Instead, relationships with others, both actual and potential, are also disturbed. The person with self-defeating patterns of feeling, thinking and behaviour needs very special forms of 'social support'. She needs love, acceptance and understanding to help challenge her self-directed emotional terrorism and extricate herself from her 'stuckness' (Nelson-Jones 1984, pp65–6 and 80–1). In some cases, the person isolates herself, withdrawing from or avoiding relationships because she feels 'unworthy'.

---

* It should not be forgotten that many psychotherapists do not 'free' people from such sociocultural shackles, but deliberately maintain them. Masson observed that even renowned 'humanistic' therapists, like Fritz Perls, Milton Erickson and Carl Rogers, believed that they 'knew' what was right for the patient. Of Erickson, Masson noted: '. . . by Erickson's own admission . . . whether the values of the therapist coincide with the values of a patient was . . . largely irrelevant, since clearly he believed he has discovered, in his own life, the correct way to be in the world. (p274).

Masson may, however, have been blind to what 'really' was happening. Brandon offered an alternative view, using Fritz Perls as his example: 'Frequently he was, by conventional judgements, unhelpful. He tried to extend their personal awareness of the agony of Samsara – the circle of self-frustrating effort – so that their ego chains might suddenly burst in the released energy. He made them seek their own internalised guru rather than lean on him'! (p100). Masson, J.M. (1989) *Against Therapy: Warning – Psychotherapy May Be Hazardous to Your Mental Health*. London, Collins; and Brandon, D. (1976) *Zen in the Art of Helping*. London, Routledge and Kegan Paul.

In other cases, the person misattributes the reasons for her predicament either to herself or others; either way she is alienated. Those who unrealistically blame themselves or others may strain relationships beyond breaking point. Where the person is manifestly persecuting herself, friends, family and partners may be driven away, if not by the frustration of their inability to help then by their inability to cope with such 'pathological' behaviour*.

The kind of social support needed at this stage is no simple matter. Having a social network of friends, colleagues and family is not enough. People who are part of such a network do not automatically provide the support needed; they may, for the reasons given above, shirk any close contact. The depressed person needs emotional intimacy:

> Support comes when people's engagement with one another extends to a level of involvement and concern, not when they touch at the surface of each other's lives . . . The qualities that seem to be especially critical involve the exchange of intimate communications and the presence of solidarity and trust.
>
> (Pearlin *et al.* 1981; see also Brown and Harris 1978)

In the absence of such supports, the person's thoughts and feelings about her world, its meaningful disruptions and her reactions to them are given free rein. Her very real threats are projected now in stark relief. The door begins to close on any possible solution or means of escape. The nightmare begins (Styron 1991).

Hypothesis 5 **The spiralling interaction of negative self-evaluations and problems of living deepens the experience of emotional distress.**

6. The window on the world

Encapsulation

In the final stage in the process of depression the cycle is completed, or begins again, or both. This stage involves a metaphorical linkage between the person's peripheral contact with her world and her very core. This may not even be a final stage: it may be no more than a distorted mirror image of the source, from which the person's trials

---

*Rogers described the case of a woman who believed that her mother never loved her. Her relationship with two husbands failed and she was only able to see beyond her negative feelings about herself through the support of her third husband, who loved her 'for who she might become' (her potential self). Rogers, C.R. (1973) *Becoming Partners: Marriage and Its Alternatives*. London, Constable.

sprang. This 'un-conclusion' is another of depression's paradoxes. The disorder is characterized by a paradox of mood: the more the person 'feels', the less certain she is of 'what' she feels. Depression is also characterized by a paradox of thought: the more accurate is her perception, the more she appears to be disadvantaged. Finally, as the disorder gathers momentum, she constructs an image of the world which may be no more than a reflection of her image of herself: she becomes the biter bit.

Throughout the earlier hypothetical 'stages' the person was involved in a continual examination of her world and her relationship with it. It may be platitudinous to observe that the depressed person is more acutely aware of her 'existence' than the rest of us*. The various stages of development which have been described represent the person's efforts to respond to events which have produced a significant change in her life. It has been observed that, although useful in many ways, cognitive theory may pay too much attention to the person's internal world. The effect of the environment, both in setting the scene for depression and ultimately in resolving it, may be of greater import (Gilbert 1984). When we consider the cumulative effect of this 'spiral of despair' it seems logical to assume that the person's 'self-view' will be affected, if not by the very 'unfairness' of life then by her perception of her failure to deal constructively with these meaningful events. As the person becomes encapsulated by helplessness, the depiction of a 'clinical depression' becomes more apparent. This is no longer common woe or misery. This is an extraordinary event. Now, the age-old question is asked ever more impatiently: does this distress issue from 'within' or 'without'? Whichever answer is proffered, we must address one *personal* issue: what is the 'self' which, through weakness or malfunction, has enabled this crisis, or which may be damaged by the emotional havoc wreaked by a cruel world?

The schema

The 'self' considered here should not be confused with the subject of *self-psychology**. The 'person' operates on at least three cognitive levels.

---

*In Reynolds' view, people with psychological problems (in general) 'feel and think a great deal and do very little'. Reynolds, D.K. (1985) *Playing Ball on Running Water*. London: Sheldon Press.

* Self-psychology is a specific variant of psychoanalysis, where the analytic concept of the *ego* is developed, especially in relation to people with so-called personality disorders or fragile self-esteem. Kohut, H. (1971) *The Analysis of the Self*. New York, International Universities Press; and Kohut, H. (1977) *The Restoration of the Self*. New York, International Universities Press.

1. She draws information from *memory*, providing a model of past experience.
2. She uses such recollections to assist in *decision-making*; and
3. She is *aware* of these actions (1 and 2) and can *reflect* upon them.

These functions might represent the basic requirements for the definition of the 'self' or 'person' (Johnson-Laird 1988). People who are unable to gain access to memories, make decisions or reflect upon 'themselves' are often assumed to be damaged or deficient 'persons'*.

In Bartlett's (1932) view, memory had a 'personal' flavour, not because of a hypothetical self but because of the way different levels of schemata were organized. Memories were not stored like some photographic replica of the original experience. Instead, each experience was assimilated into a number of schemata, each of which was a dynamic, flexible mental structure. People did not, therefore, recall events exactly as they had occurred: every event was 'reconstructed' from these various schematic contributions to 'memory'. These schemata exist, in Bartlett's view, at different levels. These range from innate or basic schemata, which might involve 'instincts' and depend greatly on sensory input, to increasingly sophisticated schemata involving 'attitudes and ideals'. These more complex schemata which reflect knowledge, beliefs and mood are the processes which are presumed to play a key role in depression.

Primitive thinking

Bartlett's schemata represented an early information-processing model, describing 'how' experience was encoded for future retrieval (Ingram and Reid 1986; Weingartner *et al.* 1981). Our interest here focuses more upon the content of the schema: what kind of information about the 'self' and the 'world' does the person retain? In Beck's view, people who become depressed are:

> prone to structure their experiences in relatively primitive ways. . . .
> In primitive thinking the complexity, variability and diversity of human experiences and behaviour are reduced into a few crude categories. (Beck *et al.* 1979, pp14–15)

Such 'primitive thinking' is characterized by the kind of cognitive distortions reviewed earlier. These are learned in childhood and, at least in Beck's view, are not supplanted by more 'mature' models of

---

*People with profound mental handicap or advanced dementia are often deemed to be 'not quite persons'.

the world*. The negative thoughts of the depressed person derive from a set of dysfunctional beliefs. These have been represented as specific 'needs': for love, achievement, approval, perfectionism, entitlement, omnipotence and autonomy*. It is commonly accepted that the person is unaware of these 'silent assumptions' by which she construes herself and her world and which form the basis for the definition of her self-worth. This is, however, a rather simplistic viewpoint. It seems unlikely that depression-prone individuals could not develop (learn) more mature patterns of thinking. If their experience of the world rested solely on such primitive thinking, they would be in a state of constant depression. It seems more likely that primitive thinking is triggered by meaningful events, in the manner described so far in the alternative paradigm. Encountering events which are similar to situations faced at an earlier stage of development may 'reintroduce' more primitive styles of thinking, associated with those earlier experiences.

Chicken and egg?

Some evidence exists for an alternative view of the depressive self-schema. Several researchers have asserted that dysfunctional attitudes are one of the effects of depression, rather than the cause of mood disturbance*. Silverman and his colleagues demonstrated that significant changes in dysfunctional attitudes could be produced by a combination of drugs and supportive psychotherapy. In their view such 'rapid and dramatic improvement in attitudes about life' could not be accounted for by such a simple form of psychotherapy. In a related study these authors showed that when 'well', depressives (*sic*) displayed less maladaptive thinking than other psychiatric patients (Silverman *et al.* 1984). These findings tend to weaken a plausible model of depression: *viz.* dysfunctional attitudes, acquired in childhood, surface in adult life when triggered by life events, stimulating cognitive distor-

---

*For other views on the 'depressive self-schema', see Kuiper, N.A. and Derry, P.A. (1982) Depressed and non-depressed content self-reference in mild depression. *Journal of Personality*, **50**, pp67–80; Kuiper, N.A., Derry, P.A. and MacDonald, M.R. (1982) Self-reference and person perception in depression. In Weary, G. and Mirels, H. (eds.) *Integrations of Clinical and Social Psychology*. New York, Oxford Press; and Kuiper, N.A. and Olinger, L.J. (1986) Dysfunctional attitudes and a self-worth contingency model of depression. In Kendall, P.C. (ed.) *Advances in Cognitive-Behavioural Research and Therapy*. Vol. 5. Orlando, Florida, Academic Press.
*These seven core 'needs' were identified by Burns and derive from Weissman and Beck's original Dysfunctional Attitude Scale. Burns, D. (1980) *Feeling Good: The New Mood Therapy*. New York, William Morrow; Weissman, M.M. and Beck, A.T. (1978) Development and validation of the dysfunctional attitude scale. Paper presented at the meeting of the Association for the Advancement of Behaviour Therapy, Chicago.
*Schreiber was one of the first to propose this view. Schreiber, M.T. (1978) Depressive cognitions. *American Journal of Psychiatry*, **135**, p1570.

tions which lead to mood disturbance. Whether the depressive self-schema is the cause or product of depression remains unclear.

What is clear is that, when depressed, the person employs a specific set of 'internal rules'. She makes predictions about what may or may not happen if she does this rather than that. These rules play a significant part in influencing her behaviour towards others (in her external world), if not also towards herself (in her internal world). There appears to be little doubt that these 'rules' derive from her experience of the world, both past and present. These rules suggest that she has failed, on a personal level, to do all that is necessary to entitle her to the esteem, respect, love and support which others derive from their fellow (wo)men. If a 'final' stage can be reached in our hypothetical spiral paradigm, it is the metaphorical isolation of the depressed person. The feeling that she is cut off from the world is consolidated. She remains in touch with the world, its demands and satisfactions. She is isolated, however, by her own self-defeating rules, which contaminate both her vision and interpretation of her world. It is as if her window on the world was glazed with a distorting lens: try as she might, she cannot see what is so meaningful to our eyes.

Hypothesis 6 **The person who is depressed begins to see the world from an extremely negative viewpoint, which stimulates further negative interpretations of 'life' and her interaction with the world.**

A TENTATIVE CONCLUSION

Reviewing the problem

Core assumptions of the alternative model

In Chapter 2 I summarized the psychological models which I considered offered the most plausible psychological descriptions of the development of depression. I believe that these offer meaningful options for the helping process. Although differing significantly from one another, these perspectives provide singular views of depression. In this chapter I have tried to place the psychosocial contribution in a wider perspective; that of a hypothetical, integrated model of depression. This paradigm rests, however, upon some core assumptions, which may prove its undoing.

If science has a cross to bear, it is the assumption that understanding is possible only through reduction and experiment. As Williams (1976) has noted, *science* involves a theoretical 'knowing'. This can be distinguished from con*science*, which implies a knowledge based on conviction or commitment. The knowledge of the sufferer from depression, clearly, is a valuable knowledge; albeit more of conscience than science. The alternative paradigm acknowledges the two-pronged nature of knowledge. The paradigm assumes that understanding depression is possible only by blending levels of experience; the person's experience of herself and her world combined with the world's experience of her.

If a single theme could be identified as the most apposite metaphor for depression, it would probably be that of *loss*. Loss is experienced through the person's psychological construction of events which are part of her social experience. Loss is akin to the sides of a coin: on one side is represented the loss of naturally occurring positive experiences (the inherent 'enjoyment' of a relationship, for example); on the other, the unwelcome gain of the aversive experience of emotional pain, which may be part and parcel of the loss of pleasure, enjoyment, meaning, etc. The alternative paradigm assumes that loss is a developmental process, within which the loss of 'pleasure' and the gaining of 'pain' are so inextricably linked that we can scarcely distinguish them.

Emphasis has been given here to the central role of cognition: the person's perception, judgement, interpretation and classification of experience results in the construction of the 'meaning' of that experience (Statt 1981). I have noted that it is blindingly obvious that depression must, like all human experience, be a biological process. I have tried, however, to separate the 'hardware' from the 'software': distinguishing the numerous biological processes of the brain from the myriad psychosocial processes of the person's interface with the world, the interaction of which ultimately runs the depressive programme. The alternative paradigm assumes that such a distinction is both tenable and constructive.

That people experience both 'internal' and 'external' worlds is another important assumption of the paradigm outlined here. It would appear that people with severe or long-standing depressive experiences own specific expectations about their world. In particular, they appear to develop a 'fatalistic' outlook; expecting that their depression will recur or follow a certain (chronic) course. It has been suggested that such fatalism is an inherent, dormant weakness of the depressed person. The 'alternative' view, adopted here, is that such an outlook is fostered as part of the experience of depression: failure to deal constructively with meaningful events leads to helplessness, which in time becomes a more generalized form of fatalism.

Cogito ergo adflictus sum

The idea that people who become severely depressed either are, or become, in some way 'defeatist' is a vital concept. It raises many issues, especially concerning the kind of help they require. It should not be forgotten that the terms 'defeatist', 'helpless', 'superstitious' or 'fatalistic' are emotionally loaded. They represent judgements made about the judgement processes of the depressed person. We might ask in what way are professional judgements any more 'reasonable' than the judgements of the person who is the patient?

Leaving the judgemental issue aside, there are strong indications that some form of psychological vulnerability is at work in the development of a depressive illness. Terms like 'defeatist' connote this vulnerability, focusing upon the possible self-defeating nature of the person's thinking style. To paraphrase Descartes: 'I think (the way I do), therefore I am depressed'. However, I hope that I have made it clear in this chapter that 'psychological style' is no more likely to be the sole, overriding cause of depression than any one of the many other factors which might be involved. The manipulation of social and biological factors can, however, often prove difficult if not impossible. The way the person understands the world is part and parcel of everyday experience and is open to manipulation from a range of perspectives. Before proceeding to discuss what kind of manipulation might be recommended, let us consider briefly the kinds of interventions available.

Seeking solutions

Therapy – the lion and the lamb

Western science has long been a supporter of the adversarial system: 'fighting' illness and 'attacking' disease. Physical medicine is replete with metaphorical examples: the more dangerous the pathology, the more 'aggressive' the treatment. It is no accident that we employ the 'radium bomb' in radiotherapy or search for the 'magic bullet' in drug treatment. These represent our metaphorical (and physical) armoury against potentially fatal illness. The popularity of equally aggressive or 'heroic' forms of treatment has existed also within psychiatry. Few intelligent aliens might appreciate our widespread acceptance of electroconvulsive therapy (ECT); not because it is ineffective, but because we have no explanation for what, exactly, it does. Equally, aliens might be forgiven for experiencing alarm at the prospect of psychosurgery for some kinds of depressive illness, given that we cannot provide any clear rationale for why exactly we would wish to interfere irredeemably with the workings of the brain.

Our 'need' to develop aggressive responses to illnesses which are either life-threatening or 'life-ruining' seems to be a basic one. Threat, whether genuine or metaphorical, stimulates an instinctive defensive posture. Like our animal brethren, we tend to respond aggressively to all forms of threat, whether to our life style or livelihood. In psychiatry, the more severe the disorder, the more likely we have been to attack it aggressively.

This is by no means a new frustration. The recognition that we had failed to deal with the problems of people with severe 'psychotic' conditions:

> . . . encouraged the introduction of procedures which were reckless, drastic, traumatic and crude . . . dangerous methods inducing states of hypoglycaemia, smothering, suffocation, hypothermia, electroshock or convulsant drug intoxication.   (Critchley 1986)

In the early days of this century, the failure of psychiatry's latest offspring, psychoanalysis, to redress the imbalances of psychosis fostered the most radical 'cure' of all: psychosurgery. All these methods were employed, in the name of science, in a deliberate attempt to 'kill the enemy' that was severe psychiatric disturbance. This led Partridge to note of such psychotic disorders that their:

> . . . stubbornness and resistiveness to treatment, expose so clearly the ignorance of their pathology and aetiology that they arouse aggressive reactions in the baffled and frustrated therapist.   (ibid)

The adversarial approach is founded upon the assumption, often mistaken, that the disorder has invaded the person: it is 'in' the individual. Although perhaps not an appropriate paradigm for all disorders, I consider it more correct to assume that the disorder *belongs* to the person: it is 'of' the individual. This view seems to be most appropriate in the case of severe depression, where virtually every aspect of the person's functioning is involved.

Gentle change

At the risk of oversimplifying, the various therapies can be distinguished in terms of those which assume that the 'unconscious' is composed of unsavoury forces trying to break through into consciousness, and those which assume the existence of a more positive hidden force. The various derivations of psychoanalysis might represent the former, and all 'humanistic' therapies, the latter. Clumsy though the analogy may be, much traditional psychotherapy has functioned like a variant of exorcism: attempting to draw out negative feelings and hostile behaviour – the devils of the psyche. Whether or not such approaches are considered acceptable depends greatly on our model of (wo)man. There is little to choose between the traditional 'unsavoury forces' view and the blatant optimism of humanistic therapies. Neither model lends itself easily to empirical validation. Our adoption of one or the other appears to reflect an ideological or philosophical choice.

I have chosen to follow what might be described as a neo-humanistic approach to psychotherapy. I assume that all people, despite their life histories or present discomforts, possess a natural desire for 'growth'. Whether or not this is apparent on a conscious level is unimportant. Rather than assume that there is something hostile in the unconscious requiring 'exorcism', I assume that there are positive forces within the person, waiting to be freed, to allow further development*. This view of the person has major implications for the therapeutic relationship. The therapist is more likely to focus upon collaboration, encouraging active participation in self-examination, discovery and experiment. Working with the person in this way seems more akin to helping than treatment. It is respectful of the person: neither her difficulties nor her capacity to resolve them are in any way diminished. I assume that people are, to some extent, what we perceive them to be. What they might become depends, to a large extent, on our relationship with them. As Gaoaon the Zen Master observed:

> All people have the spirit – it is just a matter of careful guidance. It is just like jade in the matrix – if you throw it away, it is a rock, but if you cut and polish it, it is a gem.   (Cleary 1989)

It may be that Eastern psychology has been aware of the potency of this view of people for much longer than Western thinkers. It is interesting to note how many forms of combat from the Orient involve strategically using the opponent's attack against him. Such forms of self-defence are not wholly amenable to analysis by the 'positivistic' view of Western science (Columbus and Donadrian 1991). Combat without attack also involves an alternative paradigm. The notion that attack is the best means of defence is very Western in origin. Aggression is the only way to deal with the enemy: this applies also to the metaphorical enemy of illness. It may be that a gentler form of psychotherapy may represent a psychological form of jujitsu.

Where people are entrapped by a depressive experience, the assumption that they would 'grow' through their present difficulties still holds. I believe that this is so, even for people deemed to be depressed

---

*Two quite distinct therapies represent this viewpoint: the 'strategic therapy' of Milton Erickson, and Israel Goldiamond's 'constructional approach'. Haley, J. (1986) *Uncommon Therapy: The Psychiatric Techniques of Milton H. Erickson M.D.* New York, W.W. Norton and Co. Goldiamond I. (1974) Towards a constructional approach to social problems. Ethical and constitutional issues raised by applied behaviour analysis, *Behaviourism*, **1**, 1–84.

to a 'psychotic' degree: their acceptance of their fate may be seen as no more than an acknowledgement of the power of their 'captor'. It may appear presumptuous of me to assume to 'know' what are the needs of such people. Having been presumptuous enough to work with people who are depressed and to begin writing this book, it would be false though fashionable modesty on my part to feign ignorance of their needs. The person who is 'stuck' needs help to extricate herself. This is not the same as saying that she needs to be 'told' how to live. She does, however, need help to face the challenges and choices which are her life. Perhaps she can only do this thoroughly when accompanied by someone who believes that she has both the right and the motivation to follow her own life path.

The helping model

It would be relatively easy to construct a lengthy list of 'handy hints', 'suggestions' or 'pearls of wisdom'. Many examples of these are available already in the burgeoning market of self-help literature*. I am anxious not to repeat the indiscretions of other writers on depression who have tried to tell people how they should live their lives or who offer bland spiritual direction. The few rules noted below may appear limited. They are, however, all the rules of 'helping' which are readily apparent after 2500 years of study. Alternatively, we might say that these suggestions are all that is supported in any concrete way by the available research literature. I view these as four elements which might form the basis for a helping framework; simple yet vital props for the person who is 'frightened', 'lost' or 'helpless'. Much that is written, perhaps even here, which is designed to help the depressed person is often no more than words. As the Malay saying goes:

> When darkness falls and you find yourself too far down river, words have little value. (Wintle 1985)

The depressed person will know what that means.

The main frame: the person who is severely depressed needs:

1. *A well-planned rationale* She needs help to clarify the possible meaning of her depressed experience, and how it might have come about. In parallel, she needs help to detail the small steps which might be taken toward gaining more control of these specific experiences and, ultimately, her life in general.

* *Understanding Stress* (1988) Which Books, Consumers' Association, London; Cozeus, J. (1988) *Nervous Breakdown*, Piatkus, London; Burins, D. (1981) *Feeling Good: the New Mood and Therapy*, Signet, New York; Flach, F.F. (1975) *The Secret Strength of Depression*, Bautam Books, New York.

The depressed person often feels 'all at sea', like a 'straw in the wind', 'lost', 'submerged' or 'fragmenting'. All these metaphors graphically represent the 'unsupported' nature of the depressed experience. The person lacks the 'information' which might take her away from this frightening, painful place. Nor does she have the 'means' to propel herself, even if she did have an objective in mind. The well-planned rationale is akin to a map or a rudder, if not both (Barker 1990).

2. Significant skills training   Even if the person knew where she 'should' go or had any idea of what she 'must' do to resolve her situation, she might well feel ill-equipped to take up these challenges. The depressed person may not appear, to others, to be sorely disadvantaged. They think she needs advice and they offer her more and more of it. She believes, however, that she is inadequate. That she 'cannot' take good advice simply compounds her depression. The person who believes that she lacks the ability to handle the everyday 'slings and arrows' of her life, such as meeting people or making a meal, will be overwhelmed by the prospect of confronting major events: resolving relationship difficulties, overcoming loss or planning for an uncertain future. The person needs a special kind of support to discover, or rediscover, more effective ways of handling life. Careful attention needs to be paid to addressing those 'skills' which will be of most use in the short term, perhaps serving as building blocks for further development. Therapists who address 'deep-seated conflicts' first are not necessarily wrong, but offer no practical help to a person in distress.

Consider the example of a passer-by who, strolling on the promenade, catches sight of a person in obvious difficulties in a choppy sea. What does that person need to do? In my view the answer is clear: find something, anything, which might be used to fish the person out of the water – a line, a life-belt, a long pole. What the person does not need is a series of questions, hailed from the shore, asking how she came to find herself in this predicament, although such questions might be appropriate later.

There is something objectionable about suggesting that people who are depressed need to learn some technique which will help extricate them from their emotional predicament. David Smail writes caustically about the domination of everyday life by trainers in, and students of, a multitude of largely artifical 'skills'. A linguistic attack on the notion of 'skills training' seems to me to be inappropriate, especially in the case of depression. 'Skills' is a poor description of any significant personal change which might occur; one requiring enormous effort and probably representing momentous relief. Smail's alternative is a form of 'being with' the person. I fear that the person who is depressed may be difficult to reach, and we end up 'being with' her in spirit only. That may fail to recognize the seriousness of her predicament. In Stevie Smith's famous words:

> I was too far out all my life.
> And not waving but drowning. (Smith 1971)

3. *An independent skill use structure* Help for psychological problems often is presented in a specialized, clinical environment. Although this may be desirable at some stage, there is a need to ensure that the means acquired by the person 'in therapy' are extended formally into ordinary life. One way of looking at the relationship between therapy and real life is to use a coaching analogy. Coaching might be offered, for example, to advance a person's musical or sporting capabilities. The role of the coach is quite clear: it is not to develop the person directly or resolve problems or faults. Instead, the coach helps the person to appraise the activity critically, identifying those areas which might be promoted and those which appear to obstruct or impede 'good' performance. Such coaching is facilitative, helping the person discover strengths and weaknesses, and using the former to resolve the latter. The coach exerts a very indirect form of influence. Once the person has identified what needs to be done, practice under controlled conditions is required. In these examples they would be called rehearsal or training. Once these new strategies, techniques or tactics have been practised in a safe context, the person may feel ready to perform the new 'movements' in the real world.

There are strong arguments for taking a similar approach with people who are severely depressed, using therapy as a preparation for practice which will lead, eventually, to real life experience. Helpers and sufferers alike might do well to disabuse themselves of the notion that the 'golden hour' of therapy offers anything more than a preparation or rehearsal for the confrontation with the person's own privately experienced real life. The approach outlined in Chapter 6 adopts this viewpoint.

4. *Attribution manipulation* Removing the thorns which cause the depressed person emotional pain is a laudable but ultimately inadequate gesture of help. The provision of social support or antidepressant drugs, on their own, are examples of interventions which can significantly mollify intense emotional distress. They do not appear, however, to redress the imbalance which affects the overall life of the person. I have suggested that depression is an experience which is woven throughout the person's personal and social functioning. The commonest experience of the depressed person, which has been recounted in various forms down the ages, is one of helplessness to

redress the emotional imbalance which casts a giant shadow over the whole of the sufferer's life. A major aim of any 'therapy' is to help the person reach the conclusion that a change in mood can result from actions she has initiated. The person who attributes her feelings, good or bad, to chance events, luck, the actions of others, etc. is a fragile specimen. She is neither responsible nor accountable.

In the next chapter, I shall discuss further the importance of action. Although I have made distinctions between thoughts, feelings and behaviour, these are artificial. Feelings are inseparable from 'doing' and 'thinking', and vice versa. People do not act primarily to feel better. They act, feel and think at the same time, in a 'total behaviour'. The person needs to know that she can produce such 'total behaviours'; indeed she does so, unwittingly, all the time. The 'right' action now will 'feel' right because she 'thinks' it is right. She needs to acknowledge that all she can control is here and now; the future has not arrived and the past is gone forever:

> Everything we do today is in some way related to everything that has happened to us since birth. But since we can only correct for today and plan for a better tomorrow, we talk little about the past – we can't undo anything that has already occurred.
>
> (Glasser 1980)

The person who is depressed needs to acknowledge that although her difficulties have origins they exist right here and now. She needs help to act, now, and to recognize that some things that she does can have an effect upon her mood. She needs help to acknowledge also that, sometimes, no matter what she does, her feelings will not change. Emotions are like a Zen koan, they violate the laws of logic; understanding feelings is possible, perhaps, only though intuition (Wood 1977). In the context of the alternative paradigm, the person who is depressed may come to know what she can control by her own efforts, and what is beyond her control. Like the famous words of the Serenity Prayer, her wisdom will come from being able to tell the difference.

REFERENCES

Arieti, S. (1970) Cognition and feeling. In Magda, A. (ed.) *Feelings and Emotions*. New York, Academic Press.

Arieti, S. (1974) The cognitive-volitional school. In Arieti, S. (ed.) *American Handbook of Psychiatry* (2nd edition). New York, Basic Books.

Bandura, A. (1977) Self-efficacy; toward a unifying theory of behavioural change. *Psychological Review*, **84**, pp191–215.

Barker, P.J. (1990) Finding common ground, *Nursing Times*, **87**, (2), 37–38.

Bartlett, F.C. (1932) *Remembering: A Study in Experimental and Social Psychology*. Cambridge, Cambridge University Press.

Beck, A.T. (1974) The development of depression. In Friedman, R.J. and Katz, M.M. (eds.) *The Psychology of Depression: Contemporary Theory and Research*. New York, Winston-Wiley.

Beck, A.T., Rush, A.J., Shaw, B.F. and Emery, G. (1979) *Cognitive Therapy of Depression*. New York, John Wiley.

Bemporad, J. (1980) Additional remarks on the relation between cognition and depression. In Arieti, S. and Bemporad, J. (eds.) *Severe and Mild Depression: The Psychotherapeutic Approach* (Chapter 18). London, Tavistock.

Bernard, J. (1973) *The Future of Marriage*. New York, Bantam Books.

Billings, A.G., Cronkite, R.C. and Moos, R.H. (1983) Social-environmental factors in unipolar depression: comparisons of depressed patients and non-depressed controls. *Journal of Abnormal Psychology*, **92**, pp119–33.

Bliss, S. (ed.) (1985) *The New Holistic Health Handbook: Living Well in a New Age*. Lexington, Mass., Stephen Greene Press.

Booker, C. (1969) *The Neophiliacs: A Study of the Revolution in English Life in the Fifties and Sixties*. London, Collins.

Bronowski, J. (1973) *The Ascent of Man*. London, BBC.

Brown, G.W. and Harris, T. (1978) *Social Origins of Depression*. New York, Free Press.

Capra, F. (1988) *Uncommon Wisdom: Conversations with Remarkable People* (Chapter 7). London, Flamingo/Fontana.

Charlton, B.G. (1990) A critique of biological psychiatry. *Psychological Medicine*, **20**, pp3–6.

Chesler, P. (1972) *Women and Madness*. Garden City, New York, Doubleday.

Cleary, T. (1989) *Zen Lessons: The Art of Leadership*. Shaftesbury, Shambhala.

Columbus, P.J. and Donadrian, L.R. (1991) Psychological research on the martial arts: an addendum to Fuller's review. *British Journal of Medical Psychology*, **64**(2), pp127–36.

Crawford, R. (1977) You are dangerous to your health: the ideology and politics of victim blaming. *International Journal of Health Services*, **7**, pp663–80.

Critchley, M. (1986) Unkind cuts. *The New York Review*, April 24th, pp7–12.

Dohrenwend, B.S. (1973) Life events as stressors: a methodological inquiry. *Journal of Health and Social Behaviour*, **14**, pp167–75.

Dreifus, C. (1973) *Woman's Fate: Raps from a Feminist Consciousness-Raising Group*. New York, Bantam Books.

Duval, S. and Wicklund, R.A. (1972) *A Theory of Objective Self-awareness*. New York, Academic Press.

Engel, G. (1977) The need for a new medical model: a challenge for biomedicine. *Science*, **196**, pp129–36.

Fromm, E. (1982) *The Anatomy of Human Destructiveness* (pp309–39). Harmondsworth, Penguin.

Gilbert, P. (1984) *Depression: From Psychology to Brain State*. Hillsdale, New Jersey, Lawrence Erlbaum Assoc.

Glasser, N. (1980) *What Are You Doing?* New York, Harper and Row.

Greenberg, J. and Pyszczynski, T. (1986) Persistent high self-focus after failure and low self-focus after success: the depressive self-focusing style. *Journal of Personality and Social Psychology*, **50**, pp1039–44.

Gregory, R.L. (ed.) (1987) *The Oxford Companion to the Mind*. Oxford, Oxford University Press.

Guba, E.C. (1990) The alternative paradigm. In Guba, E.C. (ed.) *The Paradigm Dialog*. London, Sage.

Gutheil, E.A. (1959) Reactive depressions. In Arieti, S. (ed.) (1974) see above.

Haugh, R.L., Fairbank, D.T. and Garcia, A.M. (1979) Problems in the ratio measurement of life stress. *Journal of Health and Social Behaviour*, **17**, pp70–82.

Holmes, T.H. and Masuda, M. (1974) Life change and illness susceptibility. In Dohrenwend, B.S. and Dohrenwend, B.P. (eds.) *Stressful Life Events*. New York, John Wiley.

Holmes, T.H. and Rahe, R.H. (1967) The Social Readjustment Rating Scale. *Journal of Psychosomatic Research*, **11**, pp213–18.

Ingram, R.E. and Reid, M.J. (1986) Information encoding and retrieval processes in depression; findings, issues and future directions. In Ingram, R.E. (ed.) *Information Processing Approaches to Clinical Psychology*. Orlando, Florida, Academic Press.

Ingram, R.E. and Wisnicki, K. (1991) Cognition in depression. In Magaro, P.A. (ed.) *Cognitive Bases of Mental Disorders*. London, Sage.

James, W. (1890) *The Principles of Psychology*. New York, Holt.

Johnson-Laird, P.N. (1988) *The Computer and the Mind: An Introduction to Cognitive Science*. London, Fontana.

Kuhn, T.S. (1970) *The Structure of Scientific Revolutions* (2nd edition). Chicago, University of Chicago Press.

Laing, R.D. (1985) *Wisdom, Madness and Folly: The Makings of a Psychiatrist 1927–67*. London, Macmillan.

Layne, C. (1983) Painful truths about depressive cognitions. *Journal of Clinical Psychology*, **39**(6), pp848–53.

Lazarus, R.S. and Folkman, S. (1984) *Stress, Appraisal and Coping*. New York, Springer.

Lewinsohn, P.M., Steinmetz, J., Larson, D. and Franklin, J. (1981) Depression-related cognitions: antecedents or consequences? *Journal of Abnormal Psychology*, **90**, pp213–19.

Lewinsohn, P.M., Youngren, M.A. and Grosscup, S.J. (1979) Reinforcement and depression. In Depue, R.A. (ed.) *The Psychobiology of Depressive Disorders: Implications for the Effects of Stress*. New York, Academic Press.

Mirowsky, J. and Ross, C.E. (1989) *Social Causes of Psychological Distress* (pp125–30). New York, Aldine de Gruyter.

Neisser, V. (1976) *Cognition and Reality: Principles and Implications of Cognitive Psychology*. San Francisco, Freeman.

Nelson-Jones, R. (1984) *Personal Responsibility Counselling and Therapy: An Integrative Approach*. London, Harper and Row.

Nelson-Jones, R. (1990) *Thinking Skills: Managing and Preventing Personal Problems*. Pacific Grove, California, Brooks/Cole.

Ornstein, R. (1986) *The Psychology of Consciousness* (2nd edition). Harmondsworth, Penguin.

Pearlin, L.I., Lieberman, M.A., Menaghan, E.G. and Mullan, J.T. (1981) The stress process. *Journal of Health and Social Behaviour*, **22**, pp337–56.

Reich, T., van Eerdewegh, P. and Rice, J. (1988) The family transmission of primary major depressive disorder. *Journal of Psychiatric Research*, **41**, pp35–49.

Ross, C.E. and Mirowsky, J. (1979) A comparison of life event weighting schemes: change, undesirability and effect-proportional indices. *Journal of Health and Social Behaviour*, **20**, pp166–77.

Seligman, M.E.P. (1990) Why is there so much depression today? The waxing of the individual and the waning of the commons. In Ingram, R.E. (ed.) *Contemporary Psychological Approaches to Depression: Theory, Research and Treatment* (Chapter 1). New York, Plenum Press.

Silverman, S., Silverman, J.A. and Eardley, D.A. (1984) Do maladaptive attitudes cause depression? *Archives of General Psychiatry*, **41**, pp28–30.

Smith, S. (1971) Not waving but drowning. In Robson, J. (ed.) *Corgi Modern Poets in Focus*. London, Transworld Publishers.

Statt, D. (1981) *The Dictionary of Psychology*. New York, Barnes and Noble.

Styron, W. (1991) *Darkness Visible*. London, Jonathan Cape.

Susser, M. (1990) Disease, illness, sickness: impairment, disability and handicap. *Psychological Medicine*, **20**, pp471–3.

Szasz, T.S. (1974) *The Myth of Mental Illness: Foundations of a Theory of Personal Conduct*. New York, Harper and Row.

Weingartner, H., Cohen, R.M., Murphy, D.L., Martello, J. and Gerdt, C. (1981) Cognitive processes in depression. *Archives of General Psychiatry*, **38**, pp42–7.

Wilkinson, I.M. and Blackburn, I.M. (1981) Cognitive style in depressed and recovered depressed patients. *British Journal of Clinical Psychology*, **20**, pp283–92.

Williams, R. (1976) *Keywords: A Vocabulary of Culture and Society*. Glasgow, Fontana/Croom Helm.

Wintle, J. (1985) *The Dragon's Almanac: Chinese, Japanese and Other Far Eastern Proverbs*. London, Routledge and Kegan Paul.

Wood, E. (1977) *Zen Dictionary*. Harmondsworth, Penguin.

Yutang, L. (1938) *The Importance of Living*. London, Heinemann.

Chapter 4

Taking care

The fragrance of proper conduct lasts a hundred generations
(Chinese proverb)

WORKING WITH DEPRESSION

I was encouraged from an early age to watch and listen to the world about me. Once aware of its vastness, I learned quickly that a little knowledge can be a dangerous thing. It may be more correct to say that my limited understanding is easily obscured by the shadows of the Big Questions: what is life and why are we here? Providing that I do not forget this, what little I know seems to be very useful. I have admitted in the previous chapters that depression, in its various forms, has been studied for at least 2000 years. There is no doubt that we know much more now than once we did. I have noted also our tendency to restate old forms of knowledge in new, often more technical language. Given that history has a tendency to repeat itself, maybe we only discover what we have lost or forgotten. When we restate the problem of depression, we may adopt the cloak of competence, cleverly disguising our ignorance with the trappings of science.

A more honest position would be to admit that although we do not know what exactly depression is, we do know something of how it works. The experience of the past two millennia has confirmed this fact. Countless people have described the view from the slough of despond. The voice of the sufferer is fairly unanimous. Any confusion about what depression actually means rests with us, the observers. The debate is concerned with the 'why' rather than the 'what or 'how' of depression.

Beyond the breakpoint

The person who is severely depressed has reached, passed or returned to a personal 'breakpoint'. 'Break' implies that something in the person has reached a limit, a 'point' suggests that this limit can be defined (Harris 1979). I discussed in Chapter 1 how people might define their own experience of this breakpoint. Some severely depressed people may be like a one-legged person who collapses when her crutch gives way. Such people may have a 'constitutional' weakness which pre-disposes them to depression. We can no more 'fix' the constitutional weakness in the depressed person than we can replace the missing limb. We can, however, look at ways of providing new supports, or try out alternative ways of coping with the loss, disability or restrictions imposed by the depressive experience. Here I shall discuss how we, the observers, try to define what is happening in the worlds of the person: the world which is shared with others and the personal world of the interior. These definitions help us to explore the alternatives which might lend support; which might help her 'stand up' to the rigours of everyday life and circumnavigate the breakpoint.

Changing views

The suggestions contained in this chapter, if not the book as a whole, reflect a broadly cognitive view of depression. I assume that some, though not all, forms of depression arise from the sufferer's specific views of the world and the meaningful experiences existing within it. As noted in the previous chapter, many people have good reasons to be depressed. Having said that, I believe that one route to the resolu-tion of their depression is through a change of perspective, on them-selves and the world which may have treated them harshly. Such a change of perspective is, of necessity, cognitive in nature. The reader should not assume, however, that I am making any specific claims here for any brand of therapy. I acknowledge only that the depressed person's emotional experience is processed by complex phenomena which we have labelled *cognitions*. The central role of these complex phenomena in ascribing meaning to our world and to ourselves is increasingly recognized. People are machines. They are also the stories, accounts and dreams (waking and unconscious) which are the product of this amazing machine (Leiber 1991). I recognize only that we need to acknowledge the curious role played by one set of ideas in constructing another: the experience (or idea) of depression. We may only come to appreciate the complexity of the depressed mind through use of a wholly artificial model of the process which produces depressed thoughts*. Such is my reasoning for focusing attention upon the cognitive process of depression*.

The road to freedom

Although the experience of depression is very personal, indeed private, I believe that what is experienced is quite public. The depressed person reflects on her life, her actions, her failings; on the past, the present and the future. In all these musings she reflects upon what she did or did not do. Action – the very stuff of life. The emotional experience of depression is an expression of the stuff of one's life. All the wrongs which were committed, all the chances which were missed, all the good times, all the things which were neglected. All this: the good and the bad. Some of this is accepted by everyone as real (consensus reality); some of it may be real only to the sufferer (personal reality). All these things belong in the world. We can talk about them. We can share – through language – our construction of these events. What is beyond our reach is the person's interpretation of these events: the construction which she places upon them and the significance she gives to them. When we take care of the person, we help her to share with us her personal reality and our consensus reality. The effects of psychotherapy may be no more than to give the sufferer the courage to meet us halfway*.

The focus upon the here-and-now shares the emphasis of existential-

---

* Leiber (1991) observed that Man (*sic*) only developed an understanding of what the heart is after having built mechanical pumps. In his view the 'direction of understanding most often moves from artifice to nature' (p6).

* Many psychotherapists would pur scorn on the idea that the person can attain any significant change of perspective through the manipulation of cognitive processes. Smail, for example, singled out the 'so-called cognitive therapies' which took the view that 'psychological or emotional distress is best dealt with by learning to take an alternative view of things'. In his view this 'really amounts to nothing more than a version of the maxim "look on the bright side".' His hostility is based primarily on the cognitivist's assumption that 'people's distress is generated from a program somehow buried inside their heads, that what matters is the way they see things rather than the way things are'. Smail, D. (1987) *Taking Care: An Alternative to Therapy* (p84). London, J.M. Dent.

I make no claims to speak for cognitive theorists or therapists. What is clear to me is that there is a need to distinguish between the awfulness of the world and the 'awfulness' which we perceive within the world. Smail neglects to acknowledge that such a distinction either exists or is worth pursuing.

* I have noted in previous chapters that research findings indicate, paradoxically, that people who are depressed may possess a more realistic view of the world than those who are not. No longer can we assume, glibly, that we are reasonable and the depressive is 'irrational'; the reverse may be the case. The process of sharing experience within the helping relationship may have the effect of encouraging the person who is depressed to adopt our view of the world; not because it is more rational but because it eases the business of living.

ist forms of therapy: to grasp the nettle of choice and action. Although it may not feel like it, we need to acknowledge that we all stand on the road to freedom; we could not stand anywhere else*. I acknowledge that I take what might be seen as an optimistic view of the possibilities of personal freedom for people in distress. Smail is critical of therapists who suggest that 'patients (*sic*) may be "freed" from a past which is (magically) alterable through reinterpretation'. My experience with people in such distress leads me to believe that some can leave the past behind them, beginning to live in the present and for the future. This does not mean, of course, that the distressing experiences are erased. But neither does this mean, as Smail infers, that the past restrains them like some traumatizing anchor.

Depression, like many other illnesses, can be viewed as an unwelcome intrusion into an otherwise 'happy' life. There may be value, however, in encouraging the person to reconsider this position. One of the major deficiencies of the narrowly medical view of depression is its assumption that the disorder somehow enjoys an existence separate from the individual. Biological psychiatrists in particular tend to take the experience of depression away from the person, removing it from the personal context of her life, her relationships, her ambitions, etc.*. Families are often encouraged, albeit implicitly, to take a back seat. The 'illness' does not involve them, so no-one discusses it. No-one is encouraged to help, because no-one can. The treatment of depression should be left to the expert. The approach outlined in Chapter 6 begins from an antithetical position. Even if depression is conceptualized as a biological phenomenon, we render it meaningless by removing it from the human context. We run an even greater risk by assuming that depression can enjoy an independent existence and that experts can treat this Thing without the involvement of the person. Although the advice in Chapter 6 focuses upon the person, there is no assumption that her relationship with her world, and its reciprocal relationship with her, will not be a vital part of the helping process. How such relationships are managed is, however, beyond the scope of this book.

---

* This view is most closely associated with Jean-Paul Sartre, who believed that no state of affairs need be what it is; anything can be otherwise. As a result everyone was standing, somewhere, on the road to freedom. Sartre, J.P. (1973) *Existentialism and Humanism*. London, Eyre Methuen Ltd. Schilpp, P.A. (ed.) (1981) *The Philosophy of Jean-Paul Sartre*. La Salle, Illinois, Open Court. Warnock, M. (1965) *The Philosophy of Sartre*. London, Hutchinson.
* I acknowledge that many psychotherapists do likewise, by restricting their interest to what is going on within the boundary of the person's skin.

Facilitation and direction

It has become increasingly popular to assert that psychotherapy is a corrupt manipulation of sorely disadvantaged people (Masson 1989) or that the assumption that psychotherapy can be of any 'use' is manifestly flawed (Smail 1987). Despite having some sympathy for these critiques I believe that the analysis may be correct but the conclusion is false. Therapies of all sorts can be used against the best interest of the individual. Equally, many therapists appear unable to help people in distress to any significant degree: whether this is a function of the therapist or the method is unclear. For the moment I can only assert my belief that distressed people are unlikely to find the kind of support they need among their families, friends or wider society. As I have discussed at some length in earlier chapters, increasingly depression is being abstracted from individual experience. At the same time, many mental health support groups see a value in 'medicalizing' the phenomenon, rather than acknowledging the 'psychosociocultural' dimensions of such distress*. I have acknowledged that we know very little: I do not assume, however, that we know nothing. I remain convinced that 'helping' can be an asset to the individual, providing that some crucial criteria are met.

How helping operates depends upon a sensitive balance between facilitation and direction. The person who is lost, metaphorically, needs to be aware of her plight: this requires sensitive facilitation, or guided exploration. Once she is more fully aware of her plight, it seems appropriate for her to expect some guidance out of her maze of possibilities: this requires sensitive direction. How the practitioner chooses to move from one to the other is a complex art, which will be commented upon later.

THE CHARACTERISTICS OF HELPING

Eight needs exist within the four helping principles established at the end of the last chapter (Figure 4.1). These shape the helping relationship. You* might consider how these contribute to your therapeutic effort.

---

*Peplau suggests that mental health self-advocacy groups in the USA increasingly support the view that all serious mental disorders are biologically based, and are supportive of medical leadership of all treatment programmes. Peplau, H. (1991) personal communication.

*To narrow the focus upon these specific issues, I shall address the reader directly.

The need for:	
1. **Structure**	taking an active role
2. **Focus**	attending to significant details
3. **Nowness**	the authorship of life
4. **Development**	growing out of distress
5. **Experience**	the direct route
6. **Collaboration**	united we stand
7. **Holism**	fumbling with the infinite
8. **Flexibility**	the transtheoretical stance

Figure 4.1 The core needs of the helping relationship

The need for structure: taking an active role

People who are severely depressed are likely to be passive. Practitioners from all disciplines often refer to their difficult or resistive nature. It is important to begin by recognizing that this assessment is incorrect. The difficulty lies within yourself; your difficulty in effecting change. This can be an uncomfortable concept for would-be psychotherapists:

> Whenever a client 'resists', it's a statement about what you are doing, not about what they are doing. Out of all the ways that you've attempted to make contact and establish rapport, you have not yet found one that works. You need to be more flexible in the way that you are presenting yourself, until you get the rapport response you want.   (Bandler and Grinder 1979)

Therapists often act as if the person has some obligation to respond; if she doesn't, she must be blocking our efforts in some way. A more realistic view is to assume that our efforts are either off-target or presented inappropriately.

Concentration is a specific problem which might well block the efforts of the helper. The person's progressive withdrawal is expressed through increased rumination and reflection (internal) and reduced attention to changes in her world (external). Your efforts to communicated with her may be limited by her ability to attend to what you are saying. In this situation a non-directive approach, which many believe is the gentlest form of interaction, may simply make communication more difficult. If the person is 'hiding' or otherwise 'retiring' from the world, it is reasonable to assume that she perceives a threat, which we would be wise to attempt to reduce. One way to do this is to offer some support; taking the initiative by shaping the development of the 'therapy'. As the person shows signs of progress, the 'therapeutic reins' may be transferred gradually.

The person's active cooperation depends greatly on her understanding of what is involved in treatment (Ley 1988). Several strategies may be used to enhance understanding, especially where concentration is impaired. For example, listing in advance the categories of information you plan to discuss:

Where shall we begin? Well how about discussing . . .
What is wrong with you;
How we might work together;
What kind of help I might offer you:
What you could do to help yourself;
and what you might expect, by way of improvement.

'OK. First of all, what is wrong – well, I think that you are depressed . . . you feel guilty and sad . . . you don't feel like doing anything. . . .' (etc.)

Use direct and simple language, short sentences punctuated by brief pauses. Repetition of important points throughout the discussion will help her to pick up the key messages. Finally, if you want the person to do something, ask her directly: 'I would like you to tell me how you feel right now'. This question implies that she can tell you, but is framed as a straightforward invitation. In the early stages, you may need to take direct charge of the proceedings, encouraging her to respond to your initiatives. This structure will allow her time to gain confidence in you and in her own ability to participate in this new venture. As she learns the rules of the therapeutic process she can begin to take a more proactive role. The structure of therapy is for her comfort: to provide a base upon which to build her confidence, gain some experience of this new approach, gradually extending herself in a form of personal growth.

The need for focus: attending to significant details

The person who is depressed is likely to own a wealth of problems of living. The sessions should focus upon addressing the specific issues involved, rather than nebulous concepts. In the early stages the focus is upon the person's present understanding of these problems. Investigation of any underlying philosophies or belief systems is best left for later.

There is value in helping the person to tease out her problems, distinguishing the various threads which contribute to these complex life problems. You are involved in a sensitive form of psychological education, helping the person become aware of the different facets of a generalized problem and attach useful descriptive labels to these parts of her overall functioning.

It is worth noting at this point that depression per se cannot be manipulated. Depression is the umbrella concept which shelters a range of interacting problems of living. If these problems can be manipulated, the negative interactions will cease and the need for the umbrella concept will disappear. I would, however, caution against using this concept with the person at this stage. Many people take real comfort from the diagnosis of depression: in some way it explains their experience. It might prove useful to acknowledge that the person is 'suffering from depression', whether this diagnosis is made by you, some other professional or even the person herself. Having made this acknowledgement, you should encourage her to identify what life problems represent the tentacles of depression. Draw up discrete lists of her problems, expressed as emotional, behavioural, motivational, relationship, physical or cognitive symptoms of depression. By encouraging her to focus, you help her to identify some of the 'facts' of depression, which you can share with her. As long as the person continues to use the soft focus of depressive metaphor, it will not be clear to you exactly what her problems mean.

As the helping process develops, the person will become more aware of her contemporary problems. She will find it easier to label them and to describe their function in her everyday life; how they work for or against her interests. Should she begin to experiment with some of the rules upon which they are based, she will become more aware of whether or not these problems need exist. Having focused her attention upon the everyday 'manipulation' of her problems, you can help her shift the focus to the beliefs which might have helped create them.

The need for 'nowness': the authorship of life

Emphasis needs to be given to the person's experience of her problems as they occur in the here-and-now. Past events are addressed, but only in terms of what they mean now. The problems caused by past events are dealt with in a practical problem-solving manner. Much contemporary psychotherapy has been contaminated by restricted notions of the role of the unconscious: any 'therapy' which does not address the instinctual, deep-seated causes of behaviour is often considered to be superficial. I favour an alternative view: that suffering is constructed by the individual, albeit unwittingly, within her sub-conscious. The product of that construction is here-and-now. As Keefe (1975) commented:

Guilt and anxiety are children of the past and the future. To the extent that a person dwells upon the should-have-been or might-have been at the expense of living life in the reality of the present, he *suffers* [italics added].

Most traditional schools of psychological thought encourage people to believe that they are powerless; that their lives have, somehow, been mapped out for them. Psychoanalysis attributed life problems to unconscious or instinctual 'drives'. Behaviourism proposed that the person was merely a function of the workings of the environment. Even humanistic psychology assumed that familial or cultural influences had overcome the person's self-actualizing tendencies. Psychiatric medicine assumes, as I noted earlier, that the physiological or genetic processes largely determine the human condition. The influence of 'nature', in the form of inherited factors, cannot be discounted. This appears, however, to be the most depressing of all determinist hypotheses.

If we assume that the sole, or even the most important, influence on the development of a depressive illness is a genetic 'stamp', we risk assuming that the person does not exist. If human distress is a function of genetics, or genetic sequelae, then so also must be human achievement. If depression can be explained fully by genetics, then the 'peak experiences' of Shakespeare, Mozart, Einstein or Muhammad Ali must also be determined by their respective genetic stamps.

I take a contradictory position, that all people are condemned to freedom; we are all condemned to the responsibility of shaping our own lives. In doing so, we must use what nature and nurture have given us. In addition to biology, child-rearing practices, cultural mores, education and socialization, among others, influence the direction of our lives. Such forces conspire to bring us to this point at this time. As Sheldon Kopp observed, 'It is a random universe to which we bring meaning'. That meaning is largely made up of choices, made day in and day out. The reasoning which we use to make choices and decisions may not always be helpful; to that extent we can blame those who shaped our reasoning, our values and thinking style. As adults we can, however, choose to follow the difficult path toward new values, new ways of thinking, a more useful form of reasoning. We are the authors of our own lives (Nelson-Jones 1990).

Viktor Frankl, the founder of **logotherapy**, emphasized the need to acknowledge the role of personal choice in shaping our lives. His personal experience of people in Nazi concentration camps led him to question why some behaved like animals, others like saints. Which kind of 'person' they became depended, in Frankl's view, less on the conditions than on their personal decisions. People who are depressed often experience something akin to that which Frankl witnessed. They are physically alive but psychologically deadened. Instead of making contact with their present world, they dwell on the sadness of the past or are fearful or pessimistic about the future. Frankl believed that the ability to make effective choices depended greatly on the person's ability to exist fully in the present. Whether the present is painful or pleasant is of no consequence; it is the only true reality. A key principle of Frankl's logotherapy is, therefore:

> Live as if you were living already for the second time and as if you had acted the first time as wrongly as you are about to act now!
>
> (Frankl 1959)

Much of the emphasis of helping is geared toward identifying what needs to be done to deal with one problem or another. Lead the person, sensitively, towards the point of existential awareness. What she did and what happened to her in the past is important; what she might do or what might befall her in the years ahead also is important. What she is doing right now is most important of all:

> Now is the only time you will ever be given to begin changes that will result in your being at the place where you want to be when you die. What needs to be done? Do it.   (Reynolds 1985)

Such existential principles permeate a range of psychotherapies*. At their simplest level, they suggest that as long as one is alive one can act; therefore we should be alive to the possibilities of action. We deceive ourselves by claiming that we 'can't' do this or that, or that we can only 'try'. Action is always possible: what it might produce is, obviously, variable.

> It isn't necessary to want or to decide or to get it together or to motivate oneself, or to make the effort, or otherwise insert some step before the *doing*. It is the doing that counts.   (Ibid, p39)

Many therapies employ a variant of religious confession: catharsis will somehow bring emotional relief; getting in touch with feelings will somehow bring emotional enlightenment. The alternative paradigm is centred upon a more radical hypothesis. The person has constructed her emotional distress; therefore, she can de-construct it, or build an alternative, more satisfying reality. I acknowledge that this is an

---

* Existential principles appear to underpin a diverse range of modern therapies, from Albert Ellis' original cognitive therapy (RET) to Reynolds Westernized version of Japanese Moritist therapy.

anachronistic model of (wo)man. It harks back to age-old concepts
of (wo)man as a free agent, possessing a god-given individual freedom
and responsibility. Whether this freedom was meant to be a prize or a
curse often is unclear. Much of our sophisticated, modern knowledge
of the role and function of society, culture, interpersonal relations,
media, etc. appears to challenge this older construction of the human
condition. I believe that many of our contemporary 'models of (wo)man'
represent no more than reflections of human experience. I agree with
Frankl that they do not offer an adequate explanation of the variability
of human conduct; why people from similar backgrounds behave differently under virtually identical conditions. Models of (wo)man which
try to explain away human behaviour by reference to external forces
from the past or present de-humanize the person.

The process of choosing is individual, moral and ethical. People who
accept the notion that they are depressives have, in so doing, already
sacrificed their personalities. The have surrendered to the Western
belief that personality is fixed; that people do not change. You need to
assume that the person has the capacity for change. You need to
encourage the person to question whether or not she possesses a basic
'self': is such an idea helpful? Much of Western psychology operates on
the notion that the 'real person' lies in the subconscious, masked by
a false self which can crack under stress allowing the real 'self' to
show itself. The English word 'person' derives from the Latin *persona*:
literally, 'an actor's mask'. Although we often assume that masks
express a false image, they can be inherently revealing:

> Why do actors wear masks in the first place? Because the mask
> makes the actor's role clear at a single glance.   (Doi 1986)

In Japanese psychology the terms *omote* and *ura* mean 'face' and
'mind'. *Omote* always expresses *ura*. Changes in a person's face are
assumed to reflect different expressions of her mind. *Ura* (mind)
always performs *omote* (face): when people look at our 'masks', they
see not only the mask but the 'mind' through the mask. The American
psychologist William James (1890) expressed a similar view: the idea of
multiple selves, expressed through different masks. A person might,
however, try to keep some of these 'selves' a secret:

> ... afraid to let one set of his acquaintances know him as he is
> elsewhere; or [the multiple selves] may be a perfectly harmonious
> division of labor, as where one tender to his children is stern to the
> soldiers or prisoners under his control.

There is no question that all of the 'selves' are true, or that the process
of presenting one and withholding another involves choice. To the

Oriental psychologist, the idea that people might comprise only one or two 'selves' is unrealistically limiting, perhaps even laughable:

> We are apparently a unity, a stream of innumerable selves follow-ing one another like a series of cinematographic pictures, so quickly that they seem one continuous whole.   (Blyth 1960)

Encourage the person to consider that, from moment to moment, she writes the story of her life. She frames her experience in much the same way as an author plots a novel. Through its fixations with history and forward planning, our culture has lost sight of the importance of the moment. You need to help her recognize that the past was, and the future always will be, momentary. This is that moment within which she makes and remakes herself: she must seize it now!

The need for development: growing out of distress

The relationship is geared, unambiguously, toward helping the person learn from her experience. Try to help her recognize how she con-structs her emotional reality, and how she might acquire new ways of dealing constructively with life events. Although learning takes place within the sessions, it needs to be supplemented by notes, handouts and homework assignments to help extend these experiences to the real world.

The emphasis is upon learning how to cope with life in general. Experimentation with specific life problems can, however, be useful in clarifying common themes and how they might be resolved. You aim to help her develop personalized methods of coping with these problems, through repeated, systematic practice. These 'experiments' can be used later to frame broader, more flexible rules for living.

The goal of many forms of psychotherapy is to encourage some form of acceptance: this also has its place within this alternative model. You need to help her to distinguish between what can and cannot be changed. Many people who become depressed suffer at the hands of an unfavourable world. They may have suffered significant losses, abusive relationships, rejection or failure. The 'trick' of being in such an incomplete or hostile world involves the same kind of acceptance. This is a rule which applies to sufferer and practitioner alike. You also need to embrace these principles if you are to be of permanent help:

> What has been neglected cannot be restored immediately.
> Ills that have been accumulating for a long time cannot be cleared away immediately.
> One cannot enjoy oneself forever.

Human emotions cannot be just right.
Calamity cannot be avoided by trying to run away from it.
Anyone working as a teacher who has realised these five things
   can be in the world without misery*.

The person's list of 'therapeutic desirables' – what needs to be done
– can be reduced to two main categories: need for acceptance or need
for change. 'I need to improve my relationship with my partner', or,
'My partner shows no sign of wanting to improve our relationship. I
need to accept that this relationship has come to an end.'

The threads of her personal construction need to be teased out
carefully during this exercise. The person cannot change others.
Whether or not acceptance or change is possible will be known only
through direct experience. The exploration of the exact nature of
her thoughts about change and acceptance, and the evidence which
supports them, is used to prepare the way for experimentation. She
may find it threatening or 'depressing' to accept that some of her
perceived 'needs' might never be achieved. You might ask her to
clarify her thinking on these subjects: 'What exactly are your reasons
for thinking that you cannot . . . (accept or change)?'.

It is important to ask what her reasons are, rather than why she
thinks she cannot do something. The former assumes she has her
reasons: the latter invites an examination of personal philosophy which
may be premature. Many people who are depressed believe that they
are 'sick', 'helpless' or 'useless'. You need to guide them towards
recognizing that as long as they think they cannot, they will not. In
Wayne Dyer's (1990) famous words: 'Believe it and you'll see it!'.
Believe you can and you will – believe you can't and you won't.
Abraham Maslow (1962 and 1976) took the radical view that all people
with mental illness were 'cognitively wrong' rather than 'sick':

Neurosis, psychosis, stunting of growth – all are, from this point
of view, cognitive diseases as well, contaminating perception,
learning, remembering, attending and thinking.

Maslow's consideration of cognitive processes are not as well known
as those of other theorists summarized in Chapter 2. However, his
hypotheses provide valuable distinctions between 'adaptive' and
'maladaptive' thinking. They also provide the bridge between Oriental
and Occidental models of (wo)man, which have been lost in the headlong rush toward reductionst explanations of depression. 'Healthy'

---

*Attributed to Huitang; see Cleary, T. (1985) *Zen Lessons: The Art of Leadership.*
Shaftesbury, Shambhala, pp26–7.

people, in Maslow's view, get lost in 'doing'; they do things for their own sake, not as part of some interminable competition involving the judgement of oneself. The 'healthy' person is an end in itself; not a means to an end, something which is relative to the rest of the world, a partial success or failure. Maslow described 'unhealthy' people as owning 'deficiency cognitions': they measure themselves primarily in negative terms – qualities they do not possess, stages they have not yet reached, etc. Psychotherapies which address 'cognitive problems' by adjusting the person's thinking style to enhance conformity to the world simply exchange one set of restrictions for another. The person who becomes depressed is distressed more by what she or her world is *not* than by its positive reality. Help the person to experience herself and her world as it is, accepting and changing as she considers appropriate or possible.

The need for experience: the direct route

This approach emphasizes the person's experience of herself, her reflections upon her life and actions, and experience of alternative courses of action. Reflection alone will accomplish little. If the person owns 'self-defeating' rules she needs to generate evidence which will help her dispute their supremacy. Changes in thinking are bound up with changes in action. Both must be experienced repeatedly if change is to occur: repetition means disciplined practice.

From the outset, encourage the person to examine her feelings, thoughts and actions; what relationships exist between these three facets of the individual? Keeping a diary is the most basic way she can record the thoughts and feelings which occur through the action of her day. At first this task may appear daunting but if she is encouraged to build up this reflective record gradually, through time she will be able to amass considerable descriptive evidence of how she constructs her day-to-day experience. The authorship of her life will become more readily apparent.

Your working relationship with the person should be focused, unequivocally, upon her experience here and how. She should be invited to re-play memories of events, whether recent or distant. You need to help her re-experience those events, by encouraging her to: 'become more and more aware of where you are . . . what is happening around you . . . perhaps you can hear certain sounds . . . or are aware of a special smell or taste. As you become more and more aware of that whole experience you become aware of feelings within yourself . . . and you know what those feelings are. As you begin to feel them again . . .

what thoughts are running through your head . . . what is that 'private voice' saying . . . what did that whole experience mean to you?'

Encourage her to recall the various sensory experiences she had at that time: visual, auditory, tactile, gustatory and olfactory. Your instructions should be intentionally vague, allowing her to 'fill in the details' privately. It is not important that you know exactly what is going on. Such vagueness can also reduce any embarrassment or shame she might feel. It may also demonstrate that you have no interest in probing into the deepest emotional recesses, or otherwise 'attacking' her. This will cement your relationship*.

These replays sensitize the person to her personal construction of reality. They are used to illustrate how she might become more aware of the experiences which lie ahead of her. Such experiential sessions might, gradually, help her develop a broader sensation of the world. An important long-term objective is that the person should spend more time in the immediate experience of her world and less time ruminating, perhaps negatively, about the world*. The difficulty which she might experience in undertaking this transfer should not be underestimated. Providing that short periods of awareness, recorded briefly in the daily diary, are used as the starting point, the authorship of her life will grow in size and significance.

The need for collaboration: united we stand

The traditional emphasis of medicine, expressed by both the behaviour and language of practitioners, has focused upon a 'manipulation' of the person who is the patient. This is analogous to the scientist's manipulation of the laboratory conditions. Many doctors speak of the medical *regimen** and of the patient's *compliance* with the treatment conditions*. These suggest that the patient is literally 'under the doctor': submitting to his expert manipulation, subjugated by the rule of the physician.

*The use of such 'artfully vague' instructions allows the person to review her own sensory experience and can be a preamble to trance induction. This approach is strongly associated with Milton Erickson. Grinder, J. and Bandler, R. (1975) *Patterns of Hypnotic Techniques of Milton Erickson MD*. Meta Publications.
*Reynolds (1985) Encouraged his 'students' to keep daily diaries which distinguished between feelings and behavior. The therapist comments each week on the diary notes, encouraging the person to attend more to her actions, and to describe these in greater detail. As the person's awareness of her actions in the world increases, her awareness of internal feelings decreases.
*Derived from the Latin for *rule*. Many patients are encouraged to assume that this is *the* rule.
*Again, this implies that the patient needs to 'yield' to the doctor's wishes, rather than understand, agree and sanction the proposed intervention.

There is no doubt that the person who is depressed needs help and
may feel helpless. This does not mean, however, that she *is* helpless.
The practitioner should take the view that the person has resources,
capabilities and other non-specific strengths which she can draw upon.
This is done through the exercise of an active collaboration or partnership. In seeking the solutions necessary to resolve her life problems
and establish the route back to meaningfulness, the person needs
guidance and support. She does not need to surrender or be taken
over. She needs a partner who will help her to tread the scary path
towards recovery.

This kind of relationship has been referred to as:

> (the) working alliance . . . the complex of understandings and
> attachments that are formed when a person in a state of crisis
> . . . turns to another for his or her expert help and a contract is
> made. This contract or alliance is a subtle mixture of explicit and
> implicit understandings; and acknowledged and unacknowledged
> attachments.   (Bordin 1976)

The working alliance discourages the traditional passivity of the
'patient' and rejects the assumption that the practitioner is in any
way 'all-knowing'. Instead, the 'patient' and the 'therapist' work
together: one learning from the other, interacting like any partnership.
Of course, the kind of partnership required depends greatly upon
the person's needs and what the practitioner has to offer. Initially,
the relationship may be akin to that of athlete and sports coach; the
person needs to develop herself in some way and agrees to try out
the 'methods' favoured by the practitioner. As the person develops
(changes) the relationship develops. Gradually balance is established,
the person takes a more active role and the practitioner reduces his
input. Eventually, the person may assume a 'majority control' of the
content of any session; this does not diminish the collaborative nature
of the relationship, but merely shows how it has matured, like the two
parties involved.

I have noted the viewpoint that all professional efforts to 'treat'
people with psychological disorders are, ultimately, manipulative and
coercive (Masson 1989). A related view is that the 'sufferer' should
always be in control of therapeutic services; deciding what is or is
not desirable. There is some considerable merit to this argument. It
ignores, however, the possibility that some people may not 'know'
what they need at that time or otherwise feel unable to choose, given
the disabling nature of their disorder. Both these arguments also have
some sympathy with the view that no special 'therapeutic' knowledge
exists concerning mental disorder and health; a view I believe to be

fundamentally flawed. A wide range of psychosocial interventions are possible with people who are depressed. If these are to 'empower' an individual who is temporarily 'powerless', such forms of help should be offered within an open, sharing relationship. However, despite my advice against being 'all-knowing', nothing is gained by pretending that the practitioner knows nothing. Psychological therapy appears to have much in common with education; the 'therapist' helps the 'patient' learn about herself and the possible processes of change*. The guidelines written for the person in Chapter 6 illustrate a curriculum which might provide the person with a basis upon which to establish her process of personal change. It is not the way; it does not provide the answers; it is not the solution.

The concept of the collaborative relationship has major implications for traditional 'therapeutic' practice in psychotherapy. For several generations psychotherapists, and others who were keen to work in a psychotherapeutic mode, conceived of themselves as 'blank screens' on which the person could project the contents of her unconscious. Other psychiatric practitioners conceived of themselves, alternatively, as objective scientists, studying the pathology of mental disorder. Both these viewpoints result in the establishment of distance between the person and those who propose to help her. It seems self-evident that people who are in severe distress need to connect with whoever is helping them. Psychotherapists, irrespective of their ideological persuasion, might do well to conceive of themselves as teachers or spiritual guides, albeit of a secular nature, rather than radical inter-ventionists. In the future more mental health professions will come to:

> regard themselves as servants of larger spiritual reality – conceived of as God or nature, a higher power or life energy – of which they and their patients are a part. As such, they will see themselves more modestly, as vehicles for healing rather than its agents, as co-participants in a process that is awesome rather than as its controlling force. (Gordon 1990)

This provides an even wider, perhaps more realistic view of the therapeutic (healing) process. The therapist's task is double-edged; needing to restore both the person's and their own harmony – with nature (the world) and the inner nature (self). Those who seek help need to establish what changes they need to make and how they might make them. Those who offer help need to become aware of their capacity to enable such a process of exploration and discovery. Both are involved in defining the 'art of the possible'.

---

*The Latin root of 'doctor' (*docere*) means 'to teach'. Perhaps doctors and other health professionals should be more like teachers than therapists (healers).

The need for holism: fumbling with the infinite

Traditional 'treatment' or 'therapy' in psychiatry has had very limited aims. By slavishly following the biomedical model, many psychiatrists ended up with greatly reduced models of the person: reduced to manageable 'parts' which were assumed to interact, mechanically, to form a 'whole'. Such a reductionist approach leads naturally to the definition of pathological parts whenever the person experiences some life problem. Any fear becomes an anxiety state; sadness and loss become one form of grief or another – 'normal', 'abnormal' or 'delayed'. All such forms of psychopathology are seen as invasions of or attachments to the self. From the perspective of the alternative paradigm, the person does not suffer from anxiety, grief or depression; rather, she expresses such disturbances of mind (*ura*) through her actions or masks (*omote*). Although she may not be aware of what exactly she is expressing, to presume that what she is expressing does not belong to her (or is meaningless) is de-humanizing. This applies equally to minor and severe forms of mental disturbance. As Podvoll (1990) observed, such an attitude has major implications for the kind of help offered:

> Believing that psychosis, for example, begins and ends with idiosyncrasies of the brain nullifies it as a human tragedy, and contributes to the steadily deteriorating conditions of care that today face almost all of the chronically mentally ill.

Some theorists have emphasized the centrality of actions in the complex functioning of the individual. In doing so the idea of 'splitting' people up into emotional, intellectual and behavioural 'selves' is questioned:

> Doing, thinking, and feeling are inseparable aspects of behaviour and are generated from within. Most of them are choices.
> (Wubbolding 1988)

Rather than talk about 'suffering from a disorder', the distress the person is expressing is acknowledged:

> Thus an angry person is said to be 'angering' rather than to 'be angry'. Clients are encouraged to say, 'Today I am guilty', or, 'Last night I was depressing'. Phrases like 'fit of depression', 'anxiety attack' or 'stressful job' are meaningless.*

---

*Contrary to writers such as Podvoll, Wubbolding (1988) believes that the issue of choice applies only to certain forms of behaviour: 'psychosomatic ailments and psychoses are not choices' (p5).

It could be said that the outcome of many traditional models of mental disorder is to 'explain away' the person's experience; with the result that the meaning is taken out of the person's actions. This is true of all biomedical and psychological models of depression. A 'depressing' person is expressing what it means to 'be' at the moment: this involves thoughts and feelings which are expressed naturally through actions – *ura* performing *omote*. She expresses the whole of her experience. You need to attend to that whole; therein lies the person.

Not only have many traditional therapeutic theories failed to take account of the whole person, but most assume that only minor 'tinkering' with the self is possible. The 'damage reduction' ambitions of the psychoanalyst were defined by Freud's infamous admonition that 'neurotic' unhappiness should be replaced by 'ordinary' unhappiness. Although the attainment of 'symptom relief' alone can be very difficult, there are good reasons for trying to address the whole nature of the person rather than her isolated parts. The pessimistic notion that people cannot achieve 'real' happiness may simply generate a self-fulfilling prophecy: if nothing much can be done, the therapist will do little, and little will be the result*.

Alternatively, if you embrace the person whole this will reduce the likelihood that you will rely on single reductionist methods of helping. Everything from adjustments to the diet to meditations and prayer might conceivably be of value. I must confess that, 25 years ago, before I became a mental health professional, I accepted without question the hypothesis that 'you are what you eat'. I also assumed that contemplating death, the infinite or God was an important, daily requirement. It took me many years to unlearn the principles of traditional psychiatric practice, and to begin to appreciate once again the infinite natural wisdom of being human. That depression can be anything but a human tragedy seems so obvious that it hardly requires repeating. That people who are depressed need to consider the role of diet, prayer or contemplation as part of their 'recovery' needs to be repeated forcefully. The traditional critic will argue, for example, that there is no evidence that this 'shotgun' form of helping is of real value. The American psychiatrist James Gordon (1990) adds the wisest of caveats against such cynicism:

> Whatever the efficacy of these approaches (exercise, dietary modification, relaxation, guided imagery and meditation) they reinforce the patient's sense of control and empowerment and the

---

* At the risk of sounding uncharitable, psychoanalysis appears to offer an excess of very little.

concept of health care as partnership in which both physician and patient have responsibilities.

This is the crux of the matter. You need to be aware that many therapeutic systems can be used as a professional shield against the distress of the person. If you desire to be involved with the whole person who is depressed, you need to be ready to use the whole of your self; no more can you afford to stand back or shelter behind one or other of the 'screens' employed by traditional psychotherapists. Gordon (1985) acknowledges that:

> Medication (for example), particularly in an institutional setting, was often used as a tool for foreclosing, under the aegis of therapy, ideas and behaviour which were unconventional and disturbing to the staff.

It should be apparent that more limited forms of intervention will be less taxing for the practitioner; all forms of 'processing' reduce the need to think, feel and act along with the object of the process. In all forms of psychological distress, but especially depression, there is a need for creative engagement. The helping relationship needs to be played for real.

The need for flexibility: the transtheoretical stance

The riddle of depression has intrigued theorists down the ages. In the past century a wealth of 'explanations' have been concocted. The radical behaviourists maintained that the actions of the depressive were the outcome of natural learning: her withdrawal from 'life' was reinforced by the withdrawal of 'pain' (Ferster 1973). Ethologists saw the depressive 'display' as a fixed action pattern, stimulated by specific releasing conditions (Eibl-Eibesfeldt 1972). The psychodynamic school saw depression as a function of unresolved conflicts established in childhood (Gilbert 1984). Many other examples exist. Indeed, even within these 'schools', dispute and conflict abound. The hypothetical model of depression outlined in the previous chapter not only integrates some of the diverse functions of the person, but attempts to dovetail differing theoretical perspectives on the genesis and resolution of depression. In this chapter some consideration has been given to the practical process of this alternative paradigm: how do we go about helping the sufferer? I remain sceptical about the emergence of any one clear indication of what, exactly, should be done. I favour the alternative view that many things might be done; indeed, that the greater the range of options, the greater the likelihood of a satisfactory outcome.

What needs to be avoided is the narrow ideology of the traditional 'schools', whether biomedical, psychoanalytic, behavioural, social or cognitive*.

My suggestions for a skeleton of self-help, provided in Chapter 6, are constructed around a cognitive framework. My reason for choosing this approach is simple: the reader is thinking, constructing images, recalling events, framing and re-framing the meaning of experiences – making herself up, moment by moment. Cognition is undoubtedly at the core of everyday experience. Cognition is the medium for the messages of our everyday lives. The self-help guide is written in the first person to allow the person to experience, directly, all the questions, comments and suggested directives which might be relevant to her own experience. In addition to some of the received wisdom of traditional psychotherapy, I include metaphors, riddles and quotes from writers as diverse as Zen masters or modern humanistic therapists as part of my helping package. I assume that many, but not all, therapeutic systems can be of benefit to the person who is depressed. There is much value in cherishing eclecticism:

> ... the dilemma is whether a therapist should practice as an ideological partisan or as an eclectic. The partisan (e.g. the psycho-analyst, the radical behaviourist, the reflective Rogerian) stays with the principles and techniques of a particular mode of therapy, whereas the eclectic uses techniques as they fit, regardless of theoretical purity. Accused of theoretical sloppiness, if not contra-diction, the eclectic therapist is likely to take satisfaction and confidence from the precision of the technique-to-problem fit ... contrary to common sense and conventional wisdom, different therapies are not more effective with different problems (Lueger and Sheikh 1989).

Although the scientific purist may be upset, much is to be gained from employing an eclectic, transtheoretical approach. It seems clear that people make changes in their lives for a multiplicity of reasons. You might consider what part any of the following have played in shaping the conditions which have resulted in the choice of a specific course of action:

- A chance encounter with a friend or stranger;
- A traumatic accident;

* All psychotherapies run the risk of becoming restricting ideologies. Masson draws attention to the tendency, which originated with Freud, for therapy to become a secular religion, with all its attendant rules and obligations for those who join the 'movement'. Masson, J. (1989) *Against Therapy: Warning – Psychotherapy May Be Hazardous to Your Mental Health*. London, Collins. Masson, J. (1985) *The Assault on Truth: Freud's Suppression of the Seduction Theory*. Harmondsworth, Penguin.

- A serious illness;
- Reading a book, poem, newspaper or magazine article;
- Viewing great works of art;
- Hearing familiar or new pieces of music;
- Recalling the past;
- Contemplating the present;
- Imagining the future;
- Looking in a mirror.

This list is endless. Any or all of these everyday events shape the conditions of the exercise of personal choice. These events provide us with the materials which stimulate the idea of choosing, or help us to weigh up options. There is no reason why the helping process cannot accommodate such 'shapers'. There is no reason why 'therapy' needs to be focused entirely on talk and the expression of warm, empathic, genuine understanding. Effective helping cannot be based within any one rigid ideology: the person and her world are too complex for such reductionism.

GETTING STARTED

Dreams and possibilities

Some important practical steps need to be taken as an introduction to the whole helping process. How does the person feel about entering into this relationship? What does she think the practitioner might be able to do for her? These thoughts and feelings should be clarified at the outset. Some time should be set aside to allow the person to air these freely. If she has unrealistic expectations, it is important to clarify what exactly is on offer; what is possible, given your skills and knowledge.

The working relationship

Some discussion of practical arrangements is also necessary. How often you should meet, where, at what time and for how long are of great significance. This discussion allows the person to express preferences while allowing you to continue to clarify the 'possibilities'. This adds to the scene-setting and represents another step taken in the art of collaboration. By discussing these arrangements in an adult, egalitarian fashion, the practitioner 'validates' the sufferer. She is a full person who needs to be consulted, but whose every wish it may not be possible to meet. Hopefully, she will gain the impression that this will be an equal and dignified relationship.

Making introductions

Although the helping process has already begun, there is value in repeating some of the features of the 'alliance' before the first faltering steps are taken. The approach outlined in Chapter 6 is heavily structured. It makes demands upon the sufferer and the practitioner. The nature of these demands should be re-stated, without being overly dramatic. The helper needs to emphasize the belief that the person can be helped, but this is most likely to happen through her active collaboration. It may be of value to illustrate the vital nature of the partnership by reference to notable partners: Sherlock Holmes and Dr Watson solving a mystery; Fred Astaire and Ginger Rogers personifying rhythm; Tim Rice and Andrew Lloyd Webber creating 'pop' opera. Each has their part emphasized by using the coach and athlete or master and pupil analogy, whichever seems most appropriate. Even within these relationships, partnership reigns supreme.

Within this introduction, acknowledgement should be paid to the importance of homework assignments (learning in the real world), keeping diaries (reflection), and generally using oneself as an experiment (self-study). An agreement may be made at this stage to tape record each session. The person can take away a copy of each session for further study at home*.

THE STRUCTURE OF THE INDIVIDUAL SESSION

You should aim to create an atmosphere of continuity of learning from one session to the next. Unlike treatments, which expose the person to some highly technical or arcane procedure, here she is an active, equal collaborator. You need to take specific steps, perhaps repeatedly, to reinforce this style of 'therapy'. This will be the case especially where the person has received more traditional forms of treatment. The key feature of this approach is the sharing of knowledge of 'what' will be done within the session: the therapeutic agenda.

Your main aim is to help the person develop an awareness of how she 'constructs her own reality'. Your key role is to facilitate that awareness, helping her make meaningful connections between her thoughts, feelings and events in her everyday life. To achieve this aim, emphasis needs to be given repeatedly to her experience within the session. What does she think of what is being done? What does this mean to her? What can she do with this new-found perception of herself and her world?

---

*This practice appears to have originated with Ellis. Ellis, A. and Grieger, J. (1977) *Handbook of Rational-Emotive Therapy*. New York, Springer.

It is common practice in therapeutic circles to allocate one hour to a session. I make no such prescription here. Where the person is very severely depressed, such a period may prove too taxing for her concentration. Shorter, more frequent periods of contact may be more appropriate. As she becomes better able to cope with the demands of the sessions, these may be extended. At all times the response of the person should be used as the gauge: abandon all 'sacred cows' such as the concept of the 'golden hour'. Of even greater importance is the need to relate everything which happens within the session to the rest of the person's life:

> There is a myth in our culture that something magical occurs during an hour of psychotherapy . . . Many people seem to believe that what happens during the golden hour is sufficiently powerful to colour the rest of the week. They seem to believe that the other 167 hours of the week have less effect than that one hour. Even some therapists agree. To succumb to this myth is to relegate 167/168ths of life to meaninglessness. Life must be lived moment by moment. Each moment brings possibilities for purposeful activity. Each moment carries a message, a lesson for us. There are no golden hours, only ready people.   (Reynolds 1985, p56)

The recent past

The person should be given an opportunity to review, briefly, what has happened since the last session. What has occurred in her every-day life, or within her personal musings or reflections, which might be addressed? Are these problems or signs of progress? A brief review of the outcome of the homework assignment is necessary. What did she do and what did she think of that? Given this addition to her self-knowledge, what can she do? Finally, as an introduction to this session, she should be given an opportunity to recall and comment upon the events of the previous session. What does she remember addressing? What does she think of that now, with hindsight?

Your aim is to promote a sense of continuity between the sessions. Encourage her to recall the past sessions so that she can reinforce the 'significance' of what has been learned. She may refer to notes or diary jottings to refresh her memory. The main aim, however, is that what has happened in the recent past is recalled, interpreted from her new 'viewpoint' and added to her growing body of self-knowledge.

Negotiation

The first step in the session is to decide about content. A realistic agenda needs to be set; one which will address the issues which you both believe represent the 'threat' from previous sessions. Alternatively, some current problem of living may be selected. This task can be left to the person's initiative in later stages of contact. Earlier in the process, however, it may be valuable to 'brainstorm', briefly, a list of possible contenders for the agenda. These should be ranked, collaboratively, in terms of their relative importance at this stage. Your role is to ensure that the person does not try to run before she can walk. Initially, the agenda will focus on developing awareness and enacting limited action-experiments. Progressively, the focus will turn to the personal rationales which underpin her thoughts, and in turn her feelings. The uncovering and 'reality-testing' of specific beliefs about herself and the world are better left until later. By that time she will have built a solid base of self-knowledge.

The core

The major part of the session is devoted to a careful examination of the item(s) on the agenda. You need to encourage the person to describe her 'problem'. Typically, she will describe problems with her feelings (sad, guilty, ashamed or fearful); her will or motivation (apathy, avoidance, inertia); her actions and interactions (slowness, coping, withdrawal, relationships) and her physical self (sleeping, eating and sex). Some specific problems may be encountered with thinking (indecisiveness, impaired concentration and memory). She may also ruminate, or think obsessively, about any of her other problems; worrying either about where these problems will lead or trying to account for their origin. Having offered a description, the person should be encouraged to defined her problem: 'In what way, exactly, is this a problem?'.

Your main aim within the core is to help the person to become aware of the personal rules which govern her perception not only of events and the actions of others, but also herself. You are trying to guide her towards recognizing that some of the 'awfulness' of her world derives from the constructions she puts upon events. Having identified how she views these problems at present, you will help her to identify and consider other viewpoints: how might others perceive these events? Finally, you will help her to assess whether these 'alternative' view-points offer any help in reducing her distress. Where these alternatives are a radical departure from her typical mode of thought, how might she go about using or developing these viewpoints?

Where the 'problem' is not one of her construction, she needs help to explore alternative courses of action. If she has not dealt successfully with this problem to date, she may have failed to acknowledge and use possible alternative courses of action. You need to help her identify such alternative solutions, and to 'rehearse' how she might implement such problem-solving strategies.

Practical assignments

In conclusion, a realistic task should be negotiated which will allow the person to explore the issues she has examined intellectually and emotionally in an interaction with her natural world. What can she do between now and the next session which may allow her to come face-to-face with the problem which has been addressed? This assignment needs to be outlined in some detail. Vague ambitions to 'speak to my mother' or 'sort things out at home' need to be translated into discrete actions: what will she do, with whom, where and when, exactly!

A brief discussion is necessary on why this is desirable. Here again, your role is to facilitate her statement of the value of doing this or that now. If she is unclear as to the 'point' of the assignment, you may clarify. You should acknowledge that any such assignment is likely to prove a daunting task. Ask her how she feels about this. Does she have any lingering doubts? What does she think might happen? What might stand in the way of carrying out the assignment? How will she record what takes place?

Résumé

Before winding up, summarize the session. What has she learned? What seem, at this stage, to be the most important 'findings'? What do these mean to her? A further dimension to the collaborative nature of the relationship can be gained by inviting her to comment upon your handling of the session. Does she see you as facilitative or directive, helpful or threatening, challenging or bullying, focused or discursive, understanding or argumentative? At first, such frank exchanges may appear threatening. Encourage her to recognize that your role is to highlight her assets and expose her weaknesses; you are merely asking her to do likewise. Finally, a few minutes should be left for any other comments, winding down from what may have been a demanding time.

STAGES OF DEVELOPMENT

The issues which need to be addressed, developmentally, across the sessions will vary from person to person. However, assuming that people who are severely depressed have some elements in common, a very general guide to ordering the content of the sessions is possible.

1. The budging process

Severe depression is characterized by its 'negativity'. The person, or more likely family and friends, will report the relative absence of all that once was considered normal. In the early stages it is wise to devote your attention to trying to dislodge her gently from her place of hiding. Given that she is unlikely to be able to cope with anything more demanding, this represents a critical area of attention. Although you may feel the need to try to ease her emotional distress, she may not think that feeling better is possible; she may even believe that her distress is appropriate. For this reason, the focus on activity may be doubly rewarding, offering the opportunity to challenge her assumption that she cannot do this or that, with the possibility that some of these actions might prove rewarding in some way.

2. Distress reduction

If her distress is not eased by the transfer of some of her attention from 'within' (feelings) to 'without' (action), now is the time to tackle disabling emotions. The same quasi-experimental approach is employed: what does she do with herself which increases or decreases her 'bad' feelings? How might she promote the use of these strategies? How might she enhance their effectiveness? The early faltering steps she has taken to re-enter the world of activity provided her with an opportunity to study herself with a degree of objectivity. This is taken a stage further in an attempt to use self-study as a means of putting some useful distance between herself (the viewer) and herself (the feeler).

3. The build-up plan

She may not be ready to pay closer attention to her thinking style, extending her awareness of how her thoughts lead her actions and implicate her emotions. Work can now begin on shaping her awareness of alternative ways of 'constructing' her world and of enacting some new patterns of behaviour. What sort of thoughts does she typically use to interpret events? How does she justify the use of such thoughts? What alternative interpretations are possible and what are her reasons, because it is assumed that her important actions are influenced by her thought processes? To what extent will thinking differently promote acting differently? If she is clearly unable to respond to important life events, careful attention may be required to help her know not only what to do but how to do it.

4. Consolidation

If she has reached this stage the person will look different, feel better and act more confidently upon her world. She might well be described by psychiatrists as being 'affectively well'. At this stage she is likely to be discharged home from hospital, or active community treatment begins to wind down in the hope that she will return gradually to everyday life.

Rather than suggesting any such withdrawal, you need to encourage the person to explore her core beliefs more closely; to take a long critical look at how she constructs the various meanings of her life. It is assumed that her discrete 'thoughts' about herself and the world in general derive from such broader constructions. Whether these predate the depression or are a function of it is largely of academic interest. Such disabling beliefs will be present. How can she become aware of such silent assumptions? How might she anticipate their re-emergence, thereby reducing the likelihood of depression in the future?

At this stage the person needs to embark on a reconstruction of herself which is of necessity looser, more philosophical. Comparison or contrast of beliefs with those of friends, colleagues or peers within a therapy group may be of immediate value. Consideration of some of the thoughts about success and failure, life and death, which have been provided by some of the great minds from the past or present may prove an even more rewarding, if longer-term exercise. David Reynolds has described his modification of Morita Shoma's Japanese psychotherapy. Once the person has built a solid foundation in the 'art of everyday living', more advanced exercises are suggested, any one of which might challenge an unhelpful personal philosophy. Reynolds' ten advanced exercises show a balance between 'contemplation', on an intellectual or emotional level, and various forms of 'meditation in life'. Included on his list are:

- Dig, plant, and care for a garden.
- Write a journal of the sounds you hear.
- Analyse the psychological advice in television shows.
- Read and compare the writings of Sheldon Kopp, Fritz Perls, Constantin Stanislavski and Dögen.
- Give away something you value to someone who can't repay you.
- Give a name to a feeling you have experienced, a feeling which has no name in English.
- Keep a journal about what you have received from others, what you have returned to them, and what troubles you have caused during that day (Reynolds 1985, pp115–16).

These exercises are exemplary for several reasons. They provide opportunities for the person to experience the relationship between what she can and cannot do – as in the patient tending of a garden, serving Mother Nature. They provide focused opportunities for comparing the advice of television pundits with those who might well have possessed true wisdom (who should be included in such a list is, of course, debatable). They provide opportunities for reviving the social self – giving things away – and acknowledging, without unnecessary judgement, that we can all give, take and be troublesome. This list also offers the person an opportunity to 'create' meaning out of distress, rather than simply suffer by coining a name for some emotion. Such an action can bring a new kind of awareness of emotional self; an awareness that much that pains us can be incorporated without suffering emotional collapse.

THE THERAPEUTIC STANCE: GAINING THROUGH LOSING

In this chapter I have outlined the structure upon which the therapeutic relationship and the learning process, for both the person and yourself, might be built. It is axiomatic that such a relationship cannot be achieved without the establishment of a human, honest, collaborative, egalitarian approach. These qualities represent the core of any positive relationship but I do not overestimate their value as an aid to the promotion of emotional independence. I believe that we need more than warmth, genuineness, empathy and unconditional positive regard to facilitate the process of change discussed here. Sadly, even love itself is rarely enough; and I suspect that love will represent too great a demand on many who strive to be therapeutic. The more ordinary human interactions are an adequate medium to express the necessary technology which I have outlined. Whether this admixture will be sufficient you must determine for yourself.

There is no room in this text for an epistle on the art of being human. In any case, I could add nothing to the available literature but I make two suggestions for your further reflection. The first concerns the concept of caring for the person. It is axiomatic that would-be therapists should be compassionate. However, I am thinking here of a different form of caring, rendered most clearly by Robert Pirsig (1974):

> . . . 'just sitting' [is] a meditative practive in which the idea of a duality of self and object does not dominate one's consciousness . . . When one isn't dominated by feelings of separateness from what he's working on, then one can be said to 'care' about what he's doing. This is what caring really is, a feeling of identification with

what one's doing. When one has this feeling then he also sees the inverse side of caring. Quality itself.

As Pirsig so astutely observed caring involves 'losing oneself' in the object of one's attention. This recalls the riddle, how does one distinguish the dancer from the dance? When two people, or a group supported by therapists, 'lose themselves', therapeutic relationships happen which transcend the original duality of 'therapist' and 'patient'. How you find the therapist within by 'getting lost' requires much the same kind of experimentation-in-life that has already been advocated for the person who is depressed.

Secondly, there are some things which the practitioner would be ill-advised to do, at least in my experience. The person in therapy is being coaxed out of her shell, to which she has retired to avoid the ravages of an unkind or disappointing world. You attempt to draw her out to experience the warmth of the sun, along with the occasional shower. Without her shell she is vulnerable. Despite this, you attempt to undress her in the cold light of day; disrobing layer after layer of dysfunctional belief. Even allowing for the melodrama of the metaphor, this is not an exercise to be undertaken lightly. In the spirit of paradox, I offer some negative suggestions in anticipation of some positive outcomes.

The content of the relationship is important. What should one exclude? I would avoid:

- appearing surprised: she expects you to be shocked or revolted. Provide her with the beginnings of a model of acceptance.
- apearing narrow-minded concerning her beliefs or attitudes. What makes you think that your values are so correct?
- appearing to reject her values because they conflict with your own. What are you asking her to do – exchange one prison for another?
- disputing religious or political issues: if any of these are important, they are important. Let her discover that they are not so valuable.

The style of relating also is important. I would exclude the following:

- being dogmatic. Help her towards her own 'truth'. She does not need another parent figure.
- being moralistic. Help her to be her own judge. Sit with her, not above her.
- arguing. Her argument is with herself, not with you. If she appears not to understand or agree, watch your own 'shoulds' and 'musts'.
- appearing to ridicule. She already believes she is ridiculous. Help her decide to jettison unhelpful cognitive cargo. Avoid adding more emotional ballast.

- premature interpretations. Help her to judge the meaning of events when it is appropriate for her.
- being too confrontational. Judge carefully whether or not she is ready to shed her emotional armour.
- appearing unsympathetic. She expects you to be so: *always* disappoint her.

Finally, the nature of the relationship itself is vital. I would avoid:

- being falsely optimistic. Know the boundaries of your abilities. Promise to take the person no further.
- expressing undue concern. You are concerned. Take care not to provoke a crisis of confidence in what is already a concerned individual.
- attibuting blame. She is an expert in accepting blame. She does not need your help to reinforce this self-defeating stance.
- introducing your own problems. Remember who is in therapy.
- making her or her ideas appear small. The real problem is that her ideas are too *big* – they overwhelm her. It is you who feels small as you attempt to challenge them.
- being impatient. At least she is moving. Take up her pace – this is one of the meanings of empathy.
- unnecessary reassurance. Life is bad – let her know this. It is you who needs the reassurance.

REFERENCES

Bandler, R. and Grinder, J. (1979) *Frogs into Princes: Neuro-Linguistic Programming*. Moab, Utah, Real People Press.

Blyth, R.H. (1960) *Zen in English Literature and Oriental Classics* (p101). London, Dutton.

Bordin, E.S. (1976) *The Working Alliance: Basis for a General Theory of Psychotherapy*. Paper presented at the meeting of the American Psychological Association, Washington DC, September.

Doi, T. (1986) *The Anatomy of Self: The Individual Versus Society (p25)*. New York, Kodansha International.

Dyer, W. (1990) *Believe It and You'll See It!* London, Arrow Books.

Eibl-Eibesfeldt, I. (1972) *On Love and Hate: The Natural History of Behaviour Patterns* (trans. G. Strachan). New York, Holt, Rinehart and Winston.

Ferster, C.B. (1973) A functional analysis of depression. *American Psychologist*, **28**, pp857–70.

Frankl, V. (1963) *Man's Search for Meaning* (p173). New York, Washington Square Press.

Gilbert, P. (1984) *Depression: From Psychology to Brain State* (Chapter 2). Hillsdale, New Jersey, Lawrence Erlbaum Assoc.

Gordon, J.S. (1985) Holistic medicine; fringe or frontier? In Bliss, S. (ed.) *The New Holistic Health Handbook: Living Well in a New Age*. Lexington, Mass., Stephen Greene Press.

Gordon, J.S. (1990) Holistic medicine and mental health practice; toward a new synthesis. *American Journal of Orthopsychiatry*, **60**(3), pp357–70.

Harris, A.B. (1979) *Breakpoint: Stress – The Crisis of Modern Living*. London, Turnstone Books.

James, W. (1890) *The Principles of Psychology*. New York, Holt.

Keefe, T. (1975) A Zen perspective on social casework. *Social Casework*, March, 18–22.

Leiber, J. (1991) *An Invitation to Cognitive Science*. Oxford, Basil Blackwell.

Ley, P. (1988) *Communicating with Patients: Improving Communication, Satisfaction and Compliance* (Chapter 6). London, Croom Helm.

Lueger, R.J. and Shiekh, A.A. (1989) The four faces of psychotherapy. In Sheikh, A.A. and Sheikh, K.S. *Eastern and Western Approaches to Healing: Ancient Widsom and Modern Knowledge* (Chapter 8). New York, John Wiley.

Maslow, A. (1962) *Towards a Psychology of Being* (p189). Princeton, New Jersey, Van Nostrand.

Maslow, A. (1976) Further notes on cognition. In *The Further Reaches of Human Nature* (Chapter 20). Harmondsworth, Penguin.

Masson, J. (1989) *Against Therapy: Warning – Psychotherapy May Be Hazardous to Your Mental Health*. London, Collins.

Nelson-Jones, R. (1990) *Thinking Skills: Managing and Preventing Personal Problems* (Chapter 3). Pacific Grove, California, Brooks/Cole.

Pirsig, R. (1974) *Zen and The Art of Motorcycle Maintenance* (p290). London, Corgi.

Podvoll, E.M. (1990) *The Seduction of Madness: A Compassionate Approach To Recovery at Home* (p2). London, Century.

Reynolds, D. (1985) *Playing Ball on Running Water* (p27). London, Sheldon Press.

Smail, D. (1987) *Taking Care: An Alternative to Therapy*. London, J.M. Dent.

Wubbolding, R.E. (1988) *Using Reality Therapy*. New York, Perennial Library, Harper and Row.

Chapter 5

The gentle art of letting go

Nothing whatever is hidden;
From of old, all is clear as daylight.
(Blyth 1976)

INTRODUCTION

This chapter focuses attention on some of the practical issues involved in helping the person who is severely depressed. The emphasis is upon what needs to be done by the practitioner. These suggestions are complementary to the skeleton of self-help provided in Chapter 6, and the skills and knowledge of the reader. At the risk of sounding falsely modest, I emphasize that these are no more than slender guidelines. I profess no intention to lead 'The Way'; these notes reflect the effort I have made to find my own way*.

THE ALTERNATIVE PARADIGM

Introductions: her 'self' and your 'self'

Building rapport

The helping process must begin with a thorough assessment of the person and her world. The important area of assessment need not be addressed here, given the wide coverage of the subject elsewhere (Barker 1985; Rehm 1981; Sartorius and Ban 1986; Wilson *et al.* 1989). What can be emphasized is the need to acknowledge the terminology used by the person and to help her, from the outset, to assess her experiences.

---

*The illustrations of my approach offered here are meant to stimulate rather than to direct.

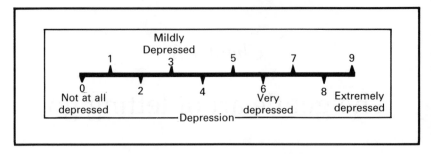

Figure 5.1

The words and phrases she uses need to be employed carefully throughout the helping process. They are the basic currency of depression. Some people will not use the term 'depressed', but will talk of feeling 'blue', 'empty', 'adrift', etc. If you wish to strengthen rapport, avoid the temptation to translate these experiences into words which mean something similar to you. Using her words and phrases is respectful. It also promotes a common language, in sympathetic connection, relating harmoniously.

Quantifying the experience

Establish, also, the depth of these experiences. To what extent does she feel 'blue', 'empty' 'adrift', 'guilty', 'fearful', 'ashamed', etc.? A variety of standardized measures of 'depression' can be used to provide a general picture (Sartorius and Ban 1986). Many practitioners use these to decide whether or not a diagnosis of depression is appropriate. People who are severely depressed often find such scales a daunting prospect, even where the questions are not too intrusive. The difficulty of concentrating and deciding which score to select can add to the person's distress, offering yet another opportunity for failure. One alternative is to focus attention upon the experiences which she has provided voluntarily: the specific feelings, thoughts or patterns of behaviour which represent her depression. Can she measure how strong these experiences are using, perhaps, some kind of linear scale or analogue? Figure 5.1 shows an example. Ask her to assess how strong any specific feeling is: at the bottom of the scale the feeling is not at all strong; at the top the feeling could not be stronger.

These measurements are personal and reliable benchmarks and can be used to evaluate changes as they occur. The 'what' and 'how' of the person's experiences also need to be placed in context: what has been happening, generally and specifically, within her recent life? Help her to outline a perspective on her life identifying what has been happening, involving who or what. How does she feel about these events and what does she think it means for her?

The role of the 'helper'

A brief introduction to the aims, process and internal 'logic' of the helping relationship is a further necessary preparatory step. This represents the introduction of 'yourself'. She needs to have confidence in her helper. Show understanding of her distress but, more importantly, be able to 'reframe' this, translating a helpless situation into one which can have a positive outcome. Begin by validating her experience; acknowledging what she thinks and feels, encouraging her to recognize that these are, for the moment, right and fitting*:

> Part of your 'self', or one of your 'selves'*, is telling you something very important. These thoughts and feelings are distressing; you do not doubt that. They are very real. And you may have often thought, 'But what does it all mean? Am I losing my reason, going crazy or whatever?'*. Those are very difficult questions to answer*. Perhaps you are acknowledging some very harsh realities: that you feel helpless; that you are very unhappy with yourself, your life or · your relationships; that you feel that nothing can change, or that this is no more than you deserve*. You seem to be giving yourself some very important messages: telling yourself that *some* things need to change*; and that is why you are sharing this with me now. Part of you has rung an alarm and another part of you has answered; part of you knows that something needs to be done and can be done*. The very fact that you are here listening to me now

---

*These experiences of 'self' are intuitively rational, right and fitting. The person will say that it feels right to criticize herself, be negative, think of suicide. These represent an unconscious critique of the person's life force or *raison d'être*. Acknowledge that her mind has its own reasons for making these statements; they represent her rational self, one which is proclaiming that 'something needs to be done!'

A parallel argument has been expressed by Therese Bertherat concerning our relationship with **bodyspeak**. Bertherat, T. (1977) *The Body Has Its Reasons*. London: Collins.

*It is worth encouraging the view, from the outset, that this person may be a manifold being, with many parts or even many 'true' selves.

*It is important to employ the actual fears expressed by the person; or to empathically predict what these might be.

*In truth, I do not know the answers to such questions.

*It is important to use the actual 'messages' which the person gave earlier in the assessment.

*Emphasis needs to be given to the fact that *all* is not wrong. She is acknowledging that something needs to be done; this is very important and valuable.

*You are noting that she knows this; you are not telling her!

is proof of that*. If it does not feel like that now, you will become more and more aware that your mind has its own reasons, as we begin to work together*. Depression is a very big jigsaw. We need to piece things together very carefully, but always together*.

I would like to help you*. I think I know a little about what has been happening to you*. I would like to share my thoughts with you. If you are willing to work with me we can share our thoughts. I can learn a lot about you, from you; and you might learn something which will be of use to you, from getting to know me*.

Cogito ergo sum

You need to emphasize from the outset the role played by thinking. Offer a simple analogy which might illustrate how thoughts mediate the generation of powerful emotions:

How you feel is at the very heart of your problems. These feelings are what has brought you here; it is fair to say that your feelings are the problem*. Perhaps we need to ask where these feelings came from ? In my experience, how we feel has a lot to do with how we think*. Let me give you an example: let me ask you to imagine that you are asleep in bed in the middle of the night and you waken with a start. You are sure that you heard something. Now, you think to yourself, 'That sounded like glass breaking, someone is trying to break in!'. How do you feel? (Invite her to respond). Let me ask you to clear that image from your mind. This time I would like you to imagine that it is another night. You are asleep in bed in the middle of the night when you waken with a start. You are sure that you heard something. You think to yourself, 'That sounded like glass breaking, I'll bet that next-door's cat has knocked over the milk bottle'. Tell me how do you feel?*

* You acknowledge that she has already begun to collaborate.
* You are offering her mind options; always allowing her the option of a 'positive outcome'.
* Use the term 'depression' in the right context; you are suggesting not that she has a disease but that she is experiencing something as complex as an emotional jigsaw.
* It is worth acknowledging that you do want to help her.
* It is realistic to acknowledge some professional optimism, however cautious.
* Note the emphasis upon thoughts, sharing and learning through human experience and collaboration.
* Acknowledging that feelings are central.
* The person expects, or has a right, to be helped by someone with experience. Acknowledge this and emphasize collaboration through repeated use of 'we'.
* It is important to select a likely example; this should be congruent with her circumstances and life style.

It can be safely assumed that the person's feelings about the two imagined events will differ. She should then be invited to consider how such different emotions came about:

It is interesting that you felt differently about those two events: the first time you felt. . . . and the second time . . . This is interesting because both events were almost identical: each time you were alone, asleep in bed in the middle of the night, wakening with a start. The only difference between the two examples was what you said to yourself. The first time you interpreted the noise as 'threatening' . . . the second time as 'non-threatening'. I believe that explains why you had different feelings. We often assume that feelings accompany events directly: that this or that *causes* fear or sadness. Maybe you have just shown me that it is more complicated than that*. What you think about a situation appears to influence how you feel about it.

I have often found it useful to use a 'sandwich' analogy. Our emotional life is like a sandwich: one slice of bread represents an event, the other the emotion which accompanies it. What makes the sandwich is not, however, the slices of bread so much as the filling. The filling in our emotional lives is the interpretations we place on events: these determine our resultant emotion. What kind of sandwich has the person just constructed?

Take the person through the stages of the simple rationale provided in section 1b of the self-help guide in Chapter 6, emphasizing that depression is at once simple yet complex. Alternatively, ask her to read part or all of this, as preperation for discussion at the next session.

STAGES OF DEVELOPMENT: AN INTRODUCTION

The endpoint of the working relationship involves the construction or deconstruction of notions of the self. The natural target of the therapeutic process is to help the person develop a 'functional' concept of self which enables rather than disables the process of living. The starting point is less clear and requires some consideration. If the person's emotional distress does not significantly hinder the development of a working relationship, the regeneration of activity is the natural starting point. This can be used as the basis for an exploration of her 'outward-directed' life; her engagement with the world, and all that might mean in terms of satisfaction, pleasure and distress. If she is manifestly distressed, some effort needs to be made immediately to

---

*Note that she has just shown you something important.

reduce this. Otherwise she will be unable to connect with the learning opportunities stemming from activity. Allow the person's presentation to determine the individual starting point; the conclusion is likely to be similar for most people who are depressed.

THE BUDGING PROCESS: ACTIVITY AND BEYOND

A preliminary rationale

Many traditional forms of therapy trade heavily upon 'mystique'. The patient in psychoanalytic and psychodynamic encounters is often left to construct her own perspective of what is happening and where it might be leading. Some behavioural therapists employ a different mystique, encouraging the person to think that behaviour is all and that emotion and reflection are somehow redundant. Both approaches can provoke unnecessary anxiety and, in the case of people who are severely depressed, can deepen their ontological crisis. They 'know' their experience of self but cannot express it in any purposeful fashion.

It is important to begin with a very 'open agenda': leave nothing to interpretation; clarify wherever possible; state clearly what your objectives are; what are your expectations and 'hunches' concerning the person's 'disorder'. The 'introductions' made at the outset provided a basis for presenting a model of therapy: something intelligible rather than obscure; a simple rationale for all that follows*.

An activity rationale

Before activity can be useful, the person needs to be willing to test it. Offer her a simple rationale for the experimental approach. You might ask her what she would do if she was lost on a country road and came to a fork where neither road was signposted. If she tries neither, she goes nowhere. If she takes one road there is no guarantee that it will take her where she wants to go; she will not know this, however, until she has tried it. Even if the road does not go where she hopes, it will probably lead 'somewhere', where further direction and support might be possible*.

* Care needs to be taken over the selection of the right kind of information. A study has shown that the popular leaflet *Coping with Depression* can be difficult to read and understand. The guide included in Chapter 6 was developed with this in mind. Barker, P. (1988) *An Evaluation of Specific Nursing Interventions in the Management of Patients Suffering from Manic Depressive Psychosis.* PhD thesis, Dundee Institute of Technology; and Beck, A.T. and Greenberg, R.L. (1974) *Coping with Depression.* New York, Institute for Rational Living.
* It is worth selecting an appropriate metaphor for depression: lost, alone and helpless on the road of life, badly in need of support and direction.

Purpose and attention

Encourage her to consider activity in a similar light. Action will take her away from distressing feelings and ruminations, albeit temporarily. Friends and relatives will also react more positively as she becomes more active. She will be encouraging them, as they encourage her. Arrange a simple experiment where you can accompany the person in a simple task: take a short walk, organize some books, wash and dry dishes or clean out a cupboard. The emphasis should be upon doing: discourage her from expressing negative evaluations about the activity – not having done it 'well', 'properly' or 'quickly enough'. Emphasize what exactly is on the activity agenda – turning and returning, over and over again, to the purpose of the activity: 'What exactly am I doing here – sorting out old clothes, filing papers, looking for a blue sock, etc.?'. All the time she is turning and returning her attention to the task: 'What exactly am I seeing, hearing, tasting, touching, sensing, smelling, as I do this?'. It is natural to have feelings about any activity; these are, however, separate from the activity. Encourage her to return to the activity with purpose and attention.

Encourage her to be experimental about her life rather than predicting emotional outcomes. Encourage her to be like a scientist or detective, testing out the activity hypothesis:

- Will engaging in activity change how I feel?
- Will doing something that I used to enjoy stimulate my mind?
- Will doing something I have been putting off make me feel different?

The ubiquitous diary

The ideal starting point for any change process is self-examination. Encourage her to take an objective look at herself by observing her life and her present estimate of its worth. The simplest form of self-analysis is the daily diary. Ask her to keep a simple note of what she does for the majority of each hour of the day. This record will be the first clear example of her active participation in the therapeutic process. For this reason, try to ensure its success. Ask her to record only what seems possible; if she is unsuccessful, reduce the demands until she can succeed. (An illustration of the daily diary format is provided in section 1e of Chapter 6.)

Future tense

Once she is monitoring her everyday activity, help her to plan ahead. The person who is depressed often uses her feelings to decide what she will or won't do: she is a 'straw in the wind of her own emotions'. Acknowledge this temptation – most people do this at some time. Encourage her to make plans for later in the day, the next morning, the next day, the next few days, and so on. She is transferring the reins of her life from her heart to her hands. She will decide what she wants or needs to do in the time ahead. Encourage her to make an informal contract with herself that she will at least make an attempt to fulfil her plan. Help her to recognize that 'the plan' is no more than that; no-one accomplishes every plan, there is no need to worship or fear it. Advise her against beating herself with the plan. Emphasize the need to be specific: how much of an activity will be undertaken or how long it will last. Short-term goals are infinitely better in the early stages: planning to read or write one line at a time; washing one dish, then another; walking for a few minutes, resting, and walking again. Goals which are large, distant or vague are difficult to achieve. Define these more clearly; break them down into manageable units. Help her to acknowledge that, 'Every journey of a thousand miles begins with a single step'.

Direction

Unqualified success in using her diary is not to be expected. More likely the task will be arduous, fraught with difficulties, and will serve as a stimulus for a stream of unqualified self-criticisms. This needs to be anticipated. Acknowledge these difficulties, empathizing with her and, most importantly, offering some practical advice. Encourage her to focus upon what she is doing, rather than what it might be worth. Emphasize that the record is not another demand upon her, but is something which she will use for her own ends.

Achieving and enjoying

The person who is depressed is involved in making powerful judgements, from moment to moment. These tend to be negative evaluations of herself, her world and the future. Now she needs to begin cultivating an awareness of the specific meaning of her activity plan: how does she feel about what she has done?

The activity plan is designed to help her become sensitive to the meanings which she attaches to the actions of her life. Help her to judge how much satisfaction she has gained from 'just doing something'; and how much enjoyment she obtained from other activities. Invite her to measure the amount of mastery she felt she had achieved over some difficult chore: the more difficult the chore, the more mastery she is entitled to feel. Ask her to measure how much pleasure she got from doing something she used to enjoy, or had never done before. The person with strong guilt feelings often avoids 'enjoyable' activities, on the grounds that she does not deserve pleasure. Encourage this person to plan chores or tasks, at least initially. If she clears away some of these chores she may begin to feel less guilty.

Breaking the mould

The person who is severely depressed is often 'stuck' in a tedious routine which is self-limiting and often arduous. This is not opposed, on the assumption that nothing else is possible or it is no more than her just deserts. Help her to pursue optional activities. Draw up a list of possible options to the 'daily grind'*. What did she use to do:

- *first thing in the morning*: shower, read the paper, make toast and coffee, feed the birds?
- *at midday*: listen to the news, write letters, meet a friend for lunch?
- *in the early evening*: listen to music, take a walk, water plants?
- *at this time of year*: sit in the sun, wrap up warm and walk in the snow, burn leaves, plant seeds?
- *on her own*: play music, read, knit, paint?
- *with others*: play card games, prepare meals, go to the cinema?
- *which cost nothing at all*: go to the library, watch wildlife, walk the dog?
- *which cost very little (£2)*: buy a magazine, have a cream tea in a restaurant, visit a museum?
- *when she lost her inhibitions*: sing in a group, tell people about her childhood, hug a friend?
- *which she didn't like, but needed to do*: sort out old clothes, sweep up leaves in the garden, wash the car?*

She will face a strong temptation to focus negatively upon what has not been done, or will be distracted by a stream of negative thoughts. Remind her of her 'contract'; she is aiming to become more active, to test out the value of such activity. She is aiming to do certain things and no more. Doing things completely or well is not on the agenda. Offer her a chance to discuss ways of dealing with these, wholly reasonable, reservations about her performance. Help her to return to

---

* The person who is hospitalized may be particularly aware of the daily grind of ward routine.
* It is important to emphasize what she used to do, rather than look for potential pleasures. This list can include, therefore, what she used to enjoy doing as well as what she used to need to do – chores, obligations and responsibilities.

the original agenda: experimenting with activity. (A menu of practical suggestions is offered in section 1i in Chapter 6.)

Making it stick

As she gains more experience in using the activity plan, build in extra strategies to compensate for her flagging motivation. Help her to:

- select times of day when planning and reviewing will be most convenient;
- coach herself, with appropriate self-dialogue, to confront and overcome motivational obstacles;
- deal constructively with negative thoughts;
- organize her environment so that distractions are reduced and visual cues to do this or that are clearly evident;
- acknowledge what she has done and avoid being self-punitive over apparent 'failures';
- work towards a balance of potentially demanding and rewarding activities;
- avoid 'giving up'.

Be prepared for an initial wave of hope which might dissipate quickly. Give her an opportunity to express her disappointment or despair over the 'point' of the therapy. Offer positive support by acknowledging her difficulties, emphasizing what has been done to date. It is worth repeating the rationale of the activity plan; each activity provides an opportunity for 'self-watching' – a chance to learn about the way her mind works. Degree by difficult degree, she is taking important steps on her own journey of a thousand miles. (Some ideas for making it stick are included in section 1j of Chapter 6.)

Dealing with the road blocks

Throughout this stage she is likely to have been assailed by all manner of negative thoughts: arguing the pointlessness of trying or ridiculing the foolishness or triviality of 'activity'. These obstacles have been largely ignored to date, or efforts have been made to manage them by writing them down and tearing them up, or setting fire to the paper. As preparation for the build-up phase, help her to begin challenging some of the more common negative thoughts which block her road to recovery. Identify the most common obstacles and help her construct a strong challenging statement. Encourage her to vocalize these aloud, write them down as a crisis *aide mémoire*, post them on notice boards, or practise reading them to herself in an effort to internalize them.

This is a wholly artificial procedure. Emphasize that it is similar to piano practice or training for a sporting event: she is preparing to act more spontaneously whilst remaining true to the spirit of her practice exercise. Encourage her to write down any alternative challenging statements, and to bring these to your next meeting for discussion.

DISTRESS REDUCTION: BALANCING EMOTIONS

Distraction: changing channels

If she is too distressed by her thoughts and feelings to begin the activity plan, help her to balance her emotions. This represents a change of focus rather than approach. The emphasis remains upon experimentation; focusing this time upon her perceptions of her mood state.

We are aware of how we feel because we are attending to specific emotions; we are tuned to a specific channel of consciousness. The alternative paradigm assumes that some feelings can be influenced by thinking, others come and go like clouds in the sky and we have little influence over them. There are times in the day, also, when we are not aware of any specific emotion; are people who are actively discussing or working interested; or are they simply discussing and working? You need to examine what the person is doing when she experiences a strong, overwhelming emotion. Is she 'tuning in' to a strong emotional channel and, by implication, 'tuning out' the world outside?

Invite her to conduct a short 'experiment'. Ask her to:

1. sit with her eyes closed for a moment letting herself focus on her feelings at that moment;
2. try to measure how strong the feeling is – perhaps on a scale between 0 and 100 (0 representing 'not at all', 100 'could not be stronger');
3. remain 'in touch' with the feeling, letting you know if it becomes stronger or weaker over the next few minutes.

Ask her to tell you how she is feeling and what she is thinking at that very moment. Invite her to change her attention channels by focusing on some specific memory, an imagined scene, part of the room or an outside view, or by doing some mental arithmetic. You are transferring her attention from her emotional channel to some neutral stimulus. You might ask her to:

- look out of the window and follow your detailed description of the scene, as you pick out objects, animals, colours, shapes, etc.;

- close her eyes and imagine what you look like, your clothes, face, expressions and gestures you are making as you talk, etc.;
- count backwards from one hundred in 3s;
- think of names beginning with B;
- study a photograph or painting, noting specific details;
- *not* think of a kangaroo;
- look carefully at the wallpaper in the room, checking its colours and patterns, noticing any blemishes, tears, stains, etc.*

When you think she is 'in' this exercise, ask her to tell you how she feels at that very moment. You can assume that she will not feel her previous emotion as strongly, since her attention has been adjusted. She may well 'not know' as she is 'busy trying to count (or whatever)'. This exercise should be pursued until she reports either a lessening of her original emotion or she loses her emotional attention, albeit briefly. This exercise should be used to illustrate that *she* has demonstrated how she can ease her distress by turning her attention onto something else, real or imagined.

ANCILLARY APPROACHES

This initial stage seems to ignore the emotional heart of depression. You have not encouraged her to review and explore her feelings. Instead you have directed what appears to be an active avoidance programme. This stage is, paradoxically, mounting a major offensive against the depressive core; sabotaging her underlying assumptions of helplessness. You have helped her to question her assumed powerlessness, sensitizing her to her experiences in life. By implication, her emotional experience of life has been afforded less emphasis for the moment.

Supplement this activity skeleton with strategies which will provide additional support, or perhaps meaning, to her struggle towards her goal. These should not be assigned arbitrarily; match them carefully to the person who is depressed.

Guided imagery

Help her to imagine carrying out difficult tasks. Provide her with a detailed 'dialogue', emphasizing the various sensory experiences involved in even the simplest of activities. Initially this will serve as a

---

*Avoid using imagery which can be easily interpreted negatively. If this happens encourage her to transfer her attention to some more neutral attentional task.

'mental rehearsal'; later, encourage her to use these sessions as another means of developing positive control over her mind.

Creative visualization

The depressed person is already skilled in 'negative visualization'. Help her to project, in her imagination, positive images of herself, her work, relationships, the growth and change process, and her slow yet steady treading of the path to recovery. Creative visualizations can be designed around everyday activities such as eating and drinking, grooming, washing, etc. Invite her to imagine water purifying her body as she slowly drinks from a glass, or washing negative thoughts from her mind as she carefully washes her face. Invite her to imagine herself engaging, happily or joyfully, in some favoured activity (Fanning 1988; Syer and Connolly 1984).

Relaxation

Offer her help to discover her capacity to control her body through progressive relaxation. Help her to watch herself learn to control her breathing and to observe small changes in the sensation of her physical 'self'. Gaining confidence in her relationship with her body can serve as a basis for developing the same kind of relationship with her mind. In addition to helping her feel physically more comfortable, relaxation serves as a model for the process of self-discovery (Rosen 1978; Wilson 1985).

Meditation-in-life

The activity schedule served as an experimental variable in testing the management of emotions. Activity also has its own function. All activity that 'needs' to be done is worthwhile; otherwise why do it? Encourage her to develop a closer relationship with her activities, becoming more aware of exactly what she is doing. When washing dishes, is she aware of the feel of the water, its temperature, the different sensations of hardness and softness, how her hands move in particular ways? David Reynolds suggests that few people are 'skilful' in the art of ordinary living. The Buddhist saying, 'Enlightenment is more likely to come when peeling the potatoes than meditating on the Buddha' is relevant here. Reynolds suggests that the person should perform everyday acts with attention and purpose: this is, if you like, meditation-in-life.

Diet

Food and drink are fuelling the person and need to be given some consideration. There is no dietary 'cure' for depression, but the content and presentation of the diet are important (Bliss 1985). Help her to consider the possible value of eating and drinking:

- *moderately* – eating too much overall, or at any one meal, is stressful for the body;
- *simply* – avoiding mixing too many different foods, which can also be stressful;
- *early in the day* – eating late can affect metabolism and disrupt sleep;
- *naturally* – keeping processed foods to a minimum enhances the intrinsic 'vitality' of her diet;
- *seasonally* – organizing her diet to be in harmony with the seasons.

Exercise

The activity plan also confronts the physical inertia which is so typical of depression. Some of the benefits which accrue from the activity plan are physiological as well as psychological. Sitting, ruminating, chain-smoking or lying in bed encourage a physiological listlessness which not only is unnatural but may be debilitating, 'Getting the person moving' promotes the exercise of her physical systems which, ultimately, will be refreshing.

Much evidence exists to link exercise with enhanced mood. Some of the claims for such psychological benefits are linked only to fairly strenuous, prolonged exercise programmes but even gentle exercise, such as walking, is of great potential value. Providing that her physical state does not preclude these, encourage her to experiment with walking, yoga, jogging, aerobics, dancing, weight training or martial arts, under appropriate supervision (Morgan and Goldston 1987).

THE BUILD-UP PLAN: CONSTRUCTIVE THINKING

Uncovering

As the activity plan develops, begin to consider the role of thinking in the generation of emotional experience. Remind her of your earlier discussions about the relationship between thinking and feeling Offer her a simple exposition of cognition, emphasizing how thoughts work and the importance of developing an awareness of thinking during everyday activity. Introduce her to the 'thought catching' form (see section 2c in Chapter 6) and arrange to use this to summarize a replay of a recent event. Ask her to identify a negative feeling experienced recently. Ask her to define this feeling and to gauge how strongly she felt it, recording this on the form. Ask her to recall where, exactly, she was when she began to experience this feeling. What was she doing; what was happening around her and what, if anything, was 'on her mind'? Using the information she has provided, ask her to recall the scene: Yesterday, you were in the . . . and you were doing . . . You were with . . . at the time, and you were thinking generally about . . . Let me know when you have that whole scene clearly in your mind's eye. OK, tell me what thoughts occur to you just now; what thoughts or images just pop into your head; what is running through your mind right now?'

Note her thoughts as she provides them, asking her to write these down for herself when she has finished. Using the guidelines in section 2b, Chapter 6, help her to distinguish between 'automatic' and 'conscious' thinking. A simple rule of thumb is that automatic thoughts tend to be short, pithy statements; conscious thoughts tend to be more rambling. Help her to tease out the judgements or interpretations she has made about the scene which appear to be related to the emotion she felt, asking her to assess her belief in each thought. Discuss this scenario with her, comparing it with the example in section 2c. Invite her to note, in both examples, the possible relationship between events, thoughts and feelings. Encourage her to begin 'catching thoughts' as part of her activity plan, using section 2d as a guide.

Awareness and distance

This is a vital stage in her development. You are encouraging her to face directly the thoughts and images which stimulate her distressing feelings. Give her time to practise this procedure with your support. Remind her of the value of catching thoughts; compliment her each time she elicits a different distressing thought and help her to acknowledge her own success in trapping negative thoughts. Help her to rehearse what she will say to herself when completing this independently. Prepare her to be able to face, and manage, the distressing nature of her own thinking. By preparing herself to confront, record and reframe the significance of her own thoughts, she is already beginning to put some valuable distance between her thoughts and her feelings.

Analysing thoughts

She has given some examples already of her use of negative bias. It is time to explore the evidence for such judgements: are these thoughts 'true' or does she simply believe them to be so? Remind her that throughout the waking day a stream of automatic thinking flows through our minds. Most of our actions are performed on 'automatic pilot', requiring no conscious effort. These pilots guide us through our lives, directing our actions, telling us what to do and what to avoid. They also feed us with judgements about the meaning of events, or our part in them. Now it is time to listen in to what these pilots are saying. Help her to prepare to challenge any negative views or judgements expressed by her pilots. Check that she is ready to proceed: does she recall the earlier experiment with the 'noise in the night'? Does she have any questions about what you are proposing?

Introduce her to the four main strategies which will be used to analyse her thinking (see sections 3a and 3b in Chapter 6). Help her to appreciate, through brief illustrations, how most people, including yourself, can misjudge situations. Review with her how her perceptions of events and herself can be tied to her depressed feelings.

A challenging alternative

Introduce her to the recording format for challenging her depressive thinking. Take her through the completed example in section 3d, encouraging her to note the relationship between the situation, thoughts and feelings. Draw attention to the use of 'alternative thoughts', the outcome and what the person did next. Invite her to supply a recent example of her own. Help her to record her feelings, the situation and her thoughts. Taking one depressing thought at a time, invite her to support or reject it. Use as many of the following strategies as are necessary to weaken her belief in her depressive thinking.

Facing the facts

What evidence exists to support this thought? You understand her belief in this thought – it seems plausible; but how does she know this is the case? Invite her to consider putting this thought 'on trial': what evidence could be presented to prove the case? Is there any chance that it might be dismissed as 'speculation' or 'circumstantial evidence'? Alternatively, is there any evidence against the thought? What can be said in 'defence'? Acknowledge that she feels that this is true.

Encourage her to stand back and consider more independent forms of evidence*.

Taking another look

How would someone else view this situation? What thoughts might her best friend, partner or someone she holds in high esteem have about this situation? Ask her to make a list of their alternative constructions. If she changed places with this person and they experienced the same events, what would she say? Would she judge this situation differently, if it were not happening to her? If she would, is she not guilty of employing a double-standard: judging herself and others differently? Perhaps she is thinking this because she is depressed. How would she have appraised this situation before she became depressed? What would she have said about it then? Finally, invite her to supply evidence for thinking in the alternative ways already outlined.

Judging the results

You have already discussed the possible effects of thoughts on feelings. Invite her now to consider the real effects of this particular thought on her feelings and her life in general. Does it help her or hinder her? What reason can she offer for holding on to a thought which disables her, even if she cannot prove that it is not true? If she believes that the thought is true, invite her to weigh up the advantages and disadvantage of holding this thought. Ask her to write down any 'gains' she obtains from thinking in this way. Against this, ask her to list the 'losses' which she incurs. Help her to stand back and weigh up the balance more objectively. How would friends or colleagues weigh up these options?

Trying another way

What other options are open to her? Even if her thought seems true, does this mean that she can do nothing to remedy the situation? Ask her to 'brainstorm' the options with you. Encourage her to write down every possible alternative, even those which appear silly or impossible. As you review these with her, ask if she is overlooking anything

---

*Ellis provides some valuable strategies for helping the person 'dispute' unhelpful personal rules. Ellis, A. (1980) Overview of the clinical theory of RET. In Grieger, R. and Boyd, J. (eds.) *Rational Emotive Therapy: A Skills-Based Approach*. New York, Van Nostrand Reinhold.

which might be an alternative? How does she know that any of these won't work unless she has tried them? Emphasize the need to turn alternative thoughts into action. Help her to enact, in the session, some of these alternatives. How does she feel when she does this or that? If it doesn't feel 'right' or 'better' just now, how does she know it won't feel different tomorrow or the day after? Even if these alternatives do not 'work', does this mean that she would be better off going back to her original plan: doing nothing, or repeating actions which have been unhelpful in the past?*

Independent practice

Conduct as many challenging experiments as are necessary within the session before encouraging her to complete a test challenge unaided. Suggest that she reads section 3e in Chapter 6 as preparation and carries the list of questions in section 3g as an *aide mémoire*. Once she has completed several challenges unaided she can dispense with the recording form. The form is no more than a series of columns; encourage her to draw her own columns in her notebook. Discourage her from assuming that there is some magic in the format, or in any prescribed pieces of paper. These are no more than props to help her internalize some alternative rules. Once she has learned them, she can dispense with the props.

Encourage her to build challenging practice into her daily plan, setting aside time during the day to complete this in privacy, free from distractions. Initially she may feel overwhelmed with depressive thought. Remind her to be selective, challenging only some of these whilst logging the others as she has done previously.

Developing personal rules

Many of her rules for believing in this or that will derive from significant others: parents, peers or culture. Invite her to explore where these thoughts come from. If she is particularly focused upon success and failure, when did this concern begin? Does she think that her striving for success and her despair over failure is a 'good thing'? Would she recommend this as a general rule? Often she will use these values to oppress herself. In helping her to challenge her depressive thinking you help her become aware that these are not generalized

---

*Quantity rather than quality is the rule here. Brainstorming is more likely to produce viable options than attempts to elicit quality alternatives. D'Zurilla, T.J. and Goldfried, M.R. (1971) Problem-solving and behaviour modification. *Journal of Abnormal Psychology*, 78(1), pp107–26.

rules; perhaps she is the only one in her circle who is using them. Even if the rules are widespread, she needs to decide if this rule is right for her. Encourage her to ask, 'Do *I* want or need or do this?' rather than '*You* must do this . . .'. Help her to recognize that she owns her thoughts and actions, as well as her feelings. She can choose her thoughts and her actions. Her feelings may, however, be more like the weather – often upredictable*.

Making haste slowly

A word of caution is included in section 3g. Discuss with her the importance of steady pursuit of her goal. She may experience some sudden 'enlightenment' so reassure her against despair if this begins to fade, as the effort to cope with depressive thinking becomes more demanding. Remind her that she is making her own luck: 'The more a person knows, the more luck she will have'. Suggest that there is no real luck, only good effort. When things get tough, she needs to apply more effort; the more effort she has to give, the better she will feel. She could look upon problems as an opportunity to test her 'effort'.

She should avoid turning her homework into another rod for her back. She is using the record in her plan; it is unable to make any demands on her that have not been spoken by the automatic pilots. She is travelling a hard road. There is no need to make it any harder. Of course, she might choose to be hard on herself but is this really a wise choice?

A catalogue of distortion

Section 4 of Chapter 6 focuses upon some of the more common 'unhelpful' thoughts*. The introduction emphasizes that these thoughts trouble most people: you might offer an example of their disabling effect from your own experience. This catalogue will help establish further distance between depressing thoughts and the person herself. By recognizing that she 'uses' these thoughts, she will come to realize that she is not alone. They are in no way peculiar to her. They are, in effect, the 'common currency' of despair and discord. Although simplistic, this classification system will help her become even more objective about her thinking. She has progressed from merely 'catching' depressing thoughts to critically evaluating their

---

*For more on unhelpful rules see: Dyer, W.W. (1976) *Your Erroneous Zones*. London: Sphere.
*This catalogue is derived from the work of both Beck and Ellis.

content and value. Now she can classify them further as representing one kind of unhelpful thought or another.

Each unhelpful thought is accompanied by an illustration. Encourage her to learn to recognize them; they will then become stimuli for recalling the core of a particular thought. Ask her to read section 4, identifying which of the unhelpful thoughts she uses most often. Once she has learned to recognize them, help her to categorize thoughts from her daily record. Draw up a list of those which she uses regularly and, using Chapter 6, invite her to classify them. After some experience with your support, she can begin classifying her depressive thoughts as they occur. A copy of all of the images may provide a useful visual aid. She might keep reduced copies of these pictures in her purse, inside the cover of her diary or stuck to significant points in her home – fridge door, beside electric points, on the back of the toilet door, etc.

Developing right-thinking skills

Your aim within this stage has been to help her develop a critical awareness of her thinking style and to consider alternatives which might prove more helpful in her everyday life. Although it is fashionable to pour scorn on the concept of psychological skills, this seems to be the most appropriate description: 'the ability to do something, especially as the result of long, practical experience'. Through time this 'skill' will become less uncomfortable, require less effort to enact and will hopefully, like other skills, become second nature. Encourage her to see the value in maintaining periodic checks on these alternative thinking skills*. Help her to review what this course of thinking awareness and challenging has been about.

1. Not thinking

Of necessity, some of the exercises have focused upon learning how not to think. She has developed an awareness of some of her cognitive clichés; she needs to be on her guard against allowing these to slip back into everyday usage. She may also have gained some awareness of the origins of her depressive thinking: the possible influences of her parents, or the influence of her moods upon her thoughts, and vice versa.

*For a useful guide see: The courage to think for yourself. In Nelson-Jones, R. (1990) *Thinking Skills: Managing and Preventing Personal Problems*. Pacific Grove, California, Brooks/Cole.

2. *Choice ownership*

She has also developed her ownership of the responsibility for choice. Although it has not often felt like it, she has always been a 'chooser'; she could be nothing else. She has learned that her interpretations and actions have represented one option and that there are other options, both in how she perceives events and how she responds to them.

3. *Self-instruction*

By using the self-talk format of Chapter 6, she has learned to own her thoughts, feelings and actions. 'I' talk has encouraged her to distinguish who 'she' is now from other 'selves' which are expression less mature views, or the rules of others. 'I' talk also places her at the centre of her life, where she can consider all her options. 'I' talk displaces the punitive 'you' talk which she has used previously to abuse, condemn or invalidate herself* (Passons, 1975).

4. *Personal rules*

She has begun to develop her own rules for living, rather than slavishly following those of her parents, friends or culture. She can distinguish between those rules which help to free her for positive action and those which oppress her, limiting her options. More importantly, she is beginning to listen to her own heart and has begun to live up to her own expectations.

5. *Choosing perceptions*

Throughout this stage she has focused upon a critical analysis of her own thinking – style and content. She is becoming increasingly aware of her use of distorted perceptions: failing to see opportunities or positive outcomes; tending to focus upon failings, deficits and, in general, what is not there! She has begun to dispense with the use of negative labels which stem from such distorted perceptions, and has begun to explore ways of affirming her intrinsic worth.

6. *Explaining herself*

She is beginning to become aware of other ways of 'explaining' her world. She appreciates that 'cause' is a complex idea. She plays a part

---

*Passons suggests that these approaches enhance self-awareness, bringing us closer to ourselves. Passons, W.R. (1975) *Gestalt Approaches in Counselling*. New York, Holt, Rhinehart & Winston.

in creating some events; others also are partly responsible. She realizes that blaming herself is inaccurate and, more importantly, adds to the depressing effect.

7. Future-think

She has begun to look ahead, take risks, weigh up options and become more experimental about her life. She is trying to locate her own values to use as benchmarks for assessing her options. She knows now that there is no 'going back'; she can only move forward.

8. Visualization

She has learned how to use her mind to create positive images of future events. She is learning how to use her mind to manage some of her distressing feelings, and can use her imagination to assist herself in carrying out complex or threatening tasks.

9. Decision-making

She has learned how to make decisions rather than feel swayed by the power of others, or of chance. Deciding is a complex process: she knows the value of collecting information, planning the fine detail and being aware of her negative 'road blocks', and is able to anticipate some of the possible outcomes.

10. Being herself

In general, she is moving towards being her own person, perhaps for the first time in her life. As she does so, she is beginning to value others as they really are, rather than as ideals. She is developing the ability to think for herself, rather than always employing stereotyped choices, values and judgements.

SUPPLEMENTARY STRATEGIES

You have asked the person to make a very significant effort during this stage. She has continued to pursue her activity plan, building upon this alternative constructions of her self and her world. In preparation for the final phase, when the focus will narrow upon her beliefs, now is a good time to begin broadening the base of the helping approach even further. It is important that any 'lessons' learned are maintained, become part of her personal philosophy and bring positive meanings to her life experience. The kind of approaches you select will, ultimately, depend on the person. Most of the following, however, have widespread applicability, providing that they are employed with discretion.

The developmental diary

Ask her to consider keeping another diary; one in which she records only her positive steps. This might include:

Acknowledgements: A list of everything which she did, however large or small, complete or partial. This should be prefaced with some positive acknowledgement: 'I acknowledge that, today, I . . .'. This journal will provide further assistance in resisting her traditional temptation to negate any activity, however well it is done. This journal is not, however, about success: it is about acknowledging objectively some of the facts of her life.

Personal encounters: A record of private meetings with her 'self' where she acknowledges who she is, gets on personal terms with her body and mind, holds friendly conversations and generally gets on better terms with herself. The bathroom is a good place to begin these encounters; looking at herself in the mirror, acknowledging who she is, becoming aware of her feelings, giving herself support and reassurance. These are meetings which end the psychological warfare which was characterized her relationship with her 'selves' to date.

Roots and relationships: An exploration of the origins of her depressive thinking. Where might she have 'collected' such ideas? Tracing the origins of depressive thinking adds a further dimension to its rejection – a possible explanation. This is a positive step toward issuing the final 'good riddance'.

Just being: Notes of times when she replaced her tendency to evaluate everything and just did something. This is the kind of log that deserves a published total: 'Today I just did . . . *x* times!'.

Gestalt exercises

A number of exercises which derive from gestalt therapy can be incorporated at this stage. The gestalt focus upon language has already been emphasized. This can be advanced by narrowing the focus upon the use of

'It talk': How often does the person talk about being 'frightened of *it*', or '*It* is getting me down'. What happens if she says 'I' rather than 'it'?

Questioning: How often does she ask questions to which there are no answers? 'Why should this happen to me? Why doesn't my husband love me any more? Why does everyone expect so much of me?' What happens if she asks 'What can I do to change this?, or, 'How can I find someone to love?', or, 'Who said I have to listen?'.

'*Can't talk*': How often does she say 'I can't' when perhaps she is really deciding that she 'won't'? What happens if you ask her 'What exactly are you unwilling to do?'.

Use can also be made of the empty-chair or two-chair techniques. In the former, she could, for example, talk to the individual who 'gave' her some unhelpful belief. She could tell this person how, by using this belief, she has created difficulties for herself. She might finally return the belief, thanking the person for the 'loan'. Alternatively, using two chairs, she might engage in a conversation with one of her other 'selves', making observations about the other 'person', switching chairs as she switches 'personas'. In the first exercise she has a chance to attribute the origins of some belief and to return it to its 'rightful owner'. In the second example, she can develop her awareness that she is not one single person but has perhaps numerous selves, all of which have a part to play in being 'me'.

Existential approaches

Many of the issues which the depressed person needs to address revolve around her very existence. Sartre's assertion that, 'Man (*sic*) is nothing else but what he makes of himself', is central to the alternative paradigm. Any of the following existential issues can be incorporated gradually into the skeleton structure. These issues will serve as a bridge between the narrow focus of this challenging phase and the broader consolidation phase.

Self-awareness: Much emphasis has been given already to the issue of choice: to what extent is the person choosing for 'herself' or others? This issue can be extended to incorporate questions about her awareness of 'who' she is and 'what' kinds of meanings does she attach to the events in her life (May 1961)? To what extent is she aware that she can:

- choose to expand or limit her awareness of herself?
- direct the course of her life or allow others to shape it for her?
- do something or nothing?
- build meaningful relationships with others or isolate herself?
- be her own unique self or conform to some stereotype?
- create or find meaning in her life?
- take the risk of deciding for herself or depend on security?
- accept the value of the present or hide from this reality?

Personal responsibility: As noted in the previous chapter, (wo)man is 'condemned to freedom'. Each time we do something we create ourselves through choice*. Much emphasis has been placed upon selecting from options organized by the person herself. Many people who are depressed assume that they have a responsibility towards everyone. They often fail, however, to honour their obligations to themselves. Help the person to explore everyday situations, identifying what would represent a 'vote' for or against herself. Help her to develop clear ideas as to what are her responsibilities, as opposed to those of others*.

The meaning of life: The fundamental existential questions – 'Who am I and what am I doing here?' – can be translated into some more appropriate form for inclusion here. To what extent has the person found meaning through:

- *work*: to what extent has 'occupation', whether paid or voluntary, extended the boundaries of her life?
- *love*: what does it mean to her to love her partner, friends, family, animals, her fellow (wo)man, etc.?
- *suffering*: to what extent has she encountered challenges, either physical, mental or social, which she could not avoid but faced with dignity, thereby finding meaning through growth?

The courage to be: The main thrust of the helping relationship is to help the person to define and accept who 'she' is, as opposed to who the world might want her to be (Tillich 1952). Making choices is rarely easy, given that there are no racing certainties; any choice is fraught with risk. The act of choosing demonstrates, however, that the person has control over herself: she is, in effect, establishing herself as valid (Keen 1970). Much of this validation involves acknowledging personal limits: the oft-quoted Serenity Prayer is apposite:

God grant me the serenity to accept the things I cannot change, the courage to change the things I can, and the wisdom to know the difference.

Viktor Frankl (1963) was fond of quoting a similar admonition of Goethe's:

---

* According to Russell, Sartre's view of Man (*sic*) suggests that 'Each time we act, we thereby choose and create ourselves as we want to be; and this is never finished – what we are is never settled – but is created in each of the deeds that constitute us.' Russell, J.M. (1978) Sartre, therapy and expanding the concept of responsibility. *American Journal of Psychoanalysis*, **38**, pp259–69.
*Dyer provides a simple 100-item checklist which distinguishes 'victim' from 'victor' behaviour. Dyer, W.W. (1978) *Pulling Your Own Strings*. London; Arrow.

If we take man as he is, we make him worse; but if we take him as he should be, we help him to become what he can be.

To what extent is the person able to accept herself as she is? To what extent does she rely on others to define her? Does she accept that she is valuable just because she exists, or does she believe she needs to prove her worth?

Humour: Great value can be found, also, in identifying the folly and inherent comedy of much human striving. Help the person to recognize the humour in her exaggerated demands and her dependence on others, the futility of worry, the 'awfulness' of responsibility. Here we are talking of laughing along *with* the person, not *at* her. If you have been using careful self-disclosure, some of your own experiences in life may appear fairly ludicrous on reflection: these can be meaningfully included in the session*.

CONSOLIDATION: BECOMING A PERSONAL SCIENTIST

Experiential testing

As she begins to witness improvements in her mood and life problems it is vital to maintain the impetus of the activity programme and the reconstruction of her thinking style. Much of what has been done so far involves experiments in living. In the consolidation phase the focus on experimentation is narrowed. Here, you encourage her to think like a 'personal scientist', assessing not only the actions and interactions of her life but the resultant value of the experiment for her (see section 5a in Chapter 6).

Prediction versus discovery

Discuss the rationale of the 'personal scientist', providing everyday examples of how people tend to predict rather than discover the outcomes of their actions*. After reviewing the rationale contained in section 5b, highlight the six steps which are involved in testing out predictions (5c). Invite her to offer a prediction of some impending event: what she thinks will happen when she visits a friend at the weekend or how she might manage a difficult encounter with a col-

---

*For a very useful guide to the use of humour in psychological therapy, see Twerski, A.J. (1988) *When Do the Good Things Start?* Horsham: Ravette Books.
*The concept of the personal scientist was first explored by Mahoney. Mahoney, M.J. (1974) *Cognition and Behaviour Modification*. Cambridge, Mass., Ballinger.

league. Encourage her to rehearse the experiment, helping her to imagine different outcomes at stage 5. Ask her to read over the two examples before arranging an experiment of her own.

Before concluding, it is wise to encourage her to draw up a short-list of possible experiments, ranking these in order of difficulty and possibility. Help her to select experimental situations which she can pursue immediately. Remind her of the values of preparation, planning and timely reflection on the outcome.

Troubleshooting

Some attention needs to be paid also to the management of setbacks. It is unrealistic to expect plain sailing at any time; as she makes positive changes in her life, her world may also be changing – not always for the better. Help her to develop a reserve strategy to fall back on. A simple rationale is offered in sections 6a and 6b. This emphasizes that lack of success does not necessarily mean failure; and anyway, what is wrong with occasional failure? Review some of the basic rules for coping with setbacks contained in section 6c and arrange a rehearsal: what would she do if this or that happened? Provide her with some 'catastrophic' examples and invite her to develop an A and B plan, as outlined in section 6c. Help her to focus her attention on what each option might do for her under these 'catastrophic' circumstances. This is a good time for some judicious humour; exaggerate the 'hiding and running' nature of the A plans. Arrange a 'trial' of these options, where you vigorously support the passive options: 'Yes, I think that staying in bed would be the best idea. I would stay there all day if necessary; keeping the covers pulled up tight, in case the world got in. It could get a little hot in there, in this weather, but at least I'd be out of the "heat" of everyday life. I'd just lie there all day, thinking about what might be happening outside. What do you say?'

Invite her to challenge your defence of the passive option, and to defend her more active option. Emphasize that for many situations there are no solutions; people just need to accept that. Offer her some examples from your own experience. These disclosures may not impress her. She might believe that you are simply inventing these to illustrate a point; as you are the 'therapist' you cannot possibly encounter life problems.

Alternatively, use examples from your family, neighbours or children. Invite her to offer advice on the shape of an A and B plan for that individual, weighing up the pros and cons of each option. If active, accepting or challenging options are good enough for these people, what makes her think they are unsuitable for her?

Credo

The person's belief system represents the very roots of her being. It is important to clarify her core beliefs. How do they 'open' or 'close' the frontiers of her life? Negative beliefs – 'I cannot, should not or must not do this because . . .' – restrain her; positive beliefs – 'This is good because . . . , or I can do . . .' – expand her range of living possibilities. Help her to identify her specific beliefs, and the specific rationales upon which these beliefs are based. These examinations should be pursued in much the same manner as the exploration of discrete 'unhelpful thoughts'. Encourage her to consider that beliefs are grand thoughts: more diffuse, complex, and ultimately more powerful than the single thoughts which have been dealt with previously.

The ordering of experience

It is worth emphasizing that 'reality' is largely experiential. Developments in subatomic physics suggest that what we see as continuous and solid is, in effect, almost wholly empty space. Instead of being a fixed, concrete 'thing', reality – the colour of the sky, the solidity of stone – is the result of energy exchanges between different fundamental fields. These pockets of energy appear to assume forms, but this is largely perceptual on our part.

There is no need to describe reality from this 'atomic' perspective. It is important to discuss, however, the person's construction of reality. How does she know what is or is not 'real'? Is she a solid person, or is she like the river metaphor noted earlier, the product of a stream of events, reactions and interpretations. Encourage her to consider how people learn to believe in experience; what she has learned about the world is used as the basis for validating (or rejecting) new experiences. Disclosure of some of your own beliefs, and their possible origins, might facilitate her exploration of her own value system. The relationship between your beliefs and subsequent actions might illustrate the profound influence which beliefs have over behaviour. Our actions are ordered by our beliefs; our beliefs derive from our experience; and our experience is determined by what we already believe. The complexity of this inter-relationship is important: this illustrates the difficulty of changing beliefs.

Belief categories

Beliefs are diverse and vary according to class and cultural influences, as well as being determined by individual experience. Given this diversity, it is worth trying to classify beliefs according to their nature and function. David Burns (1980) classified seven 'dysfunctional attitudes' which he believed were relevant to the genesis of psychological disorders. He defined these in terms of 'needs' which were perceived as being vital for a satisfactory life. The person who believes that she has a vital need for:

- *approval*: is dependent on others. Her emotional well-being depends on plaudits; she is vulnerable to criticism or manipulation.
- *love*: adopts an inferior role in relationships, for fear of upsetting and losing the other.
- *achievement*: is overly committed to work, in order to prove her self-worth. She has a fear of relaxation and illness, either of which will prejudice her productivity and, by implication, her intrinsic value.
- *perfectionism*: is on a constant wild goose chase, searching for the perfect self. Mistakes are taboo and failure is worse than death.
- *entitlement*: believes that she has a right to success, support, love and happiness. When these demands are not met, she becomes either angry or depressed.
- *omnipotence*: believes that she has, or should have, control over others. When things go wrong she takes the responsibility on her own shoulders.
- *autonomy*: believes that her potential for happiness and self-esteem is determined by outside forces. She is a perennial 'victim of circumstance' and is shackled to the belief that most things are outwith her control.

Burns has developed a simple Dysfunctional Attitude Scale which identifies whether the person has strengths or weaknesses on any of these factors (Burns 1980, pp241–55). Although Burns' framework is valuable, there may be merit in exploring other belief systems which might be disabling the person*. Does she, for example, believe in:

Progress: assuming that all problems are bound to have solutions. The assumption that there is no limit to growth, either on the part of people or things, appears attractive but may be inherently flawed. People who believe that their children should be able to develop this or that ability, or that a damaged relationship can always be repaired, or that recovery from a debilitating physical illness should be possible in this super-scientific age are suffering from such a progress belief.

Objectivity: assuming that 'facts' exist. This assumption fails to recog-

*These suggestions derive from Postle, D. (1988) *The Mind Gym: A new Age Guide to Personal Growth*. London, Macmillan.

nize the extent to which people colour their world by attaching emotion-laden judgements which 'make' things good, bad or indifferent. The person who labels herself a 'failure', a 'disgrace' or 'unworthy' may assume that this evaluation is based on the 'fact' that she has not succeeded, behaved badly or failed to meet others' expectations. Such evaluations are, of course, judgements which are used to create 'facts'.

Normality: assuming that patterns of behaviour which are uncommon or unusual are deviant. This assumption is very threatening for people who are in any way different from the average population. This belief terrorizes the person, obliging her to try to conform to the practices and values of the 'middle ground'. This assumption fails to acknowledge the enormous diversity of human conduct, and also the 'fact' that people who are unusual often make significant contributions to society.

Blame: assuming that by attributing blame to a person or thing, this somehow explains some unhappy event. This assumes that everything is either the person's responsibility completely or someone else's fault. Whether or not self-blame or blaming others appears right and fitting, one needs to ask how helpful is such a practice? Does it add to the change initiative, or merely depress the person further or make her feel more powerless?

Idealization: assuming that some people or institutions are overwhelmingly good or somehow beyond criticism. Authority figures, famous entertainers or popular 'heroes' are used almost like icons of worship. Such idealization can also exist in an individual's glorification of her nation, religion, family or class. To what extent do such beliefs diminish the person's belief in herself? To what extent do these beliefs serve as an alternative to just 'being herself'?

Dominance: assuming that power is the ultimate 'truth'; without power the person must of necessity submit. This assumption breeds a range of ideas concerning the importance of competition over collaboration; control rather than cooperation. The depressed person who is unable to realize such power believes in the need for submission. She must always do what she is told; that experts always know what is best for her; that nothing she can do will make any difference in her world; that nothing much can be done to change human nature. The belief in dominance/submission poses enormous problems for the practitioner in mental health, given that so many professional practices continue to revolve around the manipulation and control of 'patients' and the exercise of 'expert' professional judgement. The person needs to be asked to test these assumptions; is she really as powerless as she believes herself to be?

Pressure and inhibition

Eric Berne (1972) proposed that people's lives were directed by personal 'scripts', which were a preconscious lifeplan produced by parental programming. Some of these scripts reflected **pressurizers**: to what extent is it important for the person to:

be liked: who said that everyone must like her? What is so awful about some people not liking her?

be in control: who said that she could control what others think or feel or do? What is wrong with letting others choose and do for themselves?

be quick: who gave her this passion for time-keeping? What is wrong with relaxing or even wasting time?

be a real woman or man: what does this mean, if it does not refer to some stereotype?

be selfish: who told her that life had to be a competition? What is wrong with collaboration and cooperation?

Other beliefs act as **inhibitors**. To what extent is it important for her to:

not think: what evidence does she have that other people's ideas are better than hers?

not trust: what evidence does she have that everyone is untrustworthy, or is intent on exploiting her?

not feel: what is wrong with showing her feelings? What is the value in keeping them stifled?

not enjoy herself: who said that life was not meant to be stimulating, enjoyable, pleasurable and interesting?

not be different: who does she know who is average? What evidence does she have that people are not more different from one another than they are alike?

not take risks: how does she know what will happen – risk or no risk?

not acknowledge death: only two things are certain – we are alive now and will one day be dead. What does that say about the present?

Onward and upward

The content of these belief explorations will often be necessarily vague. For this reason, it is important to emphasize the value of the critical analysis which has characterized so much of the work to date. Help her to identify, evaluate and trace the origins of her beliefs. Help her to evaluate them critically one by one. Ask her to decide, when she is ready, to discard particular beliefs in favour of specific alternatives. It may be difficult for her to discard some beliefs. Ask her if she would be willing to pass these on to her children; offer them with a guarantee to friends or colleagues; publish them as a *Patent Guide to the Attainment of Happiness*? If not, why not? If these beliefs are not good enough for others what is her reason for holding on to them?

This concluding phase is expansive. The person is taking a wide-ranging excursion around the base of her life, collecting some of the building blocks and searching for traces of the original 'builders'. Despite her engagement in this philosophical enquiry, it is important that the substance of the earlier stages is maintained. Life has still to be 'lived'; reflection is important but is no more than an image of how she lives her life. Encourage her to extend her activities in positive, developmental ways. She might, for example:

begin a garden: this project might develop her awareness of care and attention; what she can change and what is uncontrollable. This takes place against the background of the natural developmental cycle of the seasons; a metaphor, perhaps, for her own cycle of change.
give away something valuable: she might become more aware of how she gives value to things, and that something 'unvalued' is given in the process. What is this, what is it worth and where does it come from?
keep a list of gifts, debts and troubles: noting the positive things she receives and what she might need to return; accompanied by observations on her negative interactions with her world (Reynolds 1983).

She might add meditation to her exercise programme, allowing herself time for reflection or simply 'letting go' (LeShan 1977). Reading might provide her with avenues for further self-exploration, where she can examine herself in preparation for her departure from therapy*.

GOING HER OWN WAY

I have often found it difficult to establish what exactly is the endpoint of the helping relationship. If we have not reached our objectives then, clearly, I need to step aside in favour of a fresher or more astute

---

*For examples of useful self-help material, try de Bono, E. (1979) *The Happiness Purpose*. Harmondsworth, Penguin/Pelican; Ellis, A. and Harper, R.A. (1975) *A New Guide to Rational Living*. Hollywood, Wilshire; Fensterheim, H. and Baer, J. (1979) *Don't Say Yes When You Want to Say No*. London, Futura Publications Ltd; Fensterheim, H. and Baer, J. (1989) *Making Life Right When It Feels All Wrong*. London, Futura Publications Ltd; Flach, F.F. (1986) *The Secret Strength of Depression*. New York, Bantam Books; Gendlin, E.T. (1988) *Focusing*. New York, Bantam Books; Rowe, D. (1988) *Choosing, Not Losing*. London, Fontana/Collins.

helper. Alternatively, perhaps we need to retrace our steps in search of the thread which has been lost. If the hoped-for ending is reached, the person will probably be ready to embark on her own exploration of self and her continued experimentation with life. If such a conclusion is reached, she signals her readiness to depart and it is time to collaborate on the appropriate ending of the relationship.

Although it is not necessarily fitting for therapists to offer gifts, it may be appropriate to provide a 'therapeutic gift' which might sustain her on the road ahead. Something, perhaps, which acts as an *aide mémoire* or raises the consciousness. I can think of no 'gift' more appropriate than Sheldon Kopp's *Eschatological Laundry List*, which he humorously subtitled, 'A Partial Register of the 927 (or was it 928) Eternal Truths'. These offer no real answers, for there are none. By the time you are ready to offer something like this she will be ready to take such powerful medicine. These lines embrace countless generations of wisdom, and traverse several cultures. The beginning and the end of (wo)man is to be found in their patient expression.

1. This is it!

2. There are no hidden meanings.

3. You can't get there from here, and besides there's no place else to go.

4. We are already dying, and we will be dead for a long time.

5. Nothing lasts.

6. There is no way of getting all you want.

7. You can't have anything unless you let go of it.

8. You only get to keep what you give away.

9. There is no particular reason why you lost out on some things.

10. The world is not necessarily just. Being good often does not pay off and there is no compensation for misfortune.

11. You have a responsibility to do your best nonetheless.

12. It is a random universe to which we bring meaning.

13. You don't really control anything.

14. You can't make anyone love you.

15. No-one is any stronger or any weaker than anyone else.

16. Everyone is, in his own way, vulnerable.

17. There are no great men.

18. If you have a hero, look again: you have diminished yourself in some way.

19. Everyone lies, cheats, pretends (yes, you too, and most certainly I myself).

20. All evil is potential vitality in need of transformation.

21. All of you is worth something, if you will only own it.

22. Progress is an illusion.

23. Evil can be displaced but never eradicated, as all solutions breed new problems.

24. Yet it is necessary to keep on struggling toward solution.

25. Childhood is a nightmare.

26. But it is so very hard to be an on-your-own, take-care-of-yourself-cause-there-is-no-one-else-to-do-it-for-you grown-up.

27. Each of us is ultimately alone.

28. The most important things each man must do for himself.

29. Love is not enough, but it sure helps.

30. We have only ourselves, and one another. That may not be much, but that's all there is.

31. How strange that so often, it all seems worth it.

32. We must live within the ambiguity of partial freedom, partial power, and partial knowledge.

33. All important decisions must be made on the basis of insufficient data.

34. Yet we are responsible for everything we do.

35. No excuses will be accepted.

36. You can run, but you can't hide.

37. It is most important to run out of scapegoats.

38. We must learn the power of living with our helplessness.

39. The only victory lies in surrender to oneself.

40. All of the significant battles are waged within the self.

41. You are free to do whatever you like. You need only face the consequences.

42. What do you know . . . for sure . . . anyway?

43. Learn to forgive yourself, again and again and again and again . . .

The objective of therapy is to score some kind of an own goal. By learning how to make the effort not to strive, the person learns to let go. After years of pursuing some ideal self, defined by others, she learns the trick of being ordinary. She learns the value of natural laws and those she must construct for herself. Finally, it may become apparent that all along, nothing really was hidden; just somehow out of the daylight.

REFERENCES

Barker, P. (1985) *Patient Assessment in Psychiatric Nursing.* London, Croom Helm.

Berne, E. (1972) *What Do You Say After You Say Hello?* London, Corgi.

Bliss, S. (ed.) (1985) *The New Holistic Health Handbook.* Lexington, Mass., Stephen Greene Press.

Blyth, R.H. (1976) *Games Zen Masters Play* (p15). New York, New English Library.

Burns, D.D. (1980) *Feeling Good: The New Mood Therapy.* New York, New American Library.

Fanning, P. (1988) *Visualisation for Change.* Oakland, California, New Harbinger Publications.

Frankl, V. (1963) *Man's Search for Meaning.* New York, Washington Square Press.

Keen, E. (1970) *Three Faces of Being: Towards an Existential Clinical Psychology* (p65). New York, Appleton, Century, Crofts.

Kopp, S. (1974) *If You Meet the Buddha on the Road, Kill Him!* London, Sheldon Press.

LeShan, L. (1977) *How to Meditate.* New York, Bantam Books.

May, R. (1961) *Existential Psychology.* New York, Random House.

Morgan, W.P. and Goldston, S.E. (1987) *Exercise and Mental Health.* Washington, Hemisphere Publishing Corporation.

Passon, W.R. (1975) *Gestalt Approaches in Counselling.* New York, Holt, Rhinehart & Winston.

Rehm, L.P. (1981) Assessment of depression. In Hersen, M. and Bellack, A.S. (eds.) *Behavioural Assessment: A Practical Handbook.* New York, Pergamon Press.

Reynolds, D.K. (1983) *Naikan Psychotherapy: Meditation for Self-Development.* Chicago, University of Chicago Press.

Rosen, G. (1978) *The Relaxation Book: An Illustrated Self-Help Guide.* Hemel Hempstead, Prentice-Hall.

Sartorius, N. and Ban, T.A. (1986) *Assessment of Depression.* Berlin, Springer.

Syer, J. and Connolly, C. (1984) *Sporting Body and Sporting Mind.* Cambridge, Cambridge University Press.

Tillich, P. (1952) *The Courage to Be.* New Haven, Connecticut, Yale University Press.

Wilson, P. (1985) *The Calm Technique.* Wellingborough, Thorsons.

Wilson, P.H., Spence, S.H. and Kavanagh, D.J. (1989) *Cognitive Behavioural Interviewing for Adult Disorders: A Practical Handbook.* London, Routledge.

Chapter 6

The self-help guide

This section comprises an outline guide designed to lead the person through the stages of examination, reflection and action outlined in the previous two chapters. This guide has been written in a simple and direct format, focusing upon the person's current and alternative constructions of her world*. Two features of the guide are significant and worthy of explanation.

The guide acknowledges the motivational and cognitive deficits commonly shown by people who are depressed, which might interfere with the use of such self-help literature. The self-help guide was required to have a reading level equivalent to that of a tabloid newspaper. The *Fox Index* (FI) suggests the number of years of fulltime education essential for reading a specific text (Gunning 1952). A 'quality' newspaper such as the Guardian has an average FI of 16; tabloid newspapers have averages between 7.5 and 10. The FI for existing pamphlets on coping with depression (Beck and Greenberg 1974) have an average FI of 11.5. This guide has an FI of approximately 7, so should provide a simple, solid base upon which the person can build her experiments in living.

The guide is written in the first person to encourage receptivity to the in-built instructions. This is designed to help the person assume personal responsibility for her thinking choices. It is important that she recognizes that she owns not only her feelings, but also her thoughts and actions. By using 'I' self-talk she is asserting recognition of *her* difficulties, *her* consideration of options and *her* experimentation with alternatives*.

* The author acknowledges the influence of Albert Ellis and Aaron Beck in the composition of this guide. Beck, A.T., Rush, A.J., Shaw, B.F. and Emery, G. *Cognitive Therapy of Depression*: New York, John Wiley. Ellis, A. (1962) *Reason and Emotion in Psychotherapy*. New York, Lyle and Stuart.
* For alternative views on the value of assertion in counteracting negative messages from self or others, see Alberti, R.E. and Emmons, M.L. (1986) *Your Perfect Right: A Guide to Assertive Living*. San Luis Obispo, California, Impact Press; Bower, S.A. and Bower, G.H. (1976) *Asserting Yourself: A Practical Guide for Positive Change*. Reading, Mass., Addison-Wesley; Butler, P.E. (1981) *Talking to Yourself: Learning the Language of Self-Support*. New York, Harper and Row; Steiner, C.M. (1981) *The Other Side of Power*. New York, Grove Press.

The publishers have waived the copyright on this chapter. The reader is free to copy this section if it is considered to be a useful adjunct to the helping relationship.

understanding your feelings and...... solving your problems

1A   WHAT IS THIS GUIDE ABOUT?

This guide was written to help people who are depressed. At first, you may feel that nothing can be done to help you. Perhaps you want to change things but feel that you do not have the energy. Perhaps you do not know how to.

In the following pages, I shall try to explain what is happening to you. I hope that this will help you understand yourself better. This may be helpful when you try to solve your problems.

In the first section, I offer my view of depression. What might cause depression? What might be done to overcome it? By the time you read this, we shall have begun to work on these questions – to try to solve some of your problems.

1B OVERCOMING YOUR DEPRESSION

What is depression?

Depression is best understood by looking at its effects. The most obvious sign of depression is a change in your mood. You feel different. You may cry when there is nothing to cry about. You may feel sad and alone in the world. You may lose interest in yourself or others. You may blame yourself for trivial faults or shortcomings. You may even feel guilty about things which happened a long time ago. Sometimes feelings of sadness or emptiness can change dramatically into a false sense of happiness. Sometimes you may get very excited: full of energy and fun. This may only be a mask for the sense of sadness which you feel.

How does depression come about?

These feelings are brought about *mainly* by the way that you think – about yourself, your life and the future. You become depressed because of the way you *interpret* things which happen to you. You may take trivial things too seriously. You may underestimate how well you are coping when things go wrong. You may blame yourself for things which are not your fault.

Although you see your *feelings* as your main problem, in truth the real problem is the way that you think. The way you tend to criticize yourself. The way you try to take responsibility for everything which happens to you. The way you are pessimistic about things ever changing in the future.

Because your 'thinking' is so important, it is worthwhile trying to change how you think. If you can change how you think, this may change how you feel.

Is that all there is to depression?

Thinking plays a large part in making you depressed. Other things are involved too. Things can go wrong with your body. This can make you feel depressed. Some people believe that they become depressed *just* because something goes wrong inside them. This may not be true as far as you are concerned. It may be that *physical* (or bodily) problems, *social* (or life) problems and *psychological* (or thinking) problems have *together* produced your depression.

Some people are more likely to become depressed than others. This has something to do with how their bodies work. This is similar to saying that some people are more likely than others to become overweight or tense or frightened of flying. These also have something to do with physical make-up. But people can *learn* to overcome such problems. In much the same way, you can learn to conquer your depression. It will take a lot of hard work, but it can be done.

What will be involved?

Depression can upset your whole life. The therapy outlined

here aims to help you find out what kind of life problems you have. Then you will learn *how* to solve them. This may ease your distress. It may also help reduce your feelings of depression. The therapy usually goes this way:

First, you learn how to become *more active*. Depressed people often become inactive: they feel that they have no energy, or that activities no longer give them any satisfaction. The first thing you will learn is how to become more active.

The next step helps you to get more *pleasure* and *satisfaction* out of life. Depression often takes this away. You are going to learn how to take it back.

Then you can start looking at the way you think about *yourself*, your *life* and the *future*. You will learn how changing the way you *think* can change the way you *feel*.

Once you know what kind of unhelpful thoughts you are using, you can practise changing the way you think, every day. You learn how to think more constructively about yourself and life in general.

Finally, you will learn how to use this new knowledge to deal better with your life. You will learn how to 'nip problems in the bud'. You will learn how to *avoid* making the mistakes which might bring on another bout of depression.

A word about homework

The therapy is a bit like a college course. Instead of learning about other things, you learn about yourself. Like any course of study, you will have to do some *homework*. Mostly, this will be no more than keeping a note of how you feel from day to day. However, such notes are very important. They show how things change, day by day. Progress sometimes is slow. Every little sign of change is important. Later on you will be able to jot down your thoughts and feelings. These notes will be helpful when you are trying to change the way you think.

From now on, the guidelines are written in the *first person*. I want you to read the rest of this text as if you are talking to yourself. This will help you to *reflect* on your *experience* of depression. This will help you to *consider* other ways of dealing with problems.

1C   ACTIVITY AND DEPRESSION

One of the most obvious signs of depression is that I become less active. Everything seems to be such a chore. Everything seems to be so difficult. Nothing seems to satisfy me. The simplest solution is not to bother.

In this first section, I shall look at the part activity plays in helping me to overcome my depression. I shall look at ways to get myself moving again – especially when I don't feel up to it.

1D ACTIVITY: A REFRESHER COURSE

Depression is a vicious circle. It slows me down, mentally and physically. One of the first things I may notice is that everything seems such an effort. I get tired easily; I do less than I used to, then I criticize myself for not doing enough. I begin to think I can't do anything at all, and that I'll never get over it. This makes me more depressed. It then becomes even more difficult to do anything. And so it goes on, getting worse and worse.

Stepping out

Activity is one way to break this circle. Becoming more active is important for a number of reasons:

- **Activity makes me feel better.** Activity takes my mind off painful feelings. I begin to feel that I am *taking control* of my life again. I am doing something worthwhile. I may even find that there *are* things that satisfy me, once I try them.
- **Activity makes me feel less tired.** Normally, I rest when I am tired. When I am depressed the tiredness is different. It is a sign that I need to become *more* active – not less. Doing nothing will only make me feel more lethargic and exhausted. Activity will freshen me up: making me *less* tired.
- **Activity makes me want to do more.** Depression often makes me feel like doing nothing at all. When I start becoming active again, the more I do, the more I shall feel like doing.
- **Activity helps me think better.** Once I become more active, I find it easier to solve problems. I start to think more clearly.
- **Activity makes me appear better.** People who matter to me will be pleased to see I am doing more.

Obstacles

Getting going again isn't going to be easy. This is usually because of 'negative thoughts' which stand in my way. These negative thoughts are typical of depression. When I decide to try something, I may find myself thinking:

'I *won't* enjoy it, so why bother?'
'I'll make a mess of it, I *always* do.'
'It's too difficult, I'd *never* manage.'

These *negative* thoughts block me from becoming active. Later on, I will learn to *challenge* these thoughts, to get these obstacles out of my way. For now, I shall simply find out what I am doing, and try to do more of the same.

1E MY LIFE PLAN

People who are depressed often think that they are doing *nothing*. They often think that they are achieving nothing, and enjoying nothing. This is all part and parcel of being depressed. They find it difficult to use their time properly. Often they can't find the time to do things they used to enjoy doing.

I need to start charting what I do. This will show me how I am spending my time. I can use this record to plan my day so that I become more active and my day has a chance of being more enjoyable.

An example

Here is an example which shows what a woman was doing over a whole week. She simply made a note of what she was doing *each hour* of the day. I do not need to write a lot; just make a note. When I discuss my record with my therapist, this will jog my memory. It will remind me of what I was doing at any hour of the day.

	MONDAY	TUESDAY	WEDNESDAY	THURSDAY	FRIDAY	SATURDAY	SUNDAY
8 – 9	had breakfast		B/FAST				
9 – 10	Helped with dishes	SAW DOCTOR	WENT TO O.T				
10 – 11	Talked to SARA	UPSET – SPOKE TO B.	O.T.				
11 – 12		SLEPT	O.T				
12 – 1	LUNCH	LUNCH	LUNCH – NOT HUNGRY AT ALL.				
1 – 2	TEA + SMOKE	WENT FOR WALK	BUS TO TOWN WITH JANICE				
2 – 3	PHONED J. HAD READ	WENT TO CANTEEN	COFFEE IN LITTLE SHOPS				
3 – 4	READING	PHONED DEREK	'WINDOW – SHOPPING'				
4 – 5	TOOK A WALK	WALKING	BACK TO HOSPITAL				
5 – 6	TEA	TEA (NOT HUNGRY)	TEA.				
6 – 7	DID TEA DISHES	DISHES!!	WATCHED T.V. (DOZING)				
7 – 8	WATCHED TV NEWS	READ PAPER					
8 – 9	SLEPT	LAY ON BED					
9 – 10							

Everyday things

For the first few days of this exercise, I shall write down what I am doing *just now*. Just ordinary, everyday things. I don't need to do anything *special*. I shall just practise using the record sheet.

1F   MOVING ON

Now I know how I am spending my day. The next step is to plan each day in advance. I am going to plan activities which will give me a sense of satisfaction or enjoyment.

There are three good reasons why I should plan ahead.

1. By planning *in advance*, I shall feel that I am taking control of my life again. It will give me a sense of *purpose*.
2. The plan will prevent me from being swamped by minor decisions. It will keep me going even when I feel bad.
3. When I *write down* my plan, things will look less difficult. I shall have broken down the day into little bits, each of which can be managed on its own. This will be better than trying to fill long, shapeless stretches of time.

Each evening I shall take a few minutes to plan for tomorrow. I shall pick a time when I know I won't be too busy, tired or distracted.

I shall make a note of what I plan to do tomorrow, against each hour of the day. If it's difficult to plan out the whole day, I shall just plan the morning. I can plan the afternoon at mid-day tomorrow.

I shall try to get a balance between activities which might be challenging, but not too difficult, and others which might give me some satisfaction – no matter how little.

I shall remember the golden rule – I WON'T REACH FOR THE STARS. I shall keep my plan simple and not rush myself.

1G FOLLOWING MY OWN DIRECTION

I know how to fill in the plan. Now I shall use it as an aid to overcoming some of my problems. My plan can become a *help* rather than a *hindrance*.

Here are some simple rules for me to follow:

1. **Be flexible**

   I shall use my plan as a *guide*, rather than a god. Of course, things will happen to throw me off my stride. This may make filling in my plan difficult. Someone may ask me to do something or go somewhere. I shall not let this put me off. I shall just carry on filling in the plan when next I can.

2. **Think of other activities**

   Some of my plans will be affected by things outside my control, like the weather or other people's needs. I shall have another activity ready in case my plans are disrupted.

3. **Stick in**

   If I can't do what I had planned, I shall just leave it. I shall not try to do it later on. I shall just carry on to my next planned activity. I shall plan to do what I have missed the *next day*. If I finish something sooner than expected, I shall take a break till my next activity. I can have a cup of tea or read the newspaper. *I shall prepare a menu of such alternatives to choose from.*

4. **Work to the clock**

   I shall try not to be too specific with my plan. I shall avoid being too vague also. 'Tidying up' is too vague. Listing everything I plan to dust is too specific. I need to find a happy medium. 'Read book – 20 minutes' is just right!

5. **Quantity not quality**

   I shall plan to spend *time* (like 30 minutes) on an activity. I *won't* plan how much I *want to achieve* in that time. What I achieve depends on so many other things, like interruptions or things breaking down. If I say that I *must* do all my washing, and for some reason I don't, I shall end up feeling bad. Instead, I shall simply plan to spend some time washing.

   I need to remember the golden rule – IF A THING'S WORTH DOING – IT'S WORTH DOING BADLY.

6. **Stick to the task**

   I need to remember my aim is to stick to my plan. I am *not* planning to overcome all my problems right away. If I work steadily at becoming more active, I shall eventually feel better. I do not expect to get over bad feelings just by watching TV for half an hour.

7. **Retracing my steps**

   At the end of each day, I shall look at what I have done, and what I'd like to change tomorrow. If I did not stick to my plan, I shall not worry. I shall try to find out what was the problem, and how I might change it. Did I plan to do too much? Did I feel tired? Was I aiming for too much success? I can learn from this.

8. **I am always active**

   Sitting in a chair is an activity. So is going to bed, or staring out the window. I am *always doing something*. I need to remember that these activities may not give me much in the way of satisfaction. I need to 'watch' what I am doing: how does it make me feel?

1H HOW DOES THAT MAKE ME FEEL?

I have been noting what I have been doing from day to day. My next step is to record how I feel about these activities.

From now on I shall record how I feel about what I am doing. I shall find out how much *satisfaction* or *enjoyment* these activities give me.

Activity can give me two kinds of *positive* feelings. I can feel a sense of:

Mastery – when I do something which is difficult, or which I usually avoid doing.

Or I feel a sense of:

Pleasure – when I get some sort of enjoyment from doing something.

I shall measure how much **mastery** or **pleasure** I feel from the things which I am doing each day. There is a simple way of doing this:

1. First of all, I shall write down what I do, hour by hour.
2. Next, I shall try to judge how much *achievement* I got from doing the activity: this is my sense of **mastery**.

I shall measure how much **mastery** I feel, measuring it on a scale between 0 and 10. A score of 0 means that I felt *no sense of achievement* at all. On the other hand, a score of 10 would mean that I felt *a great deal of achievement*.

3. Next, I shall mark this on my plan. I shall put the letter M beside the activity to represent **mastery** and put my score beside the letter. Here is an example below.

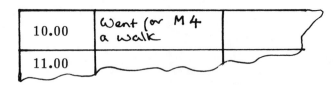

| 10.00 | Went for a walk M 4 | |
| 11.00 | | |

4. I shall now try to judge how much *enjoyment* I felt when doing this: this is my sense of **pleasure**.

I shall judge how much **pleasure** I felt, measuring it on a scale between 0 and 10. A score of 0 means I felt *no sense of enjoyment* at all. On the other hand, a score of 10 means that I felt *a great deal of enjoyment*.

5. Now I shall mark this on my plan. I shall put the letter P beside the activity and put my score beside the letter. My example looks like this:

| 10.00 | Went for MH a walk P 2 | |
| 11.00 | | |

Now my record shows *what I have done*, how much **mastery** I felt, and how much **pleasure** I felt.

I shall *remember* always to record my feelings of **mastery** and **pleasure** *as soon as I have done something*. I *won't* wait until later on. By then I may have forgotten how I actually felt at the time.

Also, I shall try to judge how difficult the activity is for me *now*. I shall try to avoid saying, 'I used to be able to do this with no difficulty'. I shall give myself credit for what I am trying to do *now*.

11 TEN COMMANDMENTS

When I am depressed I often find myself doing the same things every day. I often put off doing the things I *need* to do or would *like* to do. As a result, the pile seems to get bigger and soon overwhelms me completely. How can I start to change this?

There are some things I can do to help myself. I can begin doing what *needs* to be done. I shall:

1. Make a list of all the things I have been putting off.
2. Ask myself which of these needs to be done *first*? Which is next important? Arrange the list in order of priority. If I can't decide, I shall simply put them in alphabetical order. I could stick a pin in the list. The important thing is to do *something*.
3. Take the first task. Break it down into small steps. Ask myself what do I *need to do* to complete it?
4. Go through the steps in my mind: I shall visualize myself doing it. If I think of anything which might stop me doing it, I shall write it down. I shall try to work out how to get round this obstacle. I shall imagine a stream flowing round a rock. How might I 'flow' round this obstacle?
5. Write down any negative thoughts I have about doing things. What do I say to myself which blocks me from doing this?
6. Take each task *step by step*. I shall do it exactly as I did in my mind. I shall deal with any negative thoughts I have by putting them to one side. I shall put them in a box; I shall deal with them later. I shall tell myself just to stick to the task in hand.
7. Stop when I am *winning*. I shall avoid stopping when things start to go badly, as sometimes happens. I shall do just a little bit more – then stop when I am on top. I shall feel so much better.
8. Write down what I have done on my record sheet, as soon as I finish.
9. Focus on what I have *achieved*. I shall avoid thinking about what I still have to do. I shall keep an eye out for

any thoughts which might make my 'success' appear any less than it really is. I shall write these thoughts down also.

10. When I am ready to move on to the next task on my list, I shall acknowledge this – **Well done**.

1J   TEN HELPFUL STICKERS

Here are some hints to help me stick to my plan.

1. **Set aside some time each evening to note what I have done that day, and what I plan to do tomorrow.** I need to choose a time when I won't be interrupted and when I have time to spare.
2. **If I find doing something difficult, I shall tell my body what to do.** I shall give myself specific instructions. Saying 'Go on, do it' or 'Get on with it' is too vague. On the other hand, saying 'Legs, walk' or 'Hand, pick up a pen, hold it, now write' will get me started. I shall visualize myself going through the motions, *seeing* myself doing the activity.
3. **Watch out for unhelpful thoughts.** If I get any unhelpful thoughts I *won't* listen to them – I *shall write them down*. I shall try to answer them, and act on my answers. Once I have dealt with these obstructions, I can tear up the list or set fire to it. (The section on Road Blocks on p202–4 shows me how to do this.)
4. **Get rid of distractions.** Turning off the TV or going off somewhere quiet will help me concentrate upon what I am doing.
5. **Avoid bed.** Bed is for sleeping in, not for *hiding* in during the day. If I need to relax during the day, I shall plan another way of relaxing, like sitting in a comfortable armchair reading, listening to music or taking a bath.
6. **Treat myself for what I have done.** When I have completed an activity I might, for example, plan time for a cigarette or a cup of tea, by way of a treat. These treats are important. They help to spur on and lift my spirits. I shall be good to myself!
7. **Arrange reminders.** I can use a kitchen timer to plan the start and finish of activities. I shall put up signs to remind me what I am supposed to be doing. I shall even *tell* my family or friends what I have planned for a certain time. They can remind me if I get distracted.
8. **Give myself encouragement.** I shall always start the

day with something which will give me a good sense of achievement and which I have a good chance of completing.

9. **Try to balance my day.** I shall aim for a balance between activities which *I need* to do (tasks) and which I used to *enjoy* doing (pleasure).

10. **Do things which I found rewarding or fulfilling in the past.** If I enjoyed things once before, there is a good chance that, once I get going, I shall enjoy them again.

1K   ROAD BLOCKS

When people are depressed, their *unhelpful thinking* keeps them depressed. If depression doesn't just 'pass by', then it is safe to assume that *unhelpful thinking* is keeping me depressed.

To overcome my depression I need to 'catch' my unhelpful thoughts as they happen and then *challenge* them. These thoughts are telling me depressing things. That's why I stay depressed. The way to handle these thoughts is to *answer them back*.

Below are some examples of these thoughts. Beside each unhelpful thought is a *suggestion* about how I might answer it back. This is not the *right* answer – or the *only* answer. Just a suggestion. As I practise 'answering back' I shall be able to come up with answers which suit me.

Unhelpful thoughts	Answer
'I can't seem to do anything. It's just too difficult.'	There are problems in doing anything – that's life. How would I deal with this if I wasn't depressed? Is there anyone who can advise me?
' I can't stick to this plan.'	Keeping a plan is a skill. I haven't done this before – doesn't meant that I can't do it if I try. After all, I've used lists before – like for shopping. I could start just by making lists.
'I can't cope any longer.'	I just *think* that because I'm depressed. If I write down what I've got to do, it won't seem so difficult. I don't have to do it all at

Unhelpful thoughts	Answer
	once. I can take one bit at a time.
'It's too difficult.'	It just seems that way because I'm depressed. I've done more difficult things than this before.
'I don't know how to tackle this.'	Have a go – don't try to be perfect. Better to try and see how I get on than not to try at all.
'I don't want to.'	I don't want to do it *now* – but I did earlier on. Anyway, that doesn't matter. The point is, it would be better for me to do it. I *need* to do it.
'I don't think I'm up to it just now. I'll wait till I'm feeling better.'	I won't know if I'm up to it if I don't try. If I wait till I feel like it, I'll never do it. Anyway, doing it will make me feel better.
'There's no point – it'll only make me think of the time I've wasted. I should have done it before.'	I can't waste time. I have just done something else with the time. The point is – what am I doing now? Am I going to repeat myself, or do something different?
'I can't decide.'	The important thing is to do *something*. I could do things in alphabetical order if necessary. Once I get moving, I'll have a clearer idea of where I'm going.

Unhelpful thoughts	Answer
'I'll only make a mess.'	How do I know? I won't know till I try. Anyway, nobody's asking for a star turn. Even if I made a mess of it, it's not the end of the world. I can learn from my mistakes.
'I won't enjoy it.'	How do I know? Since when was I a fortune teller? Try it and see. Be experimental with life.
'I'm not doing anything.'	I shall write down what I do and see if this is right.
'But I'm not doing anything worthwhile.'	Nobody's asking me to judge what I'm doing, *just do it*.
'I don't deserve good things.'	Doing things makes me feel better. That's good in itself. It'll also help me to do things better.
'OK, so I washed the dishes.'	Once, that wouldn't have been very difficult. Now it's very difficult. But in spite of that, I did it. I need to give myself credit for that. My mastery score *should* be 10.

1L WHAT'S THE POINT OF ALL THIS?

Sometimes I may think, 'This is stupid. What's the point in doing all this? This isn't going to make me feel better. What's this got to do with me being depressed?'

Sometimes it is difficult to see how some of these things are going to help. I shall try to overcome this by reminding myself of these 'good reasons' for keeping going.

1. When I am depressed, I often feel that I can do *nothing*. Or I feel that when I do something I *won't enjoy it* or that I *haven't done it well*.

   These records give me a very accurate picture of *what I have done* and exactly *how I felt* about it.

2. Depressed people often tend to see only the black side of things. They see faults very clearly and ignore the good points.

   This is another reason why I should keep these records. If someone asked me tomorrow what I did today, I would probably say: 'Not much' or 'Nothing worth speaking about'.

   This is a natural answer for someone who is depressed: I tend to think in this *negative* fashion. By keeping these records, I can *look back* on what I *actually* did – rather than on what I *think* I did.

These are two very good reasons for keeping these records:

- They give me an honest picture of what I am doing and how I am feeling, during each day; and
- They will be helpful in challenging my *belief* that I do nothing, or that I enjoy nothing.

It is natural to find all of this difficult to do. It may also be hard to understand. I need to remember these points:

- I am trying to find out more about myself – so that I can understand myself and the reasons why I get depressed. The easiest way to do this is by taking 'notes' on what I am doing, and how I react to what I am doing.
- Overcoming depression can be slow at the start. I need to

try not to be too impatient. I need to remember, Rome wasn't built in a day.

- I should remember that much of my present problems stems from my *negative* view of things. I am working towards a more positive view of life and of myself. Even if it doesn't appear to be giving good results, I need to **keep on trying**.

2A I THINK – THEREFORE I AM DEPRESSED

Thinking and depression

Now that I have begun to be more active, I can take a look at my feelings of depression in more detail. What sort of feelings am I getting? What sort of thoughts are related to these feelings?

At the beginning of the guide, I read that my feelings of depression were brought about by the way that I think. In this section, I shall take a close look at the way that I think. What do I think of the things which happen to me? What effect do these thoughts have upon the way I feel?

2B   UNHELPFUL THOUGHTS: THE TRUE STORY

Depressed people tend to think in a negative sort of way. They tend to have a negative view of *themselves* ('I'm no good'), their *world* ('Life has no meaning'), and the *future* ('Things will never get any better').

These thoughts make me depressed, and stop me from dealing with my problems. I am now going to look at ways of coping with such thoughts.

Unhelpful thoughts have a lot in common:

1. They are *automatic* – they just 'pop' into my head, without any effort.
2. They are *distorted* – they do not match up to the real facts.
3. They are *very negative* – they keep me depressed and make it difficult for me to change things.
4. They are *plausible* – they appear genuine: I just don't think of challenging them.
5. They are *involuntary* – they are very difficult to switch off.

The more depressed I am, the more unhelpful thoughts I shall have. The more depressed I am, the more I am likely to believe them, and the more depressed they will make me. This is a 'vicious circle'.

Negative thinking has an effect on how I feel and what I do. Now it is time to do something about this.

I shall now take a look at ways of 'catching' my unhelpful thoughts: ways of recognizing *when* I am thinking negatively. Once I can do this, I shall learn how to look for more positive, or helpful, ways of looking at the things which happen to me.

At first, I may find it difficult to 'catch' and answer my unhelpful thoughts. I won't be discouraged. This will get easier with practice. Soon it will become more natural. Catching and answering negative thoughts is a *skill* – something I need to learn. Once I have learned the basics, I shall practise 'catching and answering' my thoughts, as part of my 'homework'.

On the next page is a form which helps me find out what kind of thoughts I have in different situations. It also helps me find out how these thoughts affect the way I feel.

I shall use this form in the first part of this exercise. This will help me become aware of *how* I think.

The self-help guide

2C THOUGHT CATCHING

The way I feel is influenced by the way I *think*. I shall practise finding out what sort of thoughts I have when I feel bad. I shall recall the last time I felt bad; I might have felt sad or angry, guilty or frightened. I shall try to remember how I felt and what was happening around me, and answer the following questions.

How did I feel? _____ Embarassed _____

How bad was the feeling – measure it by using a scale of 0–100 (100 is the very worst).

_____ 60 _____ **Score**

Situation

Where was I? In supermarket

What was I doing? Shopping - knocked jar off shelf

What was going on around me? Assistant stopped to help

Was I thinking about anything in particular? How can I pick this up without dropping my basket?

What thoughts just "popped into my mind" at that time?

Automatic Thoughts		Score
She thinks I'm stupid	100	
Why do I always drop things?	95	
Now I look flustered	90	
I'm just hopeless	80	

Did I *believe* these thoughts? I shall measure to what extent I believed them using a scale 0–100. (0 means I did *not* believe them at all; 100 means I believed them *completely*).

2D HOW YOU THINK

The first step in dealing with my unhelpful thinking is to know *how I think*, and its effect on *how I feel*.

Unhelpful thoughts make me feel bad. They make me feel sad, anxious, hopeless, angry or depressed. Instead of being overwhelmed by these feelings, I can learn to use them as a *signal* for taking some action. I can start taking notice of *when* my mood changes. I can note what was happening and what was running through my mind. If I do this, I shall become more aware of changes in my feelings. I shall also become more aware of the thoughts which spark off these changes in mood. I may find that the same thoughts occur over and over again.

Becoming aware

On the previous page is an example of the form which I can use to practise 'catching' my negative thoughts. This is how I shall use it.

1. Whenever I feel *bad* I shall make a note of 'how I felt', using the scale 0 to 100. The score of 0 means that *I didn't feel bad at all*; 100 means that *I couldn't have felt any worse*.
2. Now I shall make a note of *where I was* when I started to feel bad. Also, I shall write down *what I was doing*, e.g. reading or talking to someone.

   I shall note, also, *what was going on around me*: e.g. people were arguing or the radio was blaring.

   Finally, I shall make a note of any *general thoughts* I was having: I might have been worrying about something or planning a shopping trip.
3. Next, I shall make a note of any *thoughts which 'popped into my head'* just before I started to feel bad. I shall write these down, word for word.

   Some of my thoughts may take the form of 'images'. For instance, I may imagine myself being unable to cope with something or 'going to pieces'. If that happens, I shall just write down what I saw in my mind's eye.

Sometimes I may not be able to identify any thoughts. If that happens, I shall try to imagine what the situation *meant* to me. What does it tell me about myself, my life or the future? This may give me a clue as to why a situation makes me *feel* sad or angry or anxious.

4. Lastly, I shall try to judge how far I *believe* these thoughts. I shall use the same 0 to 100 scale. (0 means that I don't believe them at all, 100 means that I believe them completely.)

Remember, I can score anywhere between 0 and 100.

Take time

It may be difficult to record my thoughts *as they happen*. I won't worry about that. I shall simply make a mental note of the things which have distressed me during the day. Then I shall set aside a few minutes later on to write these down. If I can't remember exactly what happened and what I thought at the time, I shall try doing an 'action replay'. I shall try and remember *what happened*, how I *felt* and what I *thought* at the time.

Take care

I need to beware of 'excuses' for *not* watching my thoughts. I may say 'I'll do it later' or 'I'd better just forget about that'. I may be tempted simply to avoid looking my thoughts in the face. It is quite natural to want to avoid thinking about unpleasant things. I need to remember that, in my case, *confronting* my negative thinking is the best way of fighting my depression.

If I find myself making excuses, it is probably because I have been thinking something really important . . . so I shall *write it down*, I won't hide from it. Once I have done that, I can then practise some distraction to ease my feelings of distress but remember, just ignoring my thoughts won't make them go away.

How many – how often?

Another way of making me more aware of my thoughts is to *count them*. Counting can also make them less distressing. When I count thoughts, this gives me a chance to stand back from myself. It is almost like counting cars which pass me in the street; I would stand to one side in order to count – I would not stand in the middle of the road.

I can count negative thoughts any way that I like. I could tot them up on a knitting counter, or simply tick them off on a card in my pocket or handbag as shown here:

At the end of the day, I can add up how many unhelpful thoughts I have had. I might find myself having more than ever. This is probably just because I am getting better at 'catching' them. In the long run, they will become less frequent.

I need to remember *not* to blame myself for having so many unhelpful thoughts. This is *not* a sign of any weakness or inadequacy on my part.

3A CONFRONTING MY THOUGHTS AND FEELINGS

I have spent some time looking at how I think and how this affects my feelings. Now I need to look at how I can deal with these thoughts. In this section, I shall begin to challenge some of my more common thoughts: thoughts about myself or my life in general. I shall deal with my feelings by practising different logical ways of thinking.

In the next few pages, I shall take a look at some general hints about 'thinking'. I need to acknowledge a simple word of warning. I have been thinking 'unhelpful thoughts' for a long time, perhaps for most of my life. I should not expect to change this pattern easily; the change I desire may take a little time.

3B CHALLENGING MY DEPRESSING THOUGHTS

Now I am more aware of my depressing thoughts. The next step is to take a closer look at them. Are they really 'true'? Are they really 'helpful'? Is there a more helpful or realistic way of looking at my life?

Questioning my thinking

There are four ways of altering my depressing thoughts. I can ask myself:

1. **What is the evidence?** Why do I think the way I do? What *facts* back up what I think? Do these facts support what I think, or contradict it?
2. **What other views are there?** There is more than one way of looking at a situation. How else could I look at what has happened? I could list other viewpoints. What evidence is there for and against these views? When I look at these objectively, which view appears to be the more correct?
3. **How do these thoughts affect me?** The way I think affects how I feel. How exactly do these thoughts affect how I feel and what I do? How helpful is it to think this way? What are the disadvantages of thinking this way? Can I think of thoughts which might have a better effect upon me?
4. **Am I mistaken?** Depressed people often distort things. They can jump to conclusions; blame themselves for things which are not their fault; exaggerate the importance of things, and so on. Am I making such mistakes about this situation?

Shortly, I shall look more closely at questioning as a way of challenging my negative thinking. Before I do this, I need to look at the record format which will help me do this.

3C   A CHALLENGING RECORD

It is important to write down and challenge as many depressing thoughts as I can, each day. When I write them down, I
become more objective. Soon I shall be able to challenge such
thoughts in my head. At first, it helps simply to write them
down. My answers will be stronger if I can read them in
black and white. I need to spend some time working out
'challenges' to my thoughts on paper before I can deal with
them in my head. The more I practise, the easier it will get.

Over the page is an example of a challenging record. I shall
keep this like a daily diary. I shall use it to *confront* my
thoughts.

In the first four columns, I shall write down the day and
date, how I *felt*, what was *happening* to me, and what I was
thinking, just as I have done already.

Challenge   In the next column I shall write down as many
challenges to those thoughts as I can imagine. Then I shall ask
myself how much I believe these 'other views'. If I don't
believe the answer at all, I shall give it a score of 0. If I believe
it completely, I shall give it a score of 100. I could score
anywhere between 0 and 100.

Outcome   In the last column, I need to do three things:

1. Look at my original thought. Now that I have tried to
   confront it, do I still believe it to the same extent? How far
   do I believe it now? I shall give it another score out of 100.

   I should find that my belief in the depressing thought
   has weakened. If it hasn't, perhaps I am ruling out my
   'answer' in some way. Maybe I am saying that this may
   apply to other people, but not to me, or that I am just
   fooling myself. If I am doing this, I shall write down these
   new 'depressing thoughts' and try to answer them in the
   same way.

   I won't expect my belief in the depressing thought to
   disappear right away. I probably have been thinking such
   thoughts for some time. The 'answers' which I have come
   up with are new. It may take some time for me to believe
   in them completely.

2. Now I shall take a look at my *feelings*. I shall check how I felt before I challenged my negative thoughts. How do my feelings compare now? Do I still feel *exactly* the same? I shall give *each* of the feelings I listed another rating of 100 for severity.

 I should find that my painful feelings have lessened a little. I won't be discouraged if they have not gone away. This will take time and practice. I shall be patient.

3. Lastly, I shall ask what I can *do* to make things better. How might I test out some of the 'helpful answers' I offered as challenges? I need to think about *how I would like to handle that situation* next time it happens. What will I do if I find myself thinking and feeling this way again? I need to work out a plan to stop the same thing happening again. I need to remember to write down exactly what *needs to be done*.

3D   A CHALLENGING EXAMPLE

Here is an example of a form which might help me challenge some of the thoughts I commonly use.

			CHALLENGING MY DEPRESSIVE THINKING		
DATE	FEELING(S) How do I feel? How bad is it (0–100%)?	SITUATION What was I doing or thinking about at the time?	DEPRESSIVE THOUGHTS What exactly were my thoughts? How far did I believe each of them (1–100%)?	HELPFUL ANSWER What alternatives are there to my depressive thoughts? How far do I believe each of them (0–100%)?	OUTCOME 1. How far do I now believe my depressive thoughts? (0–100%)? 2. How do I feel now (0–100)? 3. What can I do now?
Mon 15th Sept.	Jealous Angry (80)	Got a letter from my sister saying she had just got a new house	How come she has all the luck? My whole life has been a disaster! I'll never get out of the rut (95)	She is lucky to have a new house Everyone can't be so fortunate. I'm not starving am I? I just think my life is a mess (75)	1) Thoughts (50) 2) Feelings (40) 3) I could list my successes. I could save some money. I could list things I'd like to change.

On this illustration, I can see that this person had some bad feelings on Monday 15th September. She received a letter from her sister. She felt angry and jealous. These feelings were about 80% of the *most* she could ever feel. She had *three different thoughts* about this letter. First, 'Why does my sister have all the luck?'. Second, that her 'whole life has been a disaster': and third, that she will 'never get out of the rut'.

At the time, she believed these thoughts about 95%: very strongly indeed.

When she challenged these thoughts, things weren't quite as she thought:

- She said to herself, although her sister was 'lucky to have a new home, everybody can't be so fortunate'.

- She recognized that she just *thought* that her whole life was a mess.
- Finally, she realized that 'never' is a very long time. Perhaps she should try to change her life gradually.

She did not believe these thoughts completely (only about 75%). However, this kind of alternative thinking did reduce her beliefs in her depressing thoughts. After reasoning things out, her feelings of jealousy and anger weren't quite so bad. Finally, she planned to start changing things which she was unhappy about, in a gradual way. Doing what needed to be done!

3E   TEN HELPFUL QUESTIONS

Finding 'other viewpoints' can be difficult. Here are ten questions which might help me challenge my negative thoughts.

A. Face the facts?

1. Am I confusing a *thought* with a *fact*? What evidence *supports* these thoughts?
2. Am I ignoring other ways of looking at the situation? What is the evidence *against* these thoughts?

B. Take another look?

3. How do I know my view is the *only* view? How would someone else look at this?
4. Is this just *depressed* thinking? How would I have looked at this before I became depressed?
5. What evidence do I have to support these other ways of thinking?

C. Judge the results

6. Does thinking like this help or hinder me from getting what I want?
7. What are the pros and cons of thinking this way? Would I advise others to think this way – or some other way?
8. Am I asking questions which have no real answers?

D. Try another way

9. Am I overlooking simple solutions? Am I assuming they won't work?

10. How can I test my 'other viewpoints'? What can I do to change my situation?

I shall use these ten questions as an aid to 'challenging' my depressing thoughts.

3F LOOKING FOR ANSWERS

The ten questions in section 3E will help me find 'other viewpoints'; other ways of thinking about my life. I shall use them as a memory aid. Here are some examples of how these questions can help me think more clearly.

A. Face the facts?

The first thing I need to tackle is the *evidence* for thinking the way I do. Just because I *believe* something to be true does not mean that it *is* true. Would others accept my thought as true? If my thought was put 'on trial', would it stand up in court? Or would it be dismissed as irrelevant or circumstantial?

1. The key question here is, 'Am I confusing a *thought* with a *fact*?'. What is the *evidence* for thinking the way I do? It is not enough to say 'Well, that's what I think!'. What evidence do I have to support this thought?

Automatic thought	Possible answer
(I passed Sally in the street today and she ignored me.) I must have done something to upset her.	Just because she ignored me doesn't mean that I have upset her. Maybe she had something on her mind.

In the example above, the 'depressing (or upsetting) thought' is that someone has hurt me *on purpose*. The assumed 'reason' is that she must be *paying me back* in some way. There is at least one other way of looking at this. Sally may not have seen me, or she might have been thinking about something else.

2. This example shows the need to tell the difference between what I *think* and what is *fact*. The second ques-

tion on my list can help me to look at the situation differently. I need to ask myself, 'What is the evidence *against* these thoughts?'. In the 'possible answer' above, I have done just that.

In challenging my negative thoughts, it may be helpful to remember the idea of the 'court-room battle'. I need to ask myself, 'What is the evidence *for* thinking this way?', then ask myself, 'What is the evidence *against* thinking this way?'.

B. Take another look

The next three questions involve the way I am *looking* at the situation.

3. I need to ask myself if this is the only way of looking at the situation. Often it is difficult to 'step outside myself'. Often it is difficult to be objective. One way to do this might be to ask how someone else (a friend or neighbour) might react to the same situation. How would they look at what has happened? What would they say? If this is still difficult, I could try switching places with my friend. Imagine that what happened to me has happened to a friend. She comes to me for advice or consolation. What would I say to her? *Would I look at the situation differently if it wasn't happening to me?*

Automatic thought	Possible answer
(I went to the shops, I couldn't remember what I wanted.) I'm going off my head!	OK, so I forgot what I wanted. It's hardly the end of the world. My friend Edith is always forgetting things. She just laughs and makes a joke of it.

If my friend said, 'I can't remember things – I'm going off my head', what would I say to her? Would I *agree* with her?

Or would I come up with another way of looking at this problem? Sometimes it is easy to give good advice to our friends; taking my own good advice is often more difficult.

4. In much the same way, our view of things can be another example of depressed thinking. I may *only* be thinking these thoughts because I am depressed. One way to overcome them is to remember how I would have dealt with the situation *before* I became depressed.

Automatic thought	Possible answer
(I picked up a book today. I couldn't concentrate.) This shows how I am getting worse. My mind is deteriorating.	If I wasn't depressed, I'd probably just have moved on to something else. I would probably have said, 'I'll come back to this later, when I feel like reading'.

5. The last question in this section echoes what I have already covered. I need to ask myself what is the evidence *for* thinking in these different ways? Is it *true* that forgetting things isn't the end of the world? Is it *true* that my friend would probably shrug off such a problem? Would I previously have just gone and done something else? If my answer to any of these questions is *yes*, maybe I should swap these thoughts for my negative ones. What would happen if I started to believe in these alternatives?

C. Judge the results

Here are three more questions. These ask how useful are my depressing thoughts.

6. The first question is, 'Does thinking this way help or hinder me from getting what I want?'. Like most people, I simply want to be *happy*. I need to ask myself if thinking

this way helps me to become happy? Or does it stop me from becoming happy? Does this kind of thought make me miserable?

Automatic thought	Possible answer
My life has been a complete mess. I've messed up my own life and now I am messing up everyone else's.	Brooding about what has happened just makes me depressed. What is done is done. I need to put that down to experience. The important thing is to ask myself, 'What am I going to do *now*?'.

Often I feel that I *deserve* to be miserable. Maybe I even feel that I deserve to be *punished* more for things I have done in the past. It is important to challenge these thoughts. These thoughts keep me feeling depressed. Indeed, they may make me feel even more depressed. They also hold me back from getting what I want.

7. In the same vein, I need to consider the pros and cons of thinking in this way. Sometimes depressing thoughts *appear* to be helpful. They may keep me on my toes. But they also have lots of disadvantages. These outweigh any advantages.

Automatic thoughts	Possible answers
'I *must* always try and make a good impression on people.'	Telling myself that I *must* always do anything isn't realistic.
ADVANTAGE = 'I'll go out of my way to be friendly. If they like me in return I'll feel good.'	This just puts more pressure on me. I become more tense and find it even more difficult to relax, concentrate and enjoy myself.
DISADVANTAGE = 'If someone appears not to like me, I'll feel terrible and shall think badly of myself.'	Instead, I shall try thinking, 'If people like me that's nice. If they don't, 'it's not the end of world. It's not realistic to think *everyone* should like me.'

8. Lastly, it may be that I am asking questions which have no real answers. Depressed people often ask themselves, 'Why aren't things different?', 'What is life all about?', 'Why is life so unfair?', 'Why is this happening to me?', or 'What can I do to undo the past?' Brooding over these questions is sure to depress me further. Like it or not, these questions have *no* real answers. I need to try turning these thoughts into a question I *can* answer. If I can't do something, I won't waste any more time on it.

Automatic thought	Possible answer
'When will I get over this depression?'	Sorry! There is no answer to that. Going over and over this just upsets me further. I'd be better asking myself what I can do to make myself *feel* a little better *right now*?

D. Try another way

All of these questions try to change the way I think. They also ask me to do something different as well, like telling myself to stop brooding or to go and do something else for a while.

9. The last two questions ask *how* I can change things. I need to ask, 'Is there a fairly simple solution to my problem? Perhaps one which I have overlooked?' Often, trying to think how a friend, or someone I respect, might handle the situation can help me find such a solution. Or I may know of a 'solution' but have argued that 'It won't do any good. It won't work'. *How will I know unless I try?*

Automatic thought	Possible answer
'I feel awful. I have no energy. I can't stop going over and over things in my mind.'	I know I feel bad. That's what it's like to be depressed. I shall take a short walk in the park. I'll see if a bit of fresh air will refresh me.
'There's no point. Nothing will help me. Anyway, I haven't got the energy.'	Look, I know that I *feel* bad. And I know that I *feel* that nothing is going to change this. But I won't know if this (taking a little walk) is any good until I try it. I shall stop telling myself things won't work. I shall try it and see.

10. In the same way, I shall ask *how* I can *try out* some of these 'possible answers'. I shall start planning *how* I can try 'shrugging things off with a laugh' (instead of worrying if my mind's going). *How* I can deal with my lack of concentration. *How* I can tackle the question of 'What I am going to do with my life now?'.

It is not enough to *think* differently. I need to turn this into **action**. I need to do something different. If I do something different, perhaps I shall *feel* different. *I won't know until I try.*

In the next stage, I shall take another look at the way I think and the effect this has upon my feelings. For the time being, I shall use these ten questions as an aid to challenging my negative thoughts. If I use these questions, I shall begin to bring my depressing thoughts under my control.

A WORD OF CAUTION

Before I leave this section, I should warn myself against expecting too much. There are five problems I might run into when I begin to challenge my negative thoughts.

1. Firstly, 'confronting thoughts' is unusual. Normally we don't stand back, question and 'challenge' our thoughts. What I am asking myself to do is difficult. At first I may find it near impossible to be objective. I may find that my 'answers' do not appear to affect my feelings very much. **I shall not despair**. This is quite normal. I need to give myself the chance to practise this challenging approach. I need to give myself time to get the hang of it. I won't be discouraged if I can't master it straight away. After all, I wouldn't expect to be able to drive after only a few lessons. *Practice, practice* and more *practice*.
2. I may also find it difficult to come up with alternatives when I am feeling upset. The feelings may be so bad that I may think that I cannot think at all. If this happens, I shall write down what is distressing me as a *distraction*. When I feel calmer, I shall come back to notes. Now I shall be in a better position to look for more helpful answers.

   I need to beware of making matters worse by telling myself that this means that I am a failure, or that this isn't working.
3. I need to remember that my record is just a record. It does not have to be good, well-written, or anything special. I am using it to confront my thoughts and feelings. It is not using me! There are no 'right' or 'wrong' answers – I am working out what will change things *for me*! What will weaken my faith in these depressing thoughts?
4. I need to beware of criticizing myself when I am writing down my thoughts. I might find myself thinking, 'I must be stupid to think that' or 'This just shows how bad I really am'. I need to *remember* that these are more examples of depressing thoughts. This is part and parcel of my depression. My negative thinking is the problem: not my intelligence or my goodness. I am good just because *I am*.

5. Lastly, I shall not get upset if I find the same thoughts cropping up over and over again. My depressing thinking is well established. My thinking has become a bad habit which will take some time to break, like giving up smoking or trying to stop biting my nails. I shall take the view that the more often a particular thought occurs, the more chances I have to challenge it, and break the habit.

4A   UNHELPFUL THOUGHTS

I have been introduced to the idea of unhelpful thoughts and the part they play in negative thinking. In this section, I shall focus upon these unhelpful thoughts in more detail. Here, I shall develop my awareness of the kind of unhelpful thoughts *I* make, as I make them.

If I can learn to 'catch' my unhelpful thoughts, I may be able to prevent patterns of unhelpful thinking becoming established.

CLEAR, COOL THINKING

Over the next few pages are some of the common unhelpful thoughts which trouble depressed people. It is worth noting that they trouble *most* people, but they trouble depressed people more seriously. These are examples of *unhelpful* thinking. When I use them I say something to myself which is not true, is an exaggeration of the truth, or is not supported by any evidence. These ways of thinking put me down in some way. They make me feel bad. They are very unhelpful. I intend to study these so that I can recognize them better. It's like the old saying: 'To be forewarned is to be forearmed'. If I can catch these ways of thinking early on, I may be able to confront them more quickly. As a result, I may be able to avoid feeling distressed, or I may be able to reduce the extent of any bad feelings.

I shouldn't be surprised if I find that I don't use all of these thoughts. I may use some more often than others. I may not be aware of some of these at all. However, it is only to be expected that I shall use some of them quite often. These are the real culprits as far as my depression is concerned.

These unhelpful thoughts have been illustrated with little pictures and symbols. I shall make a copy of these to keep in my pocket or handbag to help me recognize the unhelpful thoughts, and to challenge them.

At this stage, I am learning how to recognize these unhelpful thoughts so that I can catch them all the more easily. Now I am becoming more knowledgeable about what *influences* my feelings of depression, I am becoming more able to catch the unhelpful thoughts which influence my feelings of depression.

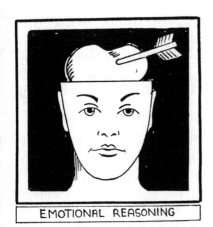

EMOTIONAL REASONING

Human beings tend to be emotional. Our hearts rule our heads much of the time. However, I need to watch that such 'emotional reasoning' doesn't lead me into trouble. Do I ever think, 'I feel guilty. This must mean I've done something wrong.' Or, 'I know that I can't prove it but I just *feel* that it's true.' These are both examples of *emotional reasoning*: letting my heart rule my head.

Again, it is important that I search for the evidence to support feeling this way. If I can't find any, I shall have to try to accept that I am being 'emotional'. I am putting myself down for no good reason. I have a choice. I can continue to 'feel' guilty or let down (or whatever) for no good reason, or I can say there is no reason *why* I should feel this way. Then I can try to work out how I should be feeling and what I should do next!

Do I ever say, 'I *should* be able to pull myself together', or, 'I *must* always try to appear cheerful', or, 'I *should* always want to be with my family'? These kind of thoughts make heavy demands upon my emotions. They make me feel I am a failure (if I am not always cheerful); or they make me feel guilty (if I don't always want to be with my family).

SHOULDS + MUSTS

It is one thing to try to be positive, cheerful or loving. It is quite another to say that I *should* or *must always* be like that. When I find myself using 'should and must', I shall simply tell myself to *stop trying to be perfect*. I can go ahead and try to be positive or loving or cheerful. But I won't punish myself if I can't always keep it up.

JUMPING TO CONCLUSIONS

Often, I may tell myself that things are 'bad', although I have no evidence to support this. This is a bit like crystal-ball gazing. I am predicting that certain things *will* happen – a bit like a fortune teller. I may tell myself that, 'I'll never get over this' or, 'I'll never be able to do that'. How do I know? Can I foretell the future? At other times, I may say that, 'Everyone is fed up with me' or, 'People don't like me any more'. How do I know? Can I read their minds? Jumping to conclusions is a very common error – all people tend to do this from time to time. The easiest way to challenge this error is to look for the evidence. How do I *know* that this or that will happen? How do I *know* that people don't like me or don't want me? There is no point just saying, 'Well, I feel that way'. This is a sign that I am *jumping to conclusions*.

Lots of people tend to exaggerate. Maybe I do this as well. If something goes wrong, do I ever say, 'Oh, this is terrible, and there's nothing I can do about it'? I may well be *magnifying* the problem – almost as though I was holding a magnifying glass over it. I make it look worse than it really is. At the same

CATASTROPHIZING

time, I can *underestimate* my ability to deal with things – almost as if I was looking at my own abilities down the wrong end of a telescope.

I make them appear much *smaller* than they really are. I minimize myself – I make myself appear less able or less competent.

When things go wrong, I shall try to avoid turning a small problem into a disaster or a complete 'catastrophe'. I shall search for the evidence. How bad is it *really*? Is it really so terrible? Is it really the worst thing which could happen to me? Am I really not able to do anything? I shall make a list of the sort of things I might at least try.

MENTAL FILTER

Most things which happen to me will not be all bad. They will be made up of 'bad bits' and 'good bits'. Do I tend to think only of the bad bits? This is a bit like making coffee with ground coffee. However, instead of keeping the water which passes through the ground beans, I keep the grounds instead. Even when making coffee, there is a 'good bit' (the coffee liquid) and a 'bad bit' (the coffee grounds). When I find myself saying, 'I didn't have a minute's happiness today' or 'My life has been just one problem after another', I may well be using the *mental filter*. I may be concentrating only upon the bad bits – throwing away any 'good bits'. I can start tackling this error by checking the evidence. I can make a list of all the 'bad bits' and then try to list the 'good bits' – no matter how small they appear by comparison. I need to beware of 'filtering' out the bad experiences, and then focusing all my attention upon them.

DISCOUNTING THE POSITIVE

In a similar way, I might be telling myself that some 'good bits' *don't count* for some reason. I might say, 'OK, so I did some work today. So what? I do that every day. It's hardly a success'. I may be telling myself that certain things don't count as positive experiences. I reject these and end up dwelling upon negative experiences (the 'bad bits'). This error is another version of the mental filter. If I am obliged to recognize something which isn't really *bad*, I discount it by saying that it's not really good either. It's nothing. I need to remind myself that filtering out good experiences only worsens my depression. *Discounting the positive* is another way of focusing on bad experiences and another way of deepening my depression.

Do I tend to see things in 'black and white'? For instance, am I either a *total* success or a *total* failure? If *one* thing goes wrong, does this mean that *everything* is wrong? This error can be called 'all-or-nothing thinking.' I seem to be saying to myself, 'If I am not perfect, I must be a complete mess', or, 'If everyone doesn't love me, then nobody loves me'. I am making it a case of *all or nothing*.

BLACK + WHITE THINKING

I need to check this error by asking myself, 'What is the evidence for saying that *everything* is wrong, or that *nothing* is right?'. It may be true that *some* things are wrong, or that *some* improvement could be made in a situation. This is not the same as saying that everything is wrong, or nothing is right. I need to remember that reality is made up of a thousand shades of grey. I am not all good or all bad, all right or all wrong. *There is no black and white.*

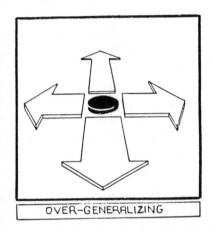

OVER–GENERALIZING

Do I tend to use one bad experience to colour other parts of my life? Do I ever make a mistake, or fail at something and say to myself, 'I never get *anything* right'.? This is an example of *over-generalization*. Just because I fail at *one* thing doesn't mean that I shall fail at *everything*. Maybe I fall out with a friend and end up saying, 'Nobody loves me'. I am taking my feelings from one situation and colouring other situations in an equally bad way.

The best way to tackle this is, once again, to ask for the evidence. How do I know that nobody loves me or that I never get anything right? There is no need to pretend that there is *no* problem. But there is no value in transferring my unhappiness from one situation to the rest of my life. I need to tell the difference between things which are really 'bad' or unpleasant and those which I have 'coloured' black, by over-generalizing.

LABELLING

When things go wrong, I may find myself sticking labels on myself. When I have a quarrel with someone, this may *mean* that I am a 'rotten person'. When I try to tackle something but give up, this *means* that I am 'hopeless' or 'useless'. I find it difficult to recognize that I am made up of 'good bits' and 'bad bits' – like other people. The label I apply usually suggests that I am *completely* bad, hopeless or useless.

To check this error, I need to ask for the evidence. How do I know that I am *completely* bad? How do I know that I shall not succeed next time round? How do I know that other people wouldn't have found this equally difficult? I need to beware of *labels* – they usually hide the truth.

The last error involves thinking that 'Everything always happens to me.' I may think that bad things – like a sudden downpour on a sunny day – only affect me. This is just another example of my bad luck, or I may think that in some way it is my fault. If people have an argument, it may be as a result of something *I* have said. Or, if someone is unhappy, it is

PERSONALIZATION

because I must have upset them. Although it is difficult to accept, the truth is that I am not really that important. Nobody is *that* important. Unless I can *prove* to myself that it is my fault – by pointing to some evidence – I shall have to accept that I am making the error of *personalization*. I am tricking myself into thinking that things always happen to me, or are my fault. This simply is not true.

5A PUTTING MY THOUGHTS TO THE TEST

I have now learned to 'catch' my negative thoughts. I have some practice in arguing them into submission. I have learned a bit about replacing depressing thoughts with more reasonable 'answers'.

I have begun to use these 'possible answers' to change the way I act. In this section, I shall go a stage further. Now I shall learn how to become my own 'problem solver'. I shall learn how to put my depressing thoughts to the test. Now is the time to start experimenting with my life. Through these experiments, I can find the real value of my 'possible answers'.

5B ACTION STATIONS

In the last two sections, I focused on arguments *against* my negative thoughts. Changing the way I think can do wonders for the way I feel. Just arguing with myself is, however, not enough. I can tell myself that these depressing thoughts are unhelpful, *but do I really believe it*? I really need to test out some of my 'possible answers'. I need to take some of my own advice, by changing the way that I act. In this section, I shall look at this in more depth. I shall consider how I can *challenge* my depressing thoughts further, by *discovering* how wrong they are.

I have already considered some ways of 'collecting evidence' which contradicts my negative thoughts. Now it's time to *act* on my 'possible answers'. Action will help me to break my old thinking habits. It will also help me to strengthen my new (more positive) ways of thinking.

Testing! Testing!

I may not think it, but I am a bit of a scientist. I make predictions about my world. Then I act on these predictions. For instance, I might predict that, 'If I press this bell, someone will come to the door'. I might predict that, 'If I stood in the pouring rain, I would not only get wet but would also catch cold'. When it comes to dealing with people, I might predict that, 'If I argue with my husband, he will stop loving me'. The important thing about such predictions is that I act on them *automatically*. Very rarely do I ask if my predictions are true or not. *I do not test out my predictions.*

A person who is depressed is a bit like a scientist gone wrong. Instead of finding out if her predictions are true or not, she distorts her view of the world to fit her prediction.

Most of the depressing thoughts I have considered involve prediction. I might tell myself that, 'I shall *never* get over this', or, 'People *won't* like me', or, 'If I do that, people *will* be upset'. In the last two sections, I have been trying to develop the idea of thinking like a 'personal scientist'. I have been *helping* myself *question* my depressing thoughts. Instead of accepting these thoughts, now I am looking for alternatives.

Taking action

Six steps are needed to *test* my predictions. I need to:

1. Think of my prediction (or depressing thought).
2. Ask what is the evidence *for* and *against* thinking this way.
3. Think of how I can test out my prediction. This will be a small-scale *experiment*.
4. Try out my experiment.
5. Make a note of what happens *as a result*.

   - If my prediction is shown to be false, so much the better. I have reason to believe my 'possible answers' even more strongly now.
   - If my prediction is shown to be true, *I need not worry*. This is still useful. I now have a chance to see where I was going wrong. I can work out how to think *differently*. Once I have worked out an alternative, I can test this again, in another *experiment*.

6. Draw some conclusions. I have learned something from my experiment. What *exactly* have I learned? I need to make a careful note of this, for future reference.

Here are a couple of examples to illustrate the process of being a 'personal scientist'.

Harriet

Harriet finds it difficult to talk to the other women on the ward. She thinks that she doesn't have anything to say. She regrets her lack of education. For this reason, she usually avoids mixing with the other women.

1. **Prediction** If I talk to people, they will find out how stupid I am. They will laugh at me and I will get upset.

2. **The evidence** I only *think* that they are smarter than me. Anyway, there are lots of things I am interested in which I could talk about. Other people say 'stupid things' and laugh *along* with everyone else. How do I know that people aren't laughing just because they are happy? Anyway, what's so bad about having a poor education? There are more important things about a person than whether or not she can talk clever, like being honest, or loyal or friendly.

3. **The plan** I shall listen and say *one* thing, anything, and see what happens.

4. **The test** How do I know I *shall* get upset if I don't try? I shall sit in on the group. I'll just listen at first and talk when anyone speaks to me. I'll try and relax and show an interest in what's being said. I need to remember to smile at people. Look interested and other people might like it.

5. **The result** It was easier than I thought. By listening to everyone else, I was less self-conscious. I said something and everyone laughed. At first I blushed and was about to worry but I checked myself. 'See', I said, 'I've cheered somebody up.'

6. **What I learned** My prediction was quite wrong. I won't say it was easy, but it wasn't half as bad as my depressing thoughts said it would be.

Mary

Mary is depressed. She can't seem to do anything to shift it. She tries reading but can't concentrate. She tries to watch television but her mind wanders on to 'negative depressing thoughts' again. She despairs of ever getting better.

1. **Prediction** I am never going to get any better. My mind is going. I can't do anything at all. I'm going to get worse. I know I am.

2. **The evidence** I know I *feel* that I'm never going to get better. But that's just depressive thinking. My mind isn't really going. This difficulty in concentrating is all part of depression. Maybe I'm trying too hard. And there are

some things that I do. However, I only think about things I find difficult.

3. **The plan** I'll tackle something *small* and see what happens.
4. **The test**   I shall try reading just a little bit – maybe just a page. Just to see if I can do it. Then I'll try watching a short TV programme, like the news.
5. **The result**   Well, I read the page. But what's a page? Wait a minute, that's another depressing thought. Putting myself down again. Yes, I said I would try a page and I did that. *Good*. Watching TV was more of a problem. The room was a bit noisy. I found it difficult to concentrate. But I kept my attention on the TV at least. *Good*. Someone said, 'Aren't you waiting for the next programme?' and I just said, 'No, I've got something to do'.
6. **What I learned**   I found out that my predictions were quite wrong. I *can* do things as long as they are realistic. Rome wasn't built in a day. I need to take things in smaller steps. And I need to give myself more encouragement.

This is a very important stage for me. Although challenging my depressing thoughts is important, putting them to the test is *the big step*. At the start of this guide, I found out that my problems stemmed from how I think about things which happen to me. Here, I have thought about putting my negative thoughts to the test. Are these thoughts really *true*? Or am I *talking myself into believing they are* – without any evidence?

Sometimes things will happen which will be unpleasant. I can use these experiences to learn that life is not always pleasant. Often it can be very unpleasant. I need to be able to tell the difference between things which *are* unpleasant and things which *I think* are unpleasant. Often there is not much I can do about *really* unpleasant things. But there is a lot I can do to change my negative thoughts. Those which make me *feel* unpleasant. Putting my thoughts and predictions to the *test* is an important part of this change.

6A   SETBACKS

I am at the stage where I am dealing directly with the
thoughts which made me feel depressed. I have learned a lot
about the kind of unhelpful thoughts I can make and how to
challenge them. Will it now all be plain sailing? Probably not.
The road to recovery is likely to be strewn with all sorts of
obstacles. Some will stop me in my tracks. These obstacles
might knock me back a bit. They might be distressing. **I won't
despair**. Such setbacks are only to be expected. They are all
part of my stages of recovery.

   In the next few pages, I shall think about ways of handling
these setbacks. Here I can learn how to deal with setbacks
when they have happened. I can also learn how to try to
ensure they don't get any worse.

6B   BOUNCING BACK

Getting over depression means making changes in my life. When making such changes things rarely go smoothly all the time. At times things go well. I think that I am almost over my problems. Then I hit some 'black spots'. I think that my depression is overtaking me again. Things start to go wrong. Maybe *everything* seems to be going wrong. I wonder if things will ever get better. I may even wonder if there is any point in going on. Perhaps something has upset me. Or I may just wake up one day, feeling like this.

One thing needs to be said about this. **It is absolutely okay to have days like this!** This is just another stage on the road to recovery. They are not a sign that I shall never overcome my depression. Although unpleasant, setbacks have a good side. Setbacks let me learn more about myself. They give me a chance to practise the skills which I have learned about dealing with depression. Maybe I should go as far as trying to make myself depressed. By doing this *consciously*, I learn that I can push myself down into a deep depression. Once I have done that, I can pull myself out again, *by my own efforts*. Getting over setbacks is the stage where I learn to build up my confidence. Confidence in *my* ability to control *my* depression. This is the ownership of *me*!

Here are some basic rules about dealing with these set-backs. First, I shall consider how to deal with a setback when it catches me unawares. Then, I shall consider how to develop my own plan for dealing with problems in the future.

6C SOME BASIC RULES

Avoid the panic button

Getting caught by a setback can be upsetting. I need to remember that they are an acceptable part of getting over depression. Even people who are not depressed have their 'ups and downs'. When I am depressed, however, the downs seem to go deeper. They seem more difficult to climb out of. This is only how it *seems*. I need to tell myself very firmly – *'No need to panic'*.

Use what I have learned

People often take a setback to mean that they are 'back to square one'. They often take this as meaning that they have failed. I need to ask myself, 'Have I been able to work things out in the past? What evidence have I to show this? Does this not mean that I can use these skills again, this time round?' I need to try out what I know. I need to stick with these new skills. What have I got to lose?

Change the frame

I shall look on setbacks as being useful. I shall try to put them in a new context. Instead of being scared, I shall look on this as a challenge. This is giving me a chance to show my stuff! By changing the 'frame', I am turning a problem into an opportunity. I am getting a chance to learn more about myself.

Go back to basics

By the time I read this, I shall have made some progress. I may be at the stage of challenging depressing thoughts as they crop up. I have worked through several 'stages' of the therapy. That doesn't mean that I can't go back to using some of the more basic methods to control my feelings. Maybe I find it difficult to answer certain negative thoughts. This may make me feel 'down'. I need to get myself moving again by *going back to basics*. I need to use distraction: steer my thoughts away from my painful feelings. I need to start using my life plan again. I need to plan for tomorrow. I need to use the M and P rating to help me 'rediscover' some of my satisfying activities.

Why don't I try writing down my thoughts again? If something is proving difficult to do, why don't I *write down* what it is I have to do; I could break it down into stages, the way I used to do. Even people who have never been depressed find this a useful way of dealing with difficult problems. I need not be embarrassed that I have to go back to basics. It's the easiest way to get going again. It makes sense.

Watch my black and white

As I make progress, the worse my 'down' spell will seem by comparison. In a strange way, my 'setback' is a sign of progress. I am upset by the fact that I have 'slid back' or I am 'running into difficulties'. I only think this because I have *something better* to compare my depression with. I need to remember that 'ups and downs' are part of everyday living. I need not let my 'black and white thinking' add to my depression.

Add up my gains

When I fall into depression again, it often seems as though everything is lost. **This is not true**. Nothing can take away the gains which I have made. Even if they seem to have gone now, they will come back as my depression lifts again. I can help to speed this up by remembering all the things I learned to do, or picked up again recently. Why don't I write them all down? Make a list of all the challenges I faced, no matter how small. There is no need to stint myself. Why don't I add up each and every gain I have made recently?

Don't blame myself

One of the easiest mistakes to make when I am feeling depressed is to blame myself for what has happened. Is blaming myself going to help? Earlier I found out that setbacks are just a part of recovery from depression. Instead of heaping blame on to myself, why not look upon it as a problem to be solved, another challenge? I won't use my setback as a stick to beat myself with.

Let's hang on!

If I don't seem to be able to solve the problem, I don't need to despair. I don't need to give up. Time and a little sustained effort on my part is what is needed. I need to remember the times in the past when I thought that all was lost. Things looked black then, didn't they? But I got over it. This time will be no different. I can bring myself through. I just need to remember, when the going gets really tough, it's time for me to get tougher. **Hang on in there!**

Confronting setbacks

A good way of learning to handle setbacks is to develop my own plan for what to do when one happens.

To help me do this, I shall sketch out *two* plans:

Plan A tells how I can make myself as *miserable* as possible. This can be used to keep me miserable for a long time. The idea behind this plan is to help me be-

come aware of how I act or think in ways which
make me depressed. The sooner I know what I am
doing, the sooner I can do something to change it.

Plan B   is just the opposite. This plan shows me how I can
take steps to overcome my depressive thinking. This
plan helps me to work out ways of challenging these
thoughts, and changing the way I feel.

On the next page are examples of these plans. Each plan is
made up of thoughts and actions. Things I could say to
myself, and things to do. These are not the *only* thoughts and
actions which I could use. They are just examples of what I
might try. I might want to work out some plans of my own,
based on my own experiences. I could ask myself what sort of
things I have thought about or done in the past which have
made me feel more depressed? What sort of thoughts or
actions have I used which have made me feel less distressed,
or even a little better?

Example

Plan A	Plan B

Plan A

Plan B

Stay in bed.

Get up and get busy. I know from experience that it will be an effort to start with, but it will get easier as I go along, and I will feel better for it. Hiding in bed won't help at all.

Spend as much time as possible brooding and feeling miserable.

Involve myself in something. Use distraction techniques. Do something active that needs a bit of concentration. I shall come back to answering thoughts later, when I feel better.

Leave the day shapeless and vague, and tell myself it's all too much for me.

Plan, in detail, exactly what I am going to do. Record what I do, and give myself marks for **mastery** and **pleasure**.

Don't do anything I enjoy. Tell myself I don't deserve it.

Make a point of doing things I enjoy, and noticing small pleasures. It will help me to get out of the depression and I will end up doing the things I have to do more efficiently.

Example

Plan A	Plan B
Don't give myself any credit for anything.	Acknowledge *everything* I achieve. Remind myself that when I am feeling really bad, even the simplest activity is an achievement. If I can, I shall try and do one extra thing beyond my normal routine. It will make all the difference to the way I feel.
Tell myself that I am weak and pathetic for being this way.	Remind myself that self-criticism does nothing to help me overcome my depression – in fact, it will make me feel worse. Give what is happening its proper name – it is a *setback*. It is nothing to do with me being weak or pathetic. I need to remind myself that it is OK to have setbacks. I need to try to see this one as a problem I can tackle. It is not a reflection of my inadequacy as a person.
Tell myself I should be over my depression by now.	Remind myself that there is no *should* about it. I need to think of all the things I have been doing to overcome this very tough problem and allow myself credit for what I have achieved.

Example

Plan A	**Plan B**
Think about all the things I have done wrong in my life. Blame myself for them and tell myself what a horrible person I am.	I need to tell myself that I am only human. Of course I have made mistakes in my life – who hasn't? I need to remember that I wouldn't expect that kind of perfection of anyone else. I need to ask myself if, in fact, a lot of the things I have done wrong were done in good faith – they seemed the best possible alternative at the time. I need to remember that I've done millions of things in my life, good, bad and indifferent. It is not fair to judge myself only on the basis of the bad ones. I need to think about some of the good things I have done instead.
Tell myself this approach is not going to work. I might as well give up. I'll always be this way.	I need to remind myself of what I have already achieved with it. If this has worked before, it will work again, even though it may be difficult to get started. A setback does not mean all is lost – it's a passing phase, and I can learn from it. I must remember the times when this has happened in the past.

WHAT DO I BELIEVE, ANYWAY?

Different people see the world in different ways. Some people are optimists, others are pessimists. Some people are philosophical about life – others see disaster at every corner. How people judge things which happen to them in their lives depends upon their beliefs and attitudes. What things do they value? What do they consider important?

What are my basic values, beliefs or attitudes? The thoughts I have about my world and myself are based upon these. I assume that certain things are important – why else should I get concerned about them? I value some people and certain things very much – that is why I get upset at the thought of losing them. I believe that certain things are necessary for me to lead a satisfactory life – this is why I so often say this 'must' happen or that 'should' have happened.

These ideas help me to judge my own personal worth – they tell me if I am doing OK or not. I have already discovered how holding very negative thoughts about myself, or things that happen, can be very unhelpful. Is the same true of extreme beliefs? If I believe that certain things must be the case, will that belief be my undoing?

Discovering my values

How can I go about finding out what my beliefs are? One way would be to ask myself what situations mean – or what they say about me. If I am upset over something, for example falling out with a friend, I might ask myself: 'What is so bad about falling out with someone? In what way is that a problem for me?'

If I tell myself it is because she won't like me any more, what does that mean to me: 'What is so bad about someone not liking me any more?'.

I might end up telling myself that I can't live without friends, or that it would be just awful if something like that happened. This might be an example of one of my extreme beliefs, that: 'I cannot be happy unless people care about me'.

Using a checklist

Alternatively, I could use a checklist or questionnaire to find out what my beliefs are. I could ask myself, do I need:

- approval from other people? Do I get angry or depressed when people do not show that they approve of me?
- love from others? Do I tend to try not to upset my friends or partner for fear that they might stop loving me?
- success to prove my self-worth? Do I get depressed when I fail at things, or things don't go the way I planned?
- to be perfect? Do I get upset over making mistakes or little failures? Am I always pushing myself to chase goals which may be unrealistic?
- to get things by right? Do I get angry or upset if I don't get the things I want? Do I get upset if I fail to get recognition for what I have done?
- to be the centre of my world? Do I tend to blame myself for everything that happens? Do I feel guilty because I cannot influence my family or friends, or feel threatened when they disagree with me?
- to be dependent? Do I tend to rely on other people, luck or good fortune to bring happiness or meaning to my life? Do I get upset when I appear to be unlucky or I am not supported by a supply of 'good things'?

Dealing with unhelpful beliefs

I need to question whether or not any of these beliefs help me to live a satisfactory life. Do they, perhaps, make my life more difficult by setting impossible demands? I need to challenge these beliefs in the same way as I confronted my depressing thoughts. I need to find alternatives which will help me to do what I need, and want to do, in my life.

Because of their hidden nature, it is difficult to unearth beliefs and attitudes. I need to commit myself to studying my beliefs over a long period of time. I shall not expect to find out all about myself in a few days or even weeks. I need to continue keeping a watching brief on all my depressing thoughts, asking myself from what extreme beliefs they might have come. In time, it may become clear to me where these ideas about life came from. Then I might be able to cast them off in favour of some new, more helpful beliefs about life and myself. Till then, I shall keep on watching, confronting and finding alternatives.

REFERENCES

Beck, A.T. and Greenberg, R.L. (1974) *Coping with Depression*. New York, Institute for Rational Living, Inc.

Gunning, R. (1952) *The Technique of Clear Writing*. New York, McGraw-Hill.

Chapter 7

An epilogue

I am gone into the fields
To take what this sweet hour yields;
Reflection, you may come tomorrow,
Sit by the fireside with Sorrow.
(Shelley, 1921)

DÜRER'S MESSAGE

It is increasingly recognized that people who are depressed can be helped by psychosocial means to resolve this crisis of their existence. Sadly, this optimism seems to be restricted to the margins of the clinical population we might call severe depression. As I noted in the Introduction, a curious inverse relationship exists between the degree of distress and the complexity of the intervention offered. People who are assigned, albeit unsympathetically, to the 'worried well' category may be offered individual counselling, participation in self-help groups, adjunct antidepressant therapy, couple or family therapy, and telephone 'hotlines'. Those assigned to the more severe categories of depression, especially the 'psychotic' types, are offered the vaguest forms of support, either in hospital or the community, built around a monolithic drug therapy programme and the assumption that they are 'inhabited' by a disorder which is highly resistive to any treatment. This book is based on an alternative assumption: that complex problems require complex solutions. Personal complexity demands therapeutic eclecticism.

I also reject the conventional wisdom that those ravaged by depression, perhaps to a psychotic degree, are unable to learn about themselves. We are afraid to become closely involved, on a human level, with any form of severe mental disorder. We continue to pretend that the disorder is not somehow psychological, social or otherwise *human*. Having ceased to attribute such 'madness' to demons or devils, we now lay the blame on an equally distant cause – the biophysical root. This represents no more than another chapter in the catalogue of avoidance and rejection which has characterized the history of mental illness services. As we now proclaim our conviction of (mental) 'health for all', we need to evaluate the place of holistic, biopsychosocial interventions in the management of people with severe depression.

I have assumed that the person's needs are, at one and the same time, simple yet complex. She needs a form of help that is presented simply, with a clear focus, if she is to construct her own emotional rescue. Although many complex issues may be addressed, involving sophisticated psychosocial constructs, the 'therapy' can appear like just another positive human relationship, where people are confiding, sharing and seeking solutions. The overriding aim of all such conversations is to help the person abandon her position of perceieved helplessness, by building her confidence in her capacity to live with or overcome life problems. This is achieved by establishing a base for:

Positive reinforcement   Much of her depressing behaviour has involved avoidance or escape – hiding or running from the world or herself. All these are the product of negative reinforcement – patterns of behaviour which have been built up by her repeated success at avoiding *too much* pain. She has lost sight of the fact that by doing so she has also avoided any satisfaction: escape and avoidance have become the *raison d'être* of her existence. The early stages of therapy aimed to return her to the everyday world, with attention and purpose. Here she learned that different kinds of satisfactions were to be found in a very imperfect world. Among these was the satisfaction of confronting and finding a way around some of her original 'road blocks'. Through this experience she began to engage in a highly personal:

Perceptual adjustment   She explored and catalogued her thoughts about the world and herself – discovering that what she perceives is, largely, what she gets. This was no blind encounter with 'positive thinking' but the beginning of a careful consideration of her personal philosophy; tracing the roots of some of her beliefs; seeing through the mirror of what she is to the possibilities of who she might become. Through both these experiences she encountered:

Social change   Now that she has returned to her world and is interacting with the people in it, they perceive her differently. Slowly she becomes a person again, rather than a 'depressed patient'. Her activities in her world stimulate a ripple effect of relationships where mutual exchange and support enjoy steady growth. It is assumed also that all three of these changes stimulate:

Biochemical change   All these actions in the external world have implications for her internal processes. Just as learning a foreign language or engaging in strenuous activity produce change in biochemical activity within the brain, so it is expected that the myriad cognitive and behavioural events outlined will produce similar positive changes at the deepest level of the person's body. I have said least about this since much of it remains a mystery to me. I believe that it can, however, be a joyous mystery; representing the fragile pivot of the concept of psychological homoeostasis.

These strategies serve, I believe, as the basis for hope. In the introductory chapter, I described Dürer's vision of melancholy. I have long been impressed by his insight into the character and resolution of melancholy. It is genuinely sad that, with the centuries, his message has been translated, perversely, from one of hope to tragic despair. The melancholy spirit which pervades the person can have access to 'enlightenment', as Dürer intimated, providing that we can supply the necessary ladder of knowledge and magic. I have outlined much of what we know works, often for reasons which remain magical; as yet, they are not fully understood.

THE VALIDITY OF COGNITIVE THERAPY

Although I have acknowledged many of the sources, I have avoided defining the approach described as **cognitive therapy**. My reasons are few and simple. Firstly, as many of the seminal figures in the cognitive therapies have already acknowledged, the idea that we are (somehow) what we think we are is hardly a new one. In times of trial we have often looked to the past for inspiration. Albert Ellis, to his credit, did this and sparked the formation of a heterogeneous discipline which may yet prove to be a match for psychoanalysis in explaining the whys and wherefores of the human condition. Cognitive 'therapy' is therefore little more than a medium for the exploration of certain ideas about the art of being human. I have enormous respect for those who have fabricated the process of cognitive therapy. I am, however, uncomfortable with the content of some of the better-known expositions*. I think that there are great dangers in the belief that the medium contains any message. I have manipulated the structure of cognitive therapy in an effort to find a simple structure which would

---

*I am particularly uncomfortable with the assumption that people can be classified meaningfully as (for example) 'obsessionals', and that the therapeutic exercise necessarily needs to imitate a scientific experiment. Scott, J. and Williams, J.M.G. (1989) *Cognitive Therapy in Clinical Practice: An Illustrative Casebook*. London, Routledge.

support the reflection necessary for the construction of an alternative philosophy of self. I acknowledge that I am more interested in what personal experiences mean and where they relate to the wider 'meaning of life'. For that reason alone, I stand uncomfortable among the clinical trials, use of diagnostic classifications and translation of crude scientific method which is characteristic of much 'cognitive therapy'. My experience of psychiatry and life has instilled in me a deep suspicion of *processing*. One process or another will always be necessary; the important question is – what will it process?

Secondly, I suspect that, except in the work of writers like Ellis who remains in a class of his own, cognitive therapy owns no deep philosophy of life. My repeated reference to matters spiritual and philosophical will have made my position clear, at least implicitly. Having been brought up in a strict religion which I abandoned in my early adulthood I have, like many who acted similarly, spent much of my time since reflecting on various matters spiritual. I believe that there is a 'way' to some form of human enlightenment. I do not accept that such a 'way' necessarily involves escaping from distress, which is often largely inescapable, but it does involve the attainment of some knowledge which is more than knowledge *about* the world or ourselves. In reaching for our goals we should not confuse the process, such as cognitive therapy framework, with the goal itself. A finger which points at the moon should not be confused with the moon itself (Watts 1968).

Thirdly, I have noted repeatedly how so many different therapies appear to meet at critical intersections. Cognitive therapy method and principle share much with gestalt, existentialist psychotherapy, behaviour therapy, various forms of non-directive counselling, and reality therapy. I have drawn specific parallels with the less well-known but, in my view, highly significant alternative therapies which derive from a Western reflection on Oriental psychology. Since the beginning of this century, Moritist therapy in Japan has been helping people to turn their attention from rumination on their life problems to experimenting with possible solutions. As a Western style of therapy it has achieved some popularity in the USA since the end of World War II. For me, the meaning of these historical precedents and chance similarities is that there is nothing as popular as a good idea; an idea which can cross cultural boundaries and pass back and forth through generations. Just as, 25 years ago, I rejected the notion of 'one true religion', so do I reject the idea of the supremacy of any single psychotherapeutic ideology.

If I possess a 'hidden agenda' as a therapist, it is the hope that the person will find herself through not looking too intently. This is reflected in my interest in activity, and the acknowledgement that *thinking* is not all that important. I believe that many of the strategies which purport to 'deal' with negative thinking simply put distance between the person and her thoughts. In this sense they share much in common with meditation, whether contemplative or 'in-life'. When the person is meditating, or doing something properly:

> ... there will be an inevitable *bing!* – thought. At that point, you say, 'thinking'. You don't say it out loud; you say it mentally: 'thinking'. Labelling your thoughts gives you tremendous leverage to come back to your breath ... It doesn't matter what thoughts you have ... whether you have monstrous thoughts or benevolent thoughts, all of them are regarded purely as thinking. They are neither virtuous nor sinful.   (Trungpa 1984)

Perhaps one of the functions of therapy is to help the person distinguish between what is or is not. Is she one person or multiple selves; is this her voice or an echo from the past; is this truly awful, terrible or disgusting – or are these just thoughts about what has now passed into history? Thinking chains the person to the past or mortgages her to a uncertain future. Both these functions interfere with her experience of now. Perhaps therapy aims to help her to relinquish the past, suspend her impatience for the future and simply *live*.

Is such 'nowness' no more than an inflated materialism? Perhaps! However, nowness itself is no more than a process for recognizing the world for what it is: a flowing river into which we dip and then it is gone forever. We might enjoy that dip, for as long as it lasts. We merely delude and depress ourselves by assuming that such moments can last, or are in any way controllable. George Santayana (1920) echoed such age-old sentiments of Oriental wisdom when he observed that:

> Contempt for mortal sorrows is reserved for those who drive with hosannas the Juggernaut car of absolute optimism. But against evils born of pure vanity and self-deception, against the verbiage by which man persuades himself that he is the goal and acme of the universe, *laughter* is the proper defence.

For Santayana, existence was justified – in the sense of being worthwhile – only by the contemplation of the brief beauties which existence calls into being. We are all in the clutch of fate; it is vanity to assume that we can control events. The 'spiritual' (wo)man recognizes her helplessness and is content to witness events, including her own actions (Devin *et al.* 1986). Yes, this is one of the functions of cognitive therapy. I believe that I am right in saying that it is a function borrowed from disparate sources of wisdom that, by now, are ingrained upon the hands of time.

IMPLICATIONS FOR THE THERAPIST

Throughout this book, I have expressed, self-consciously, my own views of the central tenets of the helper's art. These can be summarized simply as follows:

Accept uncertainty The world cannot be predicted, it can only be experienced, evaluated and responded to. This is as true for you as it is for the person you aim to help. Experience the person – avoid trying to predict her patienthood.

Accept responsibility – This is your life, in which you must act for your own reward or suffering. If this is not obvious to you, by what magic will you convey this to the person? By acknowledging your responsibilities it may become easier to accept the basic freedom of the person.

Avoid bad-faith choices Chasing more leads to less, envy leads to bitterness, power is the ultimate weakness, revenge is never sweet and the martyrdom is satisfactory only if others choose to watch. Making good-faith choices is a lively, lifelong apprenticeship, for the person and therapist alike.

Cherish the whole, lose the parts This applies to the wholes which you and the person represent, as well as the whole which you both become within the therapeutic relationship. You can come to cherish loss and, as a result, can gain.

How these are enacted is, traditionally, referred to as 'therapy' although I have grave misgivings about the appropriateness of the term. 'Therapy' derives from *therapeutike*, the Greek for the art of healing. The original meaning implied remedial action in both health and disease; we have translated this, until recently, to mean only the treatment of sickness, whether metaphorical or actual. Despite the efforts being made to redefine areas of medicine, such as 'rehabilitation', in more holistic terms, psychiatric therapy has always had very limited aims: easing distress or suffering. The palliative nature of such conservative interventions often looks more like 'care' than 'cure'. Since my original discipline was nursing, I have never felt inhibited by disease the way, for example, doctors often are. I have always felt at home with the people in my care; their experiences and their judgements curiously echoing some of my own. Given that, why should I distance myself from them?

The biomedical *objectification* of mental disorder appears to me to represent a defensive strategy on the doctor's part. It adopts a resolutely Cartesian position concerning both the doctor's relationship to the 'patient' and her relationship with her disorder. The mechanism of such reductionism is designed to offset the potential for anxiety and despair when faced by the truly disturbing individual. I have emphasized the need for involvement in an approach which is concerned to promote growth and development, rather than simply escape from the clutches of illness. Indeed, I would rather conceptualize the helper's approach as care than therapy. As analogy with gardening may be apposite. The gardener or nurseryman exercises serious attention, concern and protection over his plants. He cares by ensuring that the soil is irrigated and aerated, and that the plants are exposed appropriately to the elements. His care plan varies according to different plants but each embraces the same broad aim: the good gardener promotes growth and development. The definition of care in this context is functional. It is not enough to talk to plants, to love them or to have other caring feelings. The meaning of care is expressed by the function of the relationship. A good gardener will rear plants which will, gradually, need less and less care. This needs a formal *structure*, within which are expressed certain *skills*, always with proper *attention* and acknowledgement of their *purpose*. Little wonder that the Zen garden is seen as one of the pathways to enlightenment.

Within the context of mental health I have called this approach **trephotaxis**, from the Greek meaning 'the necessary conditions for the promotion of growth and development' (Barker 1987). Such care is not intended to heal people or otherwise make them whole: they are whole already. Instead it projects an ecological awareness, acknowledging the interaction of biological, cultural, social and personal 'selves' (Barker 1985). This approach is about helping people to meet their own 'needs'. In the context of the person who is depressed, three main need areas emerge, involving thought, feeling and behaviour:

- A need to learn how to *think* in a manner which promotes adaptive, accepting, everyday function.
- A need to learn how to be aware of the complexity and diversity of *feelings* which can be drawn from her world.
- A need to learn how to handle (through *behaviour*) the slings and arrows of outrageous fortune.

Some people, like some plants, may have been damaged at some critical stage of development. They will bear the scars of such traumas, which are unlikely ever to disappear. This does not mean, however, that growth and development, within the limitations of the trauma, cannot take place. It may be unrealistic to expect that people who have experienced damage in their lives should somehow erase these events. Some of the women I have worked with were abused sexually, physically and emotionally in their youth. Such scars cannot, should not, be erased. I would go as far as to say that they should be worn with pride: not pride in the events, but pride in the resilience in still being here, despite these attempts to nullify their existence. It is both impertinent and unrealistic to assume that the person who is depressed does not also possess great capacities for development which, through appropriate nurture, will relegate such historical traumas to a position of diminished importance in the framework of her life. To depict the person as overtaken by some emotional stereotype echoes our age-old fears of demonic possession. It provides us with an excuse for not getting closely involved. The person does not need to trust the therapist; the therapist needs to trust himself.

> Leone was forty-two, married with two teenage sons. She had been hospitalized with an endogenous depression on four occasions over the past five years. Her psychiatric history extended over a 15 year period. Her husband had been unfaithful on numerous occasions, most recently with a neighbour. He also drank heavily, incurring major debts which Leone had always struggled to repay, usually with assistance from her older brother. On this occasion she was described as withdrawn and paranoid; reluctant to talk to any of the staff; 'furtive and suspicious'. She was given drug therapy and ECT. Leone was detained under a section of the Mental Health Act; consent for the ECT was provided by her husband. No specific counselling or psychotherapy was arranged. The ravages of Leone's domestic life were not addressed: her illness was of biochemical origin.
>
> When I interviewed Leone she 'watched' my eyes constantly. Eventually, I confided in her the discomfort which her 'watching' aroused. Could she explain what she was looking for? Leone talked cautiously about the 'silver lenses' which she could detect in the staff members' eyes. They were not what they pretended to be. Was I one of 'them'? Such admissions were taken by the staff to represent a gross delusion on Leone's part. At the time an American science fiction series was running on television. In this programme aliens assumed human shape and were seen to insert contact lenses to cover their 'alien' eyes. This coincidence did not escape the team's notice, but was deemed of little relevance. The delusion did not come from the television; it was part of the psychotic process.

This unfortunate woman no longer existed within the psychiatric milieu. Many different people cared in different ways for the patient. I suspect, however, that Leone's suspicion was grounded on the realization, perhaps unconscious, that no-one really cared for *her*. The sum total of the psychiatric intervention, through diagnosis and treatment, was to disempower Leone: to invalidate her as an individual; to betray her. As a result, she did not trust them, the form of her distrust almost excusing them their actions. The lay reader might be forgiven for assuming that it was only 'right' that Leone should be depressed after having been abused in such diverse ways. The professional reader will have had similar experiences where the 'wisdom' of psychiatry can appear so blind to the truly, painfully obvious.

The only certain implication of all that I have said in this book is that the therapist must accept the full ownership of the professional life. I believe that it is no mere slip of the tongue when therapists talk of 'a patient of mine'. We assume that ownership of the people in our care is not only possible but desirable. In doing so we often fail to accept our personal responsibility, which demands that such people be freed to be themselves and that we are bound to help them. This responsibility demands that the therapist lies awake at night in sympathy, if you like, with the person who is somewhere suffering her life. Empathy does not end with the closure of the therapeutic day.

THE SOCIAL IMPLICATIONS OF THERAPY

If growth and development are possible, what might be their outcome in more general, social terms? It has become increasingly apparent that any therapy must, of necessity, be socially disruptive. There is no question that the behaviour, feelings and thoughts of people can be manipulated to fall within some concept of 'normal limits'. Such a perverse concept is far from my mind. I recognize that the goal of therapy is to help people realize that they are no longer someone's son or daughter. The influence of parental control, proffered for good or ill, no longer represents the hub of their existence. They are themselves. Alone, perhaps, but themselves nonetheless. In a more contemporary vein, some people need to acknowledge that they are not someone's wife or mother; they are themselves, pure and simple. Such a realization can have a profound effect on more than just the person.

I recall one year of my practice which was characterized by the behaviour of four women whom I had been seeing for some months or years. Each had been diagnosed as severely depressed. Each was described as possessing 'low self-esteem' and, at least initially, presented various problems involving their roles as wives or mothers. Each woman discontinued their involvement in therapy. Each made their decision known, in person, to the receptionist. Each time this occurred the receptionist, who had known them well, failed to recognize them. Such was the extent of their physical change they were virtually unrecognizable. All four women had been successful in therapy; each had become, more or less, her own woman. The only other common denominator was that each woman had, in one way or another, rejected her husband; deciding to make a new start, alone . . .

These women illustrated the extent to which people can change. The combined result of their change of heart – experienced through changes of behaviour and thinking – was to enact the rejection of their husbands; an issue which had long been burning them and finally burned the men in their lives. The icing on this therapeutic cake was that once free of their bondage, they could become what they had always had the potential to be.

No doubt the husbands took a different view of the situation. They might well have interpreted events as further signs of the instability of their spouses. Who was I to take sides? I recall a similar group of women who were involved in couple therapy. The husbands were patient and, to all appearances, supportive of their depressed partners. As each woman grew stronger, the husband – almost by hydraulic action – grew weaker. In every case, the men all progressed to report physical problems: gastric, orthopaedic or cardiac. I draw no unnecessary conclusions. What was clear was that as each woman bloomed, her formerly strong husband withered.

Change, even on a personal level, is socially disruptive. My examples pertain only to intimate relationships. I believe that their corollary is to be found in a wider social network. I illustrate these examples only to suggest the possible disruptiveness of therapy. The same can be said of the ideas associated with it.

Like most parents, my wife and I aimed to bring up our daughter to recognize and respect the values which we held dear. One of these was that all people were equal, regardless of their colour, creed or social standing. At a tender age, she refused to join in a class song on the grounds that 'it was racist'. Our ideologically correct daughter was asked to stand in the corridor 'as a punishment'. Later she attained a similar notoriety for refusing to dissect a frog, on the grounds that she was a vegetarian. These reminiscences are amusing now, given that acknowledgement of ideological difference is almost *de rigeur* in schools. In 1970s Scotland, such ideas were socially divisive, and educationally disruptive.

Fifteen years on I believe that such distressing events served only to strengthen the development of a remarkable young woman. I am, of course prejudiced. I have experienced a similar experience of prejudice where women in therapy have been involved. These women did not live in a social vacuum; their problems may not have been caused directly by their social situation but they were reinforced strongly by a set of values which determined that women were second-best. It is to our eternal shame that our therapeutic institutions continue to maintain mysogynist values, however thinly veiled and whether expressed by women or men.

If people are to become themselves the existing social order – which set the scene for their disorder and so pitifully purports to treat it – must take the inevitable consequences. For therapy to be effective on an individual level, we must expect that women and men will no longer fulfil the restrictive roles which families, culture or society map out for them. The ripple effect of change, for one person, will be felt proportionately throughout the land. If this does not happen, our tinkering will end up reinforcing some of the myths that define men and women.

At the time of writing, two books appeared at my local bookstore which reflect an effort to tinker with the definition of men and women on a grand scale. Naomi Wolf's *The Beauty Myth* (1991) provides a fitting counterpoint to the core argument of this text. The media now serve as vehicles for the instillation of dysfunctional ideas of self which once were engineered only within dysfunctional families. In Wolf's view, a multi-billion dollar empire now spawns images of 'beauty pornography' which socially engineers the control of highly literate women whom we might have assumed, in thist post-feminist age, would be its harshest critics. A decade ago I described this set of ideas as 'cosmetic fascism' (Barker 1982). I assumed then that such ideas would by now have gone the way of other forms of totalitarianism. Instead, we now have to develop the concept of 'pre-pubescent anorexia' to describe the retarded state of our children who are entrapped already by the beauty myth.

Wolf's critique does not spare men's blushes. There is no doubt that this perversion on a grand scale serves as a vehicle for the male ego. After the brief flurry of freedom enjoyed by some women in the 1970s, the 1980s became the seedbed for their humiliation.

At the same time, Robert Bly's *Iron John* (1990) is attempting to raise the consciousness of men in Britain, after phenomenal success in the USA. Bly is thought by many to be representative of the 'new man': able to cope with the emancipation of women without becoming a wimp. Bly's thesis stands uneasily beside Wolf's treatise. Whereas she aims to slay a modern myth, Bly builds his case for the 'new man' around a host of ancient myths. I suspect that the prospect of groups of men engaging in communal hugging and grunting in an effort to rediscover their primitive roots will become no more than a fringe sport in these conservative islands. Alternatively, we could say that, as the home of rugby, we pioneered such open sharing of the male gender and all that it implies. I suspect that Bly's ideas, though well-intentioned, will serve, like rugby culture, as more ammunition for the defence of male insecurity rather than its own emancipation.

To free people from their emotional shackles, most of which are invisible, we need a new concept of warriorship: one which does not involve the continuation of the old battles between the sexes, the classes, or between parents and children. Aggression has always been the source of our problems and never its solution. This book has outlined the battle lines which people draw for themselves, against themselves; all of this aggression deriving from the hostility of their parental figures or their culture. Such a concept of warriorship involves the fearlessness to be who we are (Trungpa 1984, p28). We need to help people who are depressed to be who they are, so that they can go out into the world and fearlessly make their own contribution to a better world.

I noted in Chapter 1 how the escalation in depression is arguably a disease of modernism. Its progress has been charted by a chain of societal upheavals over the past 50 years. We may well be witnessing a universal culture which is in rapid decline. What value exists in helping people to 'feel a little better' if their only exit is to a world in pending chaos. One way to establish a more enlightened society for others is to discover what inherently we have to offer. By taking a fearless look we may:

> ... find that, in spite of all our problems and confusion, all our emotional and psychological ups and downs, there is something basically good about our existence as human beings. Unless we can discover the ground of goodness in our own lives, we cannot hope to improve the lives of others.   (Trungpa 1984, pp29–30)

SUICIDE

I have made little specific reference to suicide, despite its strong relationship with severe depression. This is for two reasons. Firstly, the therapeutic management of suicide differs little from the approach outlined for depression. The person who proposes suicide as a solution for her problems possesses a similar unwillingness to accept herself or her world as the person who is severely depressed. Although some might consider her unsympathetic, Dorothy Rowe (1990) defines the dilemma of suicide concisely:

> All of us can die, and do die, when every part of us gives up struggling and accepts death. If you have to harm yourself in order to die, you do not want to die. What you want is a painless way of being yourself without having to battle against a world which hurts or ignores you.

Secondly, suicide is such an emotive topic that it requires more room to breathe than would be possible in this text. Many of us struggle interminably to come to our own sense of the experience of the depressed person. The impact of the suicidal person is so much greater that we risk oversimplifying her rationale if we do not consider sufficiently the specific details of this ordered death.

> Hector was a retired architect who had planned to renovate a majestic old house for the twilight years of his marriage. Suddenly, his wife died and Hector was devastated. He tried to kill himself twice in the two years following her death. I met him as he was recuperating from major orthopaedic surgery to repair multiple fractures produced by his last attempt. The common consensus was that Hector needed some help to deal with his unresolved grief. He listened to me sympathetically, said how positive he felt after seeing me, and looked forward to our first session a few days later. The next night he walked out of the hospital as the staff changed over. It was assumed that he jumped into the estuary from the rail bridge: his body was washed ashore further down the coast a week later.

Hector illustrates one kind of suicide, typical of men: the dramatic leap into the beyond from which there is no turning back. He also illustrated Rowe's thesis of a person who wanted a painless way of being himself, alone. My way of confronting loss, of fearless acceptance, is far from painless, and I know that he knew that. It was, however, the only way I knew. The original Hector was the hero of Homer's *Iliad* who, ultimately, was killed by Achilles. The Hector I knew also was a hero within his own life. He died at the hands of his own Achilles; his only significant weakness was his belief that he could no longer stand alone. My respect for Hector's decision was disturbed only by the coroner's judgement that his death was a function of an 'imbalance of mind . . .'. I suspect it was one of the sanest decisions he had taken in his life. It may have been, however, unnecessary:

... for every life there is a season, and when the season comes to an end there is no need to take active steps to bring life to an end. Nature simply takes its course ... We do not have to swallow pills, or cut our throat, or drown ourselves, or fling ourselves in front of a train, or off a high building, or put a noose around our necks. We simply die.   (Rowe 1990, p263)

THE PURSUIT OF FAITH

I have made reference to the relative infancy of the 'science' of psychiatry. In reviewing some of the models of treatment of the oldest clinical population, it is apparent that the science of psychiatry has often made haste slowly. Although this may be frustrating to those of us who would wish to have our darkness lightened, to the seeker after genuine enlightenment 'not knowing' may constitute a vital source of knowledge. I observed also how down the centuries we have enriched our glossary of emotional terms. The origins and function of such 'affectivity' is little clearer now than it was in Aretaeus' day. Is it not ironic that we are now entertaining the prospect of re-labelling severe depression *melancholia* and are attacking it with the new psychological technique of cognitive therapy, which employs a concept of affectivity which derives from the Ancient Greeks – that emotion is a consequence of thinking. When will our new-found knowledge cease to be that which we have forgotten?

Much of our scientific understanding of the experience of happiness, sadness, anxiety and other expressions of the emotions derives from cultural sources: often mass reports by sociologists and anthropologists. These stand uneasily in front of the personal reflections of poets and writers who, to the scientific mind, represent an unacceptably subjective account of the disorder. I have tended to emphasize such literary accounts of depression in the belief that these also represent data sources which, with appropriate analysis and synthesis, can inform the science of psychiatry and may hasten the enlightenment. In Chapter 1 I alluded to the fact that writers were just as prone to examine cognitive variables and to attribute significance to their thinking as a precipitant of emotional distress as were psychiatrists, psychologists and sociologists. Indeed, the evidence demonstrates that art has consistently informed science on this subject.

Two writers representing different literary cultures and styles have offered insights into the cognitive basis of emotional distress which rival anything which the psychologist has offered. The writings of Franz Kafka are widely accepted as metaphorical or symbolic statements depicting the powerlessness and frustrated despair of the depressive character. In Bemporad's view (1980) these writings afford 'a rare and unforgettable glimpse into the inner world of melancholia'. Kafka's biographer described a troubled childhood development against the background of family tragedy and a wholly unsatisfactory relationship with his father and mother which may have served as the basis of his adult melancholy. The seeds of Kafka's disturbance by existential philosophical questions, which were expressed through the inherent dilemmas of his writings, may have been sown in childhood (Brod 1973).

Beck's cognitive model of depression attributes the origins of contemporary negative thinking to dysfunctional schemas which originate in negative experiences of childhood and puberty. In a letter written to his father, Kafka recounted his early experience of his relationship with his father and the lasting effect it had upon his personality. Kafka found his father to be all-powerful, critical and unfeeling; disparaging the very weakness he demanded in his son:

> In all my thinking I was, after all, under the heavy pressure of your personality . . . All these thoughts, seemingly independent of you, were from the beginning burdened with your belittling judgements. (Kafka 1973)

This letter provides ample support for Beck's hypothesis, echoed, as I have noted, by other theorists such as Berne and Ellis, that the script of one's life is often written by unhelpful parents.

A no less hostile criticism of parental influence on adult thinking style is offered by the American humorist, Garrison Keillor. In his novel *Lake Woebegone Days*, he enters a lengthy footnote representing the alleged transcript of a 'thesis' written by a fictitious member of his boyhood town. The thesis details 99 critical statements made by the adult of his mother and the effect of her parenting on his emotional self. In the final section the author writes of the mother:

> Now you call me on the phone to ask, 'Why don't you ever call us?' . . . I didn't call because I don't need to talk to you any more. Your voice is in my head, talking constantly from morning till night. I keep the radio on, but I still hear you and will hear you until I die, when I will hear you say, 'I told you so'. (Keillor 1986)

If we were in any doubt that early experiences, especially at the hands, or mouths, of parents, played any part in shaping our view of ourselves and the world, these two short quotations might dispel some of our uncertainty. Often the intrusion of the past into the person's everyday life possesses an almost hallucinatory quality. I recall a woman called Miriam who, after a lifetime of depressions, became seriously depressed after nursing her husband to his eventual death. As she began to be more philosophical about her loss she began to pick up the threads of a new life, albeit alone. Each week, as we reviewed her 'lifeplan', I would invite her to comment constructively on what she had done, alone and unaided. Each time I did so, she would drop her head, retiring into a lengthy silence. One day I made the same request, adding: '. . . and tell me what you are saying to yourself when you drop your head like that!'. Miriam looked up immediately; 'Why, I'm not saying anything . . . all I can hear is my mother saying, "self praise is no praise at all" '.

Kafka's experience seemed to sour his whole adult life: his bitterness toward his father was unrelieved by the open expression of his letter. If the fictitious 'emotional cripple' in Keillor's book is the author himself, his humour is a thin disguise for outrage and protestation at parental influence over adult affectivity. Keillor appears, however, to have resigned himself adaptively to the folly of the human condition, and may be all the happier for that. In Miriam's case, at 70 years of age, after more than 40 years of repeated hospitalization, she gave her long-since departed mother back her 'voice' and settled down to the business of finding her own. These examples remind us of (wo)man's effort to make sense of the world which is threaded through with words. We should not forget that much of the understanding we seek may be found in the words of wise women and men, but also in the bald expressions of those entrapped by affective disorder. In striving to seek resolution for emotional pain, we should not reject the hypothesis that such pain may be the inevitable sequela of earlier life experiences. We cannot turn back the clock; there is no going back. The aim of all our strivings may be to help the person express what she experiences and then to learn how to find her own faith, through doing what needs to be done.

REFERENCES

Barker, P. (1982) *Behaviour Therapy Nursing*. London, Croom Helm.

Barker, P. (1985) *Patient Assessment in Psychiatric Nursing*. London, Croom Helm.

Barker, P. (1987) *Trephotaxis: The Medium is the Message*. Unpublished manuscript.

Bemporad, J. (1980) *Severe and Mild Depression: The psychotherapeutic approach* (eds. S. Arieti and J. Bemporad) London, Tavistock, 402–3.

Bly, R. (1990) *Iron John: A Book about Men*. Shaftesbury, Element Books.

Brod, M. (1973) *Franz Kafka: A Biography*. New York, Schocken Books.

Devin, E., Held, M., Vinson, J. and Walsh, G. (1986) *Thinkers of the 20th Century: A Biographical, Bibliographical and Critical Dictionary.* London, Firethorn Press.

Kafka, F. (1973) *Letter to His Father* (orig. 1919). New York, Schocken Books.

Keillor, G. (1986) *Lake Wobegon Days.* London, Faber and Faber.

Rowe, D. (1990) Suicide and death. *Changes,* **8**(4), pp262–9.

Santayana, G. (1920) *Little Essays: Drawn from the Writings of George Santayana by Logan Pearsall Smith.* London, J.M. Dent.

Shelley, P.B. (1921) *To Jane: The Invitation,* in The Oxford Book of English Verse 1250–1900 (ed. A.T. Quiller Couch), Oxford, Clarendon Press.

Trungpa, C. (1984) *Shambhala: The Sacred Path of the Warrior.* Shaftesbury, Shambhala.

Watts, A.W. (1968) *The Way of Zen.* Harmondsworth, Penguin.

Wolf, N. (1991) *The Beauty Myth.* London, Vintage.

Subject index

Author index